THE INTERNATIONAL FRAMEWORK FOR MONEY AND BANKING IN THE 1980s

Gary Clyde Hufbauer, Editor

The International Law Institute
Georgetown University Law Center
600 New Jersey Avenue, N.W.
Washington, D.C. 20001

Library of Congress Catalogue Number
81-84609

Copyright © 1981 by Georgetown University
International Law Institute

ISBN: 0-935-328-04-1

Printed in the United States of America
October 1981

Price $30

CONTENTS

Note: Detailed contents are set forth in each chapter.

PREFACE

At its June 1979 meeting, the Institute's Board of Trustees decided to undertake a series of conferences focusing on the international regulatory frameworks that govern a variety of economic sectors. These conferences were to be organized with a view toward the design of an effective international economic order. After careful consideration, it was agreed that the first conference would deal with "The International Framework for Money and Banking in the 1980s", and a grant was generously provided by the Mary and Daniel Loughran Foundation to underwrite the research of recognized scholars.

As originally conceived, the Conference was to address five major topics:

(1) The current condition of the international monetary system and the international regulatory machinery now in place (e.g., the International Monetary Fund, the Bank for International Settlements, and the Organisation for Economic Co-operation and Development);

(2) The role of the international commercial banks and the euro-currency markets;

(3) Developments in national regulation of the international financial system;

(4) Recent reform measures and pending proposals, such as the European Monetary System, new national regulations, a possible expanded function for the SDR or new reserve currencies, or a return to a more fixed system of exchange rates:

(5) The design of future international regulatory institutions, with special emphasis on the leadership role of the United States.

A careful reading of this book will show that the deliberations in Washington last spring were not quite what we had originally conceived: the papers placed more emphasis on market forces and less on regulation. In any event, the quality of discussion far exceeded our expectations.

The second "Frameworks" conference is planned for April 1982, and will address policy issues in the transportation sector. We expect it to build on the strong foundation of this first endeavor.

Don Wallace, Jr.
Director, International Law Institute
October 1981

FOREWARD

The International Law Institute sponsored a Conference
with the same title as this volume on April 30 and May 1,
1981 in Wasington, D.C.   The Conference brought together
leading scholars, financiers, and government officials.
Their collective purpose was to identify key issues that
will shape the world of international money and banking in
the 1980s.   By the year 1990, we can assess whether the
Conference succeeded in its mission!   Meanwhile the edited
Conference papers and comments are published here so that
they may be read by a wider audience.

The Conference deliberations (apart from the luncheon
address by Jacques Van Ypersele) were summarized on the
second day by Richard Cooper, and his remarks serve as a
useful introduction for this volume.   After the Conference,
many of the speakers revised and updated their papers.
Accordingly, there is not always a perfect correspondence
between the remarks of the commentators and the themes of
the main papers published here.

Both the Conference and this volume were financed by a
generous grant from the Loughran Foundation.   Much of the
organizational work for the Conference was done by my
colleagues, George Spina and George Berry.   The manuscript
was typed by Sandra Fells.

The International Law Institute records its appreciation to the authors, the commentators, the conferees, its own staff, and the Loughran Foundation for making this endeavor possible.

Gary Clyde Hufbauer
Editor
October 1981

CHAPTER ONE

INTERNATIONAL BANKING IN THE 1980s:

SUMMARY REMARKS

Richard N. Cooper

Maurits Boas
Professor of International Economics
Harvard University

CONTENTS

I.   INTRODUCTION

The organizers of the conference have put together an extremely interesting array of topics, varying from quite specific and technical issues such as the tax treatment of banking earnings and the question of official export credits, to very broad-reaching issues such as the future direction of the international monetary system and what might be done to shape it. My unenviable task is to summarize and to distill wisdom from seven papers and the remarks of eighteen discussants, not to mention the often stimulating remarks from the floor.

I have been struck by the sobriety of these sessions. It is true that we heard this afternoon about the velocity of a public speaker -- "200 words a minute gusting to 250" -- and yesterday we learned about the caution of bankers, which was likened to the fellow who, when asked by his optometrist to describe the color of a car across the street, said it was green -- at least on this side. We have also had international banking likened to common-law marriage -- a very sensible arrangement which however gives rise from time to time to accusations of living in sin. But apart from those few remarks it has been a very sober group. That is perhaps fitting not only for bankers but for those who discuss the role of banking in the world.

I propose to go seriatum through the seven topics that we have taken up and to indicate briefly what I distilled by way of consensus or sharp, well defined, differences of

view. At the end I will try to put the discussion into a
somewhat more general framework which I believe helps to
interpret the specific topics.

II. MULTIPLE RESERVE CURRENCY SYSTEM

Yesterday morning we heard from Fred Bergsten on the
movement of the world toward, and the problems arising from,
a multiple reserve currency system. Bergsten sees a strong
tendency in that direction and in his conference remarks, if
not in his final paper, he was alarmed by it. He feared
that multiple reserve currencies would increase both the
frequency and the amplitude of changes in exchange rates,
with consequential disturbance to national economies. It
would greatly complicate control over the creation of
international reserves. And at least the smaller reserve
currency countries would experience a substantial loss of
autonomy in the exercise of monetary policy for domestic
economic purposes. That is less of a problem for the United
States simply by virtue of its size, although some loss of
autonomy is implied even for the United States.

An important distinction was made between the problems
created both by moving from a single reserve currency to a
multiple reserve currency system, and in having such a
system. The complications are much greater in the period of
transition than in a fully established system. But Bergsten
countered by arguing that in practice the distinction blurs.
In a growing world economy we are always in a state of

4

transition so that some of those transitional problems are with us forever.

The course of action Bergsten suggested contained a variety of elements. One was to create target zones for exchange rates and to have key countries -- perhaps through the IMF, perhaps bilaterally -- coordinate the management of exchange rates within those target zones. He conceded that if that could be done successfully some of the worst features of a multiple reserve currency system would be greatly mitigated. Another element involves rules regarding acquisition of reserves by monetary authorities, with greater emphasis on Special Drawing Rights as the ultimate reserve asset. The movement to a single asset could take place gradually, and would involve the creation of a substitution account into which all reserve currencies -- not merely the dollar -- would be exchanged for SDRs. This would permit some degree of control over reserve creation.

My own view of this question, which was reflected in the remarks of several of the discussants, is to appreciate the possible disadvantages of a multiple reserve currency system, but to believe action to head it off is not so urgent as Bergsten argued in his oral remarks, and to entertain considerably more skepticism about the substitution account than he showed. With the proper kind of cooperation among a relatively small number of monetary authorities, the worst possibilities arising out of a multiple reserve currency system can be handled.

5

Moreover, as Bergsten acknowledges in his paper, it is not even clear just how strong the tendencies are toward a multiple reserve currency system. Allowance has to be made for special features, such as the fact that Japan, a heavy dollar holder, drew down its reserves sharply in 1979 which depressed global dollar holdings, and that the United States built up its holdings of marks. In addition, a large part of reserve increases in the last five years have gone to OPEC countries. The "reserves" of some of these countries are more akin to long-term investments, and the composition of their portfolios has to be assessed in that light. Long-term investment by its nature would show more diversification than true monetary reserves.

Since it came up in Bergsten's paper and again later in the discussion, I might observe that one should regard with extreme skepticism the theoretical studies on optimum reserve holdings. They reflect some very exciting work that is taking place on the frontiers of theory, but their results involve very strong assumptions which are known to be contrary to fact. So we should view those results as strictly illustrative at this stage rather than as serious estimates pertaining to the real world. This does not mean that they are wrong, only that they are unreliable.

III. THE ROLE OF COMMERCIAL BANKS AND THE IMF

Let me now turn to the second session, in which Jerry Cohen discussed several themes. First, the key international role played by commercial banks in recycling. Second, that recycling is likely to continue as an important problem in the next several years (the OPEC surplus is likely to remain large, although it can be expected to decline from current levels). Third, that the banks must continue and can be expected to continue a quantitatively important role in recycling, but a role that declines in relative importance. Fourth, that official institutions, in particular the IMF, will have to fill the growing gap.

We had quite a discussion about the various mechanisms for the IMF to raise financial resources. Joe Gold treated us to some ideas as to what further possibilities might exist. One issue that was not discussed in that session, which I think should be noted, is the question of the IMF's credit rating in the private market. Unlike the World Bank, the IMF does not have guarantees from member governments for its debt. The IMF is held in such high repute that it could undoubtedly raise several billion dollars without raising the issue of its credit-worthiness. But could it raise several tens of billions of dollars on the market without a change in its charter? That is an issue that we did not discuss, but it points to the importance of techniques that do not involve going to the private market.

Doubts were expressed about any kind of more formal relationship between the IMF and the commercial banks. But it was noted that the informal relationship is quite strong now. The banks rely on the IMF in effect to give a certificate of credit-worthiness to potential borrowers, particularly if their policies have been in question. The IMF in turn counts on new bank credits in framing its program recommendations for individual countries; it counts on the country being able to go to the commercial banking system to raise substantial funds.

IV. BANK REGULATION

The third session took up the question of bank regulation. Fred Dahl pointed out the conflicts of jurisdiction in bank regulations that exist today, and the tentative steps that have been taken among the major countries towards collaboration in bank regulation. He expressed the need for more collaboration in the future, especially on the question of disclosure. He suggested that potential investors in commercial banks will bring pressures on the banks and on the authorities for greater disclosure.

No one was willing to defend the notion that reserve requirements or other analogous requirements should be extended to the Eurocurrency market, although this issue has been discussed off and on for at least a decade. One might draw the logical conclusion that we should abolish reserve requirements within the major countries as well, but no one was willing to defend that proposition either. One might note, however, that there are some important differences between the Eurocurrency market and domestic banking even in the major countries. First, the depositors in the

Eurocurrency market are typically very large -- large firms, banks and even countries. Each bank can reasonably be expected to be responsible for the diversification of its depositors, something that cannot always be relied upon in a unitary banking system. Moreover, if a large depositor withdraws funds from a bank, the bank can borrow readily in the inter-bank market, for the market is a closed system. Withdrawals from a particular bank come back into the market or can be brought back into the market one way or another -- provided, of course, that the key central banks and in particular the Federal Reserve do not withdraw funds from the system altogether. That feature marks a big difference from national banking where there is the possibility that the public will withdraw deposits in favor of holding currency -- something we do not often think of these days but which historically played a major role in the insecurity of banking. So the usual modes of government intervention -- deposit insurance, reserve requirements and close surveillance over portfolios of banks -- would not seem applicable to the Eurocurrency market, whatever their merits may be today in national banking systems. There is, though, a tension between domestic bank regulation and the absence of regulation in international banking. That is a point to which I want to return later.

V.   TRADE IN BANKING SERVICES

In the fourth session, Geza Feketukuty explored banking services as an issue of trade policy. He characterized his paper as exploratory, rather than as a proposal, and discovered in writing the paper how hard it is to define just what banking services are, and more particularly where to draw the line between foreign trade in services and foreign investment. He reported several types of complaints that banks make about operating in other countries: restriction on entry, several kinds of discriminatory regulation against foreign-owned banks, and regulatory requirements which are onerous although not discriminatory. He suggested that, as in the trade area, the international community might have a notion of what might be considered legitimate national objectives, such as reduction of air or water pollution, promotion of industrial safety, and so forth. So long as national regulations are suited to those objectives and are fairly applied, they would be internationally acceptable even when they infringed on foreign trade, including trade in services. Attempts going beyond these objectives, for example to fiddle with banking structures or ownership, might be considered illegitimate.

The obstacles to banking that seem to be most important among industrial countries (banking in developing countries raises a whole different set of issues) reflect national anxiety about trans-border data flows of all kinds, including banking data. We are moving to an era in which high speed, high volume computers located in one part of the world may service large parts of the rest of the world. Countries are still groping toward a policy in this area that will allay their concerns and yet not impede economic transactions. This seemed to be a possible choke point in the near future against extension of international banking.

Several discussants raised strong doubts about the desirability of undertaking international negotiations with respect to trade in banking services. Banking often arouses very emotional feelings in the public at large, so that democratic governments would find it difficult to keep international negotiations in this area in a rational frame of reference.

VI.   TAXATION OF BANK INCOME

In the fifth session, Tom Horst drew our attention to the possible importance of taxation in influencing bank lending rates and hence the geographical location of banks. The foreign tax credit limitation is calculated in sharply different ways from country to country, but it is very important in determining the overall rate of taxation on bank earnings, and this creates differential incentives across countries. The panel generally took the view that tax considerations should play a more central role in bank decision making. Tom Horst observed that as competition among banks increases, the role of tax advisors will have to increase if the banks want to continue to be competitive.

VII. OFFICIAL EXPORT CREDITS

The sixth session was devoted to official export credits. It is paradoxical that in a world preoccupied with inflation and excessive budgetary deficits, governments should vie with one another for export sales by providing subsidized credits. Why do they do it? The question all the more deserves asking because the process of doing so subsidizes capital goods. This represents aid to developing countries, but it also tilts the incentives in those countries toward capital-intensive and away from more appropriate labor-intensive modes of production. Secondly, while much of the export credit goes to LDCs, much of it goes to other developed countries or to Eastern Europe, where the justification for subsidization is all the more questionable.

Export credit subsidies also need questioning because we now have a system of flexible exchange rates, under which a country whose exports are not doing well will experience a decline in its exchange rate. With a lag, its exports will improve. By the same token, a successful export promotion scheme will lead to a corrective appreciation of the currency. One may therefore ask why countries promote exports in an awkward way through export credit subsidies rather than just letting the international monetary system take care of their exports.

In this connection, I wonder whether there is something that we might call "interest rate illusion," both on the side of buyers and, perhaps for that reason, on the side of sellers. By that I mean that interest rates get disproportionate weight in assessing competitive offers for, say, a nuclear generating plant or a large-bodied aircraft or some other major capital purchase. Each offer contains a number of dimensions of competitiveness -- the price, the technical qualities and the durability of the product in question, the currency in which the loan must be repaid, the maturity of the loan, and the interest rate. Of all of these elements, the interest rate and the maturity are the easiest to understand and the easiest to boast about to your cabinet colleagues, if you are the minister in charge of transport or electric power, and you want to talk about the good deal you got in shopping between France, Germany, Japan, and the United States. Because of this illusion, I wonder how many economically costly purchases are made in which interest rates, as only one among many components of competitiveness, get excessive weight. Certainly in talking with foreign officials one frequently encounters the tremendous sensitivity they have to the interest rate, as opposed to many of the other dimensions of competitiveness. After all, who knows what the dollar-DM exchange rate will be ten years from now when the loan matures? But an interest rate at eight and a quarter percent -- that is known to be lower than nine and a quarter percent.

There is no potential limit to the fiscal competition that can go on once it starts. Moreover, both LDCs and

13

communist countries have become skillful in playing one industrial country against another. Hence the widely felt need for a consensus agreement among major exporters which constrains export credit subsidies. We had considerable discussion about the nature of the consensus and the prospects for improving it.

VIII. THE ROLE OF PRIVATE BANKS

In the final session this afternoon we had a vigorous debate on the extent of the decline of U.S. banks and the ascendency of non-U.S. banks and non-dollar transactions in the international system, centered on Robert Heller's paper. There is no doubt that on some measures such a decline has taken place. The question is how should one apportion that decline as between changes in the unit of measurement and genuinely greater activity on the part of non-U.S. banks or greater use of non-U.S. currencies. The increased dollar valuation of German marks and other currencies that we see now in the bond market, in the banking market, and in official reserve holdings came about partly because of a change in the dollar-DM exchange rate and partly because the number of securities denominated in marks actually went up. Bob Aliber suggested that the valuation factor deserved much more weight in the observed change relative to the activity factor than Heller's paper implied. We did not discuss as much as we might have what implications the two factors hold for the future. For example, even if the assets of German

14

banks have risen relative to U.S. banks largely through changes in the valuation of the mark, that still leaves them as more important competitors.

A final issue on which it would have been useful to have more discussion is the possible future role of Arab banks or banks in other members of OPEC. Just as members of OPEC are moving into downstream refining and petro-chemicals, they also have ambitions in banking. Are these ambitions likely to be realized and become quantitatively important on the international banking scene in the next decade? They are not of great quantitative importance today, but if we were having this conference in 1990 would we make the same judgment?

IX. SUMMARY

Now let me try to pull together all of these strands, diverse as they are. I will do so first by observing that improved communication and better information across national boundaries have greatly lowered the barriers to international trade and investment. Those lowered barriers in turn have had an important impact on national policies; very often the impact is to undercut the effectiveness of those policies. For example, national monetary policy, insofar as it is devoted to regulating economic activity, is much more difficult to undertake successfully if there is a lively competitive international capital market than if there is not. The moment the authorities try to push monetary variables one way or another the market adjusts and capital inflows or outflows undercut the effectiveness of the monetary authorities. Similarly with regulation and taxation. Increasingly activities can and do relocate from an area where taxation or regulation are seen to be onerous compared with the alternatives. Thus the mobility of goods and of enterprises permits escape from highly taxed and highly regulated national jurisdictions, except where the benefits to the enterprise are judged commensurate with the taxation or the regulation.

Yet we still frame policies at the national level. How do we deal with this erosion of effectiveness? There are two quite different schools of thought. There are those who welcome the relief from governmental "oppression" in the form of taxation or regulation and who see increased mobility as a way of lightening the load of government on enterprise. On the other hand, there are those who feel that the governmental control of economic activity must be restored. But since it cannot be restored at the national level in the face of increased mobility, they seek to restore it through international or even supra-national mechanisms -- agreements, treaties, or international organizations that have functional responsibilities and powers.

The extra-territorial reach of some national jurisdictions, which when undertaken by the United States is so offensive to Europeans, is part of the same fundamental process. We had a brief discussion yesterday about the

16

recent attempt by U.S. regulatory authorities to cover the home offices of foreign bank branches, at least to gain information. This extension of jurisdiction arises from the frustration of regulatory objectives that is possible in an era of high international mobility.

A final possible alternative for dealing with the problem is to take steps at the national level to reduce the mobility of firms and commerce, the source of the problem. No one at this conference recommended that particular alternative as a way to cope with these problems. But it is interesting to note that the move in 1973 to flexible exchange rates, while complex in its origins, had as one of its consequences some reduction in capital mobility across currencies and hence some restoration of national monetary autonomy. Flexible exchange rates can thus be seen in part as an effort to provide some insulation between national jurisdictions. Professor James Tobin of Yale has suggested that a tax be imposed on all currency transactions with the same objective in mind, and to reduce currency speculation.

We spent a lot of time in this conference talking about international arrangements of various kinds. That is not a mere coincidence. We heard about the need for an international money to restore control over international liquidity, and about the need for a substitution account. We heard about a greater role for the International Monetary Fund, both as a direct lender and as a provider of information or certificates of creditworthiness for various countries. We heard about the possible need to extend regulation to the Eurocurrency market, at least as far as disclosure was concerned. We heard about the possible desirability of a code to govern trade in banking services. We did not actually hear about the need to harmonize taxes, but it was implicit in Tom Horst's paper that large differences in what he called the minimum lending rate arising from tax treatment will induce harmonization of tax rates to the extent the jurisdictions want to retain their banking activities. And we heard about the importance of an export credit consensus to limit the fiscal competition among national authorities in pushing exports. So in each case there was some suggestion for international regulation. The institutional mechanisms varied. But the national level of regulation is no longer adequate in the face of extensive international mobility.

This new world into which we have been moving results in a degree of competition between national governments in favor of preferred economic activities, whatever they may be. Export credits were the clearest case in this conference. We did not talk much about investment, but the same kind of national competition for location of internationally foot-loose industries can be observed. Competition among policies may bring greater rationality to policy. That is one possibility. But at other times competition among policies may expose crucial flaws in the system. For example, there is no natural limit to fiscal competition such as takes place with export credits, and we therefore need some mechanism for limiting the competition.

Sorting out those areas of policy competition among governments that make sense from a systemic point of view from those that contain dangers for the system represents a good agenda for further work. So I conclude by observing that if one measure of the success of any conference is its ability to spawn additional conferences, this one will have to be judged a great success.

CHAPTER TWO

THE MULTIPLE RESERVE CURRENCY SYSTEM IN THE 1980s

C. Fred Bergsten

Director
Institute for International Economics

CONTENTS

TABLES

I. INTRODUCTION

"The emergence of a multiple-currency reserve system may be the least noticed, and yet the most spectacular result of the evolutionary process of international monetary reform that succeeded the abortive effort to set up a new world monetary order within the framework of the IMF in the early 1970s."

Karl Otto Pohl, "The Multiple-Reserve Currency System," Euromoney, October 1980, p. 45.

"The world is currently moving toward a multi-currency reserve system."

Fritz Leutwiler, "The Swiss Franc as a Subsidiary Reserve Currency," Aussenwirtschaft, vol. 35, No. 1, March 1980, p. 26.

"A so-called "multi-currency reserve system" is developing....A multiple currency reserve system is inherently unstable."

H. Johannes Witteveen, Towards a Less Unstable International Monetary System: Reserve Assets and a Substitution Account, Group of Thirty, 1980, p. 1.

1. The Record to Date

The evolution of a multiple reserve currency system appears to have accelerated sharply during the past few years. The dollar component of annual increases in the foreign exchange holdings of all monetary authorities[1] -- the "marginal dollar ratio" -- has declined steadily since 1977. This ratio dropped to less than 60 percent in 1978 when denominating total holdings in SDR, down from the level of 75 percent or more which had apparently prevailed in every previous year except 1973. In 1979, when the United States moved into current account surplus, official dollar

23

holdings actually declined[2] -- probably for the first time since 1949[3] -- while world foreign exchange holdings continued to rise. In 1980, and from 1978 through 1980, as a whole, the dollar accounted for only about 30 percent of the SDR-denominated growth of official foreign exchange holdings. The marginal dollar ratio recovered somewhat in the first quarter of 1981, but at 55 percent still fell well below the historical norm. The average dollar ratio, which had apparently stood at 85 percent or more for many years, dropped sharply after 1977 to 73 percent at the end of 1980 (and to 59 percent if the dollars converted into ECU are counted as ECU rather than dollars). (See Table 1 for the data.)

The corollary to the declining role of the dollar, of course, is the accelerating use of other national currencies as reserve assets. The DM absorbed about 7-12 percent of the growth of official currency holdings from 1970 through 1977.[4] From 1978 through 1980, however, it accounted for over one-third of the value growth -- a larger amount than provided by the dollar.

The yen and Swiss franc also played significant roles during 1978-80, each accounting for about 10-13 percent of the total buildup of official currency holdings. Taken together, official holdings of these three "new" reserve currencies equated to almost 60 percent of the total buildup of foreign exchange reserves in value terms. So it appears that the evolution of multiple currency usage has

24

Table 1

Shares of Individual Reserve Currencies in Increases in Total
Official Holdings of Foreign Exchange: 1973-1980 [1]
(in percentages)

	March 1973 to June 1974	July 1974 to Dec. 1975	1976	1977	1978	1979 excl. ECU	1979 incl. ECU	1980 excl. ECU	1980 incl. ECU	Memo: Share of Outstanding Total, end-1980 excl. ECU	incl. ECU
U.S. dollar											
volume	84.2	84.6	99.8	86.6	80.1	-8.5	-60.3	11.2	23.8	73.1	59.0
value	82.0	89.1	97.4	79.5	57.3	-34.8	-57.2	29.3	23.6		
Deutsche mark											
volume	8.2	7.8	7.0	8.4	14.3	29.6	10.3	50.9	50.6	14.0	12.1
value	11.8	6.8	12.4	12.1	28.2	48.7	12.3	34.2	20.7		
Swiss franc											
volume	n.a.	3.8	0.1	2.7	-1.2	27.2	9.4	15.1	15.1	4.1	3.5
value	n.a.	3.3	1.0	4.5	1.4	33.6	8.5	10.9	6.6		
Japanese yen											
volume	3.5	0.8	1.6	2.1	5.0	38.3	13.3	5.3	5.3	3.7	3.2
value	4.2	2.1	1.7	2.9	9.5	30.8	7.8	9.8	6.0		
Pound sterling											
volume	1.5	-1.3	-7.8	0.1	-0.1	7.9	2.7	9.3	9.3	3.0	2.6
value	(x)	-5.5	-11.6	0.7	-0.3	13.8	3.5	10.2	6.2		
French franc											
volume	1.8	2.5	-0.4	0.1	1.6	1.1	0.4	4.5	4.4	1.3	1.1
value	1.1	2.7	-1.2	0.1	2.9	2.1	0.5	3.0	1.8		
Neth. guilder											
volume	0.7	1.8	-0.3	0.1	0.5	4.4	1.5	3.7	3.7	0.9	0.8
value	1.0	1.5	0.1	0.2	1.1	5.7	1.4	2.6	1.6		
ECU											
volume	n.a.	n.a.	n.a.	n.a.	n.a.	n.a.	122.6	n.a.	-12.2	n.a.	17.8
value	n.a.	n.a.	n.a.	n.a.	n.a.	n.a.	123.2	n.a.	33.6		
Memo: New Three [2]											
volume	11.7	12.3	8.7	13.2	18.1	95.1	33.0	71.3	70.1	21.8	18.8
value	15.9	12.2	15.1	19.5	39.1	113.1	28.6	54.9	33.3		

(x) less than 0.05
n.a. - not applicable

Source: International Monetary Fund, Annual Report 1980, p. 62, and Annual Report 1981, p. 77.

1 The currency composition of foreign exchange is based on the IMF currency survey and on estimates derived mainly, but not solely, from official national reports. The numbers in this table should be regarded as estimates that are subject to adjustment as more information is received. They covered about 90% of total official currency holdings for the period under review; the residual includes currencies other than those listed, and amounts whose currency composition could not be ascertained.

2 DM, yen, Swiss franc

accelerated substantially over the past three years.

A more disaggregated analysis of the data -- to the extent that is possible, since very few countries publish a currency breakdown of their reserve holdings -- presents a more ambiguous picture, however. In 1979, for example, Japan's foreign exchange reserves declined by SDR 9.8 billion. Since Japan holds virtually all of its currency reserves in dollars, this decline more than explains the global decline of about SDR 2.3 billion in (non-ECU related) dollar balances which occurred in that year. The rest of the world, on balance, continued to increase its dollar holdings, at least modestly, and only the large Japanese deficit (and intervention need) triggered the decline in dollar balances. Even eliminating Japan from the data, however, the dollar's share in the increase in total cur-rency reserves (about 40 percent) would have been well below its traditional level.[5]

A second complicating factor in analyzing the increased use of non-dollar key currencies is the sharp increase in holdings thereof by the United States itself, during the period of more active intervention policy instituted in November 1978 and running through 1980. U.S. balances of foreign exchange rose (from virtually zero) by about SDR 3.3 billion in 1978 and again by over SDR 5 billion in 1980. Since the bulk of these increases was in DM, the U.S. ac-tions accounted for a sizable share -- perhaps one-half or even more -- of the global rise in DM holdings in both years.

Several interpretations are possible of this growing
reciprocity of holdings among the key currency countries.
On the one hand, it could be viewed as definitive evidence
of the emergence of a full-blown multiple currency system.
The United States now holds DM and, to a lesser extent, yen
and Swiss francs, just as the issuers of those currencies
have held dollars for many decades. On the other hand, a
major part of the U.S. motive in accumulating DM and Swiss
francs in 1980 was to cover its liabilities in those currencies generated by the issuance of DM-denominated and Swiss
franc-denominated "Carter bonds" in 1979. When those
liabilities are repaid (during 1981-83), the U.S. holdings
of DM and Swiss francs will decline sharply. Moreover, the
Reagan administration has announced that it will follow a
much less active intervention policy than did the Carter
administration during its last two years in office, so U.S.
holdings of foreign currencies may return to very low
levels. In that case, the international use of those
currencies -- particularly the DM -- will record a substantial decline.

A third factor which complicates analysis of the
evolution of multiple currency usage is the different pace
of that evolution among different groups of countries and
the different levels of the dollar ratio among these groups.
In his comments on this paper, von Furstenberg notes that

the dollar ratio of the non-oil developing countries actually rose from 59 percent in March 1973 to 64 percent in mid-1980. The dollar share of holdings of the oil exporting countries dropped by twenty percentage points over the same period and "accounted for one half the total diversification out of the dollar."[6] The rest of the decline must therefore have come from the industrial countries, although von Furstenberg adds that their dollar holdings rose in absolute SDR value from the end of 1976 through mid-1980.[7]

In addition to these differences in the _changes_ in dollar ratios, the differing _levels_ of the ratios may also be important. In early 1980, for example, the dollar ratio ranged from 67 percent in both oil-exporting countries and non-oil developing countries to over 90 percent in both EMS and non-EMS industrial countries (excluding the United States; see Table 2).[8] An even sharper distinction obtains between the dollar ratio of the five "new" reserve centers themselves (Germany, Switzerland, Japan, United Kingdom, France) and the rest of the world for which data are available (excluding the United States); already by September 1978, these ratios were 93.3 percent and 67 percent, respectively.[9]

These breakdowns suggest that the future constellation of payments imbalances between the groups with higher and lower dollar ratios may have an important bearing on the evolution of overall dollar usage. If the surplus of the oil-exporting countries substantially exceeds the deficit of

29

Table 2

Shares of Individual Reserve Currencies in Total Official Holdings of
Foreign Exchange by Major Country Groupings, First Quarter, 1980
(in percentages)

	EMS Countries	Other Industrial Countries	Oil Exporting Countries	Non-oil Developing Countries	Total
U.S. Dollar	90.3	82.8	67.1	67.4	78.1
Deutsche mark	5.6	8.9	16.7	17.7	11.7
Swiss franc	2.9	2.6	5.1	1.9	3.1
Japanese yen	0.2	4.5	4.9	3.9	3.1
Pound sterling	0.4	1.1	2.9	5.4	2.3
French franc	(x)	(x)	2.2	2.3	1.1
Netherlands guilder	0.5	0.1	1.0	1.4	0.7

(x) - less than 0.1

Source: IMF Survey, January 26, 1981, p. 28. Data for "other industrial
          countries" include the United States; excluding it raises the dollar
          ratio of this group to 91.8 per cent.

30

the non-oil developing countries, as is likely to remain the case for at least the next few years, the industrial countries will remain in deficit and reserves -- primarily in the form of foreign exchange -- will shift to countries with lower dollar ratios from countries with higher dollar ratios. As a result, the global dollar ratio is likely to continue to decline -- albeit slowly, because even significant changes at the margin produce only modest changes in outstanding totals.[10]

The underlying rate of growth of the multiple reserve currency system thus remains somewhat unclear. Its future pace is unpredictable. Nevertheless, such a system does seem to be evolving. The dollar's share has declined substantially for over three years. The shares of the "new three" -- especially the DM, but also the yen and Swiss franc -- are clearly growing. The outlook for international payments imbalances suggest that the recent trend will persist.[11]

Moreover, the continued growth of multiple currency usage in 1979-80 was based at least in part on an important shift in motivations. In 1978, as in 1973, the acceleration in the use of non-dollar currencies was largely demand-generated. Concern over the stability of the dollar triggered a degree of currency diversification, in the sense that a smaller share of the surplus countries' reserve increases was held in dollars. The United States itself also sought to acquire foreign currency reserves. The new key currency countries largely continued to resist international use of their monies.

In 1979 and 1980, however, supply factors suddenly began to play a major role in the move toward a multiple currency system. On the one hand, the United States moved into near-balance on its current account, thereby reducing the net supply of new dollars becoming available for reserve holdings in other countries. On the other hand, all three of the new reserve centers -- particularly Germany and Japan -- swung into heavy deficit (see Table 3) and anticipated that those deficits might remain for some time to come.

These new reserve centers thus began to reverse their traditional attitudes toward the international use of their currencies and, especially in 1980, began to borrow heavily abroad in their own currencies to finance at least part of their deficits. Moreover, the new key currency countries concluded that it was futile to resist key-currency status and decided to try to manage rather than ignore it.[12] Supplies of DM and yen became readily available to foreign official holders through the actions of the German and Japanese authorities for the first time.

This reversal was most noteworthy for Germany, which foresaw the longest continuation of a deficit position and suffered the largest loss of reserve assets during the early stages of its dramatically altered external balance. Switzerland, with a relatively modest deficit and loss of reserves, altered its stance the least. Japan fell more

TABLE 3

Current Account Position[1] of the Major
Reserve Currency Countries: 1971-1980
(In $ billion)

	Germany	Japan	Switzerland	United Kingdom	United States
1971	0.8	5.8	0.1	2.6	-1.4
1972	0.8	6.6	0.2	0.4	-5.8
1973	4.6	-0.1	0.3	-2.6	7.1
1974	10.3	-4.7	0.2	-7.9	-4.7[2]
1975	4.0	-0.7	2.6	-3.7	18.3
1976	3.9	3.7	3.5	-2.0	4.4
1977	4.2	10.9	3.4	-0.5	-14.1
1987	8.7	16.5	4.4	1.2	-14.3
1979	-5.5	-8.8	2.4	-3.9	-0.8
1980	-15.5	-10.8	-0.7	6.4	0.1
1981 est.	-15.3	-2.1	-0.5	9.9	4.4

Source: OECD Economic Outlook No. 29 (July 1981).

[1]   Goods, services and all transfer payments.

[2]   Excluding cancellation of Indian debt (-1993) and
extraordinary grants (-746)

closely toward Germany on the spectrum, although its current account deficit receded sharply toward the end of 1980. But supply factors, particularly for the DM, seem likely to promote continued non-dollar growth.[13]

Caution is also required in interpreting the impact of this "supply-side" shift on the evolution of the multiple currency system. It is clear that demand for non-dollar assets must exist for diversification to occur, whatever is offered by the new reserve centers; one may even ask whether the overt German and Japanese financing efforts made any difference at all. However, most of these efforts were directed toward major dollar holders in the Persian Gulf -- holders which have exhibited a high degree of concern for systemic stability. It seems that these holders, primarily Saudi Arabia, are likely to exercise their diversifi- cation demand more actively if offered off-market methods of doing so which will minimize the risk of creating market instability. Thus it is quite probable that the shift into non-dollar currencies has been accelerated, perhaps substan- tially, by the change in attitudes of the new reserve centers.

A second caveat on the results for 1979-80 also relates to the concern for systemic stability exercised by most major dollar holders. Because of these concerns, such countries were reluctant to add pressure to the exchange markets when the dollar was declining in 1978, even though they may have wished to reduce the dollar component of their portfolios. When the dollar strengthened in 1979 and particularly 1980, however, they may have taken advantage of the opportunity (and a higher price for their dollars) to carry out some shifting. The decline in official dollar holdings in 1979-80 can thus be seen, to at least some extent, as an extension of the events of 1978 motivated by standard portfolio balance considerations. Again, dollar strength can, paradoxically, produce movement out of the dollar.

Traditionally, of course, all national currencies used actively in international finance have "competed" with gold in contributing to the growth of systemic liquidity. More recently, the SDR has become a "competitor" as well (to some extent, so has the ECU, which is treated statistically as a component of total foreign exchange holdings by the IMF).

At present, however, foreign exchange holdings represent by far the most active component of international reserves. Indeed, they accounted for 95 percent of the growth in total international reserves between 1973 and 1980 when gold is valued at a constant price; SDRs accounted for only 1.5 percent, though this ratio has become higher with the resumption of new allocations in 1979 (see Table 4). The share of foreign exchange is only 35 percent for this period when gold is valued at market prices, but virtually the entire change in the value of gold holdings of course derives from price changes and gold remains "buried at the bottom of the reserve pile."[14]   Hence it seems

Table 4

Changes in the Composition of International
Reserves: 1974-1980
(in billions of SDR)

	1974	1975	1976	1977	1978	1979	1980	1974-80
With gold at market prices								
Gold	60.2	-33.2	-4.4	20.4	39.4	184.2	71.6	338.1
Foreign exchange	24.8	10.9	22.9	40.0	20.9	25.0	44.7	189.2
SDR	0.1	-0.1	-0.1	-0.5	(x)	4.3	-0.1	3.1
IMF position	2.7	3.8	5.1	0.3	-3.3	-3.2	5.1	10.6
TOTAL	87.8	-18.7	23.5	60.2	57.1	210.4	120.7	541.0
With gold at SDR 35 per ounce								
Gold	(x)	(x)	-0.2	0.1	0.2	-3.2	0.3	-2.9
Foreign exchange	24.8	10.9	22.9	40.0	20.9	25.0	44.7	189.2
SDR	0.1	-0.1	-0.1	-0.5	(x)	4.3	-0.1	3.1
IMF position	2.7	3.8	5.1	0.3	-3.3	-3.2	5.1	10.6
TOTAL	27.5	14.5	27.8	40.0	17.9	23.1	49.3	200.0

(x) - less than SDR 0.1 billion

Source: International Monetary Fund, International Financial Statistics, March 1981.

appropriate to refer to today's international monetary standard as increasingly becoming a "multiple reserve currency system."

II. AN ANALYTICAL FRAMEWORK

There is no completely satisfactory conceptual basis for analyzing the evolution of the multiple currency system.[15] We do not have a firm basis on which to judge the optimum mix of national currencies in international finance, from a theoretical let alone a practical standpoint. The most relevant analysis published to date in fact concludes that "there is an infinite set of solutions" to the problem of currency portfolio composition, depending upon which variables one wishes to emphasize.[16]

Some guidelines might be obtained from events in the private markets. BIS data indicate that the dollar's share of the foreign assets of reporting European banks fell from over 80 percent as late as 1969 to about 67 percent at the end of 1979, with the DM share rising to almost 20 percent at the end of 1979, and the Swiss franc to about 6 percent.[17] The decline in the dollar's share occurred over two relatively short periods of time when the dollar was under severe pressure in the exchange markets (1969-71, 1977-79) and actually recouped a bit in the interim. It is thus difficult to judge the slope of the trend, though its direction seems clear.[18]

On the view that public authorities usually lag the

37

private markets, one might judge that the share of the dollar in official reserves has further to decline -- at least another five percentage points or so. On the other hand, we know that the reserve asset preferences of monetary authorities -- at least in the major countries -- comprise a different mix of factors than the private sector. We turn next, therefore, to the several explicit efforts which have been made to shed light on that issue.

For developed countries, the key variables which determine the composition of official currency holdings appear to be: (1) the composition of their holdings in the past (when the dollar was dominant); (2) the nature of their exchange arrangements; (3) the distribution of their trade flows among the several key currency countries; and (4) ranking decidedly lower, profit/risk considerations.[19] For the developing countries, the normal portfolio selection criteria of profit maximization and risk minimization appear to dominate with the currency composition of imports playing an important role in that calculation.[20] In conceptual terms, the Markowitz-Tobin variance model with weights determined largely by consumption patterns (in this case, import consumption patterns) appears to apply to developing countries, but seems to be overshadowed by systemic concerns in industrialized countries.

On the basis of these propositions, several authors have in fact constructed "optimum currency portfolios" for individual monetary authorities and for the system as a

whole. Their results, which cannot be compared directly
because of differences both in the underlying models and in
the time periods from which data are drawn, are summarized
in Table 5.

Each of these authors stresses that his estimates can
be applied to the real world only with caution. Nevertheless, there is a striking consistency across different
methodologies and time periods in the suggestion that the
dollar should now be playing a substantially smaller role --
perhaps on the order of 10-15 percentage points -- than is
in fact the case. The DM, but other currencies to an even
greater extent, is under-represented in the present portfolio mix.

Heller-Knight furnish at least part of the explanation
of the over-representation of the dollar in two of their
findings. The first centers on exchange-rate arrangements.
Countries which peg their currencies to the dollar can
minimize the variance (in local currency) of the value of
their reserves by holding most of those reserves in dollars.
Perhaps more importantly, countries which intervene primarily in dollars -- even those which peg to the SDR or some
other currency basket -- maximize convenience and minimize
transaction costs by holding dollars, and minimize variance
in the value of their reserves denominated in their intervention currency.[21]

Table 5

Estimates of Optimal International
Currency Portfolios
(in percentages)

	Ben-Basset (1972-76) DCs	LDCs	Kouri-Macedo (1973-77)	Macedo (1973-78)	Assets of European Banks	Memo: Actual Share, end-1980 excl.ECU
Dollar	56.7	58.2	62.87	46-61	66.9	73.1
DM	13.6	12.5	36.93	12-18	19.4	14.0
Sterling	0.1	2.0	25.28	-1 to +4	1.8	3.0
French franc			-12.58	9-17	1.2	1.3
Guilder			n.i.	n.i.	1.3	0.9
Yen			-12.59	8-14		3.7
Swiss franc	29.6	27.4	n.i.	15-16		4.1
Canadian Dollar			n.i.	-9 to -12	9.4	n.i.
Lira			n.i.	0 to -2		n.i.

Time periods under each column heading indicate years included in each
author's analysis.

Negative entry implies net borrowing in that currency.

n.i. - not included

Sources: Ben-Bassat, op. cit., p. 294.
          Pentti J. K. Kouri and Jorge Braga de Macedo, "Exchange Rates
             and the International Adjustment Process," Brookings
             Papers on Economic Activity 1978:1, p. 129.
          Jorge Braga de Macedo, "Portfolio Diversification Across
             Currencies," Economic Growth Center, Yale University,
             Center Discussion Paper No. 321, Sept. 1979, p. 43.
          International Monetary Fund, Annual Report 1980.
          Bank for International Settlements, Annual Report 1980, p. 122.

Conversely, "pure floaters" would probably be prone to less intervention in general and thus to construct their portfolios more along Markowitz-Tobin lines; in fact, they were the only grouping to exhibit a significant decline in their dollar ratios from end-1970 (90.3 percent) to end-1976 (74.2 percent). A specific arrangement which enhanced the dollar ratio was the explicit agreement among the "snake" countries not to hold each others' currencies beyond working-balance needs; as a result, the six countries remaining in that arrangement at end-1976, which accounted for almost 40 percent of all currency reserves covered in the study, had the highest dollar ratio (almost 90 percent) of any grouping.

A second phenomenon uncovered by Heller-Knight was a sizable ratio of dollar holdings seemingly unrelated to any of their explanatory variables, including dollar-pegging.[22] On average, countries in their sample tended to hold 66 percent of their currency reserves in dollars regardless of trading and payments arrangements. I interpret this to encompass at least two factors: 1) the inertia of long-standing practice dating from the period in which the dollar was virtually the sole key currency, a la sterling's maintenance of a world financial role for decades (roughly 1925-65) beyond what was justified by underlying British circumstances; and 2) concern for systemic stability by large dollar holders conscious of the market impact of their diversifying, or even of their being perceived to be

41

interested in diversifying.

One reason for the inertial continuance of a "greater-than-justified" role for the dollar may be an inability on the part of other currencies to assume a greater share of international financial responsibility, reinforced prior to 1979-80 by the reluctance of their issuing authorities to support such a role. In an earlier study, I analyzed the criteria which are rquired for key currency status and applied these criteria to the emerging alternatives.[23] After reaching the obvious conclusion that no single currency could fully replace the dollar in international finance, I found that (in 1975):

> Germany comes the closest on most of the basic economic criteria, both external and internal. However, it still operates under major political constraints, has relatively weak capital markets, and is not sufficiently aloof to external economic and political forces. Japan suffers from the same shortcomings, particularly its lack of economic security, and also has a demonstrated proclivity to apply controls. The only other serious national possibility is Britain, based on its superior capital markets, but its political role has moved in a direction which is opposite from what is needed and its economic outlook is far more uncertain than the outlook for most of the other major countries. France, Switzerland, and the Netherlands simply have too many limitations to qualify on a national basis.
>
> Two subsidiary conclusions emerge. One is that some of these national currencies, particularly the mark, if not strong enough to fully replace the dollar, are likely to be quite strong and hence could come to play important regional roles as reserve currencies or share global reserve currency status with the dollar.[24]

These conclusions would still seem largely to hold today. However, both Germany and Japan are now in a stronger position than in 1975 to play key currency roles.

42

The primary reason is the widening of the gap between their (especially Germany's) inflation rates and those of the competition, particularly the United States. It is also due to the fairly rapid evolution of their capital markets in recent years, due in turn partly to the advent of sizable deficits in their federal budgets and thus the development of a much more active market in government securities. In the case of Japan, substantial liberalization of the capital markets has also occurred, and Japan's capacity for playing a key currency role is further enhanced by her continued rapid economic and export growth. The onset of detente further aided the key currency case for both countries by de-emphasizing the importance of security factors -- a major advantage for the United States (and Switzerland).

There is one useful proxy in assessing the possible extent to which the international position of individual currencies might develop. This is the "international liquidity position" of their countries, the comparison between their foreign assets and liabilities. Several definitions can be used on both sides of the balance sheets, including or excluding both liquid assets of the private sector and liabilities to private as well as official foreign holders. An analysis of U.S. history records a striking correlation between a decline in some of these key ratios below 100 percent and the dollar crises of the 1960s.[25]

All of the new reserve centers have substantially

higher liquidity ratios today than does the United States, even when gold is valued at market prices (see Table 6). In fact, valuing gold at market prices, ratios of reserves to foreign official holdings of their currencies for all of the new reserve centers except Germany are above the U.S. ratio of reserves to all foreign holdings in 1946; Germany's ratio is about where the U.S. ratio stood in the early 1950s.[26] The German ratio of reserves to all foreign holdings would not be as impressive, of course, but would still appear relatively comfortable.

On the other hand, these quantities now change much more rapidly than in the past. Even with the enormous increase in the market value of gold reserve, Germany's liquidity ratio (with gold valued at market) was cut by 60 percent between 1973 and 1980. Nevertheless, at their end-1980 reserve levels (with gold valued at market), the new reserve centers (plus the U.K.) could support a further expansion of over SDR 200 billion in reserve use of their currencies without letting their liquidity ratios fall below 100 percent on this particular definition.[27] For the three most important new centers alone, an expansion of over SDR 100 billion would be possible. On this measure there is thus a good deal of scope for further expansion of the multiple currency system.

TABLE 6

Liquidity Ratios[1] of Key Currency Countries: 1973-1980
(End of period, in millions of SDR)

	1973					1980				
	Reserves		Foreign official holdings	Ratios		Reserves		Foreign official holdings	Ratios	
	Gold @ SDR 35/oz.	Gold @ market[3]		Gold @ SDR 35/oz.	Gold @ market	Gold @ SDR 35/oz.	Gold @ market[3]		Gold @ SDR 35/oz.	Gold @ market
United States	11,919	27,939	75,151	0.16	0.37	21,480	134,398	167,649	0.13	0.80
Germany	27,498	34,326	5,192	5.30	6.61	40,975	81,636	32,201	1.27	2.54
Switzerland	7,063	11,893	1,075	6.57	11.06	15,191	50,768	9,332	1.63	5.44
Japan	10,152	11,377	-	∞	∞	20,165	30,516	8,425	2.39	3.62
United Kingdom	5,368	6,589	6,236	0.86	1.06	16,851	24,899	6,870	2.45	3.62
France	7,070	16,460	909	7.78	18.11	24,302	59,268	2,898	8.39	20.45
Netherlands	5,426	10,481	287	18.91	36.52	10,669	29,440	2,105	5.07	13.99

Source: International Monetary Fund, Annual Reports 1980, 1981 and International Financial Statistics.

1 Ratio of reserve center's reserve assets to foreign official holdings of its currency.

2 Reserves are as of end-1973, foreign official holdings as of March 1973.

3 SDR 93.05 in 1973, SDR 462.20 in 1980.

III. THE OUTLOOK

From the analyses already cited, we can identify some of the factors which are likely to determine the pace of evolution of the multiple reserve currency system. Several of these factors, such as the distribution of each country's trade among the principal reserve centers, change slowly and are not likely to lead to substantial alterations in the international share of different currencies except over the longer run; given the likely continuation of its dynamic trade growth, Japan will probably gain a bit on this criterion over time. Other factors, such as the relative risk-return calculus, are likely to change erratically and unpredictably; the dollar's share clearly declined in years of dollar depreciation (1973, 1978) but recouped during the intervening period (1974-77) and could do so again if the underlying strength of 1979-81 were to continue for a while.

The more decisive elements in the evolution of the multiple currency system are likely to be systemic themselves. The advent of flexible exchange rates has had two key, albeit opposite effects on the portfolio management of national reserves. On the other hand, the perceived increase in potential currency instability accompanying more flexible rates has increased the diversification incentive for monetary authorities wishing to limit their vulnerability to shifts in the international purchasing power of their assets. Moreover, countries not pegging their exchange rates to any fixed standard (the "pure floaters") may tend

46

to intervene less than they did under fixed exchange rates and hence are not motivated as importantly by the convenience and transaction cost benefits of holding dollars.

On the other hand, we have seen that the systemic shift of the early 1970s led to increased dollar ratios for many countries -- both dollar peggers and basket-peggers. This seems to have occurred in part because many dollar-peggers sought to limit fluctuations in the value of their reserves denominated in terms of both their local currency and their primary intervention currency, which under flexible rates might otherwise have become greater -- and certainly would have become more frequent. Another, perhaps more important, consideration for many countries which peg to some unit other than a non-dollar currency is that the increased level of exchange rate fluctuations that has come with floating has increased their total intervention activities, thereby enhancing the value attached to dollar holdings by virtue of the convenience and low transaction costs of dealing in dollars.

Assuming that there will be no early return to a system of fixed parities a la Bretton Woods, the single most important variable determining the future shares of different national currencies is thus probably the exchange arrangements of individual key countries. As of mid-1980, most major reserve holders fell into one of three categories concerning their exchange arrangements. There were eight members of the European Monetary System, accounting for about one-third of total international reserves excluding gold. Twenty-one countries accounting for about 10 percent of total non-gold reserves were pegging to a currency basket other than the SDR. About forty-eight countries accounting for almost one-half the total were not pegging at all.[28] It is changes in arrangements by this last group of countries that could most rapidly lead to changes in the overall composition of international currency reserves.

In principle, such changes could occur in either direction. Countries now pegging to a non - SDR basket could shift to the dollar. "Pure Floaters" might decide to re-peg, substantially increasing their dollar ratios in the process.

In practice, however, major shifts are more likely to come from another direction. The EMS countries might decide to hold each other's currencies beyond the very short-term periods in which they now do so before refinancing their intervention accumulations, or they might create and hold more meaningful ECU balances.[29] Many of the largest "pure floaters," such as Japan, now maintain very high dollar ratios anyway. Basket-peggers would seem likely, over time, to adjust their reserve portfolios in the direction of a composition akin to the composition of their pegging basket. A shift of a major country from dollar-pegging or SDR-pegging to free floating could over a few years produce a substantial shift from dollars into other currencies by that country. Even clearer would be a shift from dollar-pegging to pegging to some other national currency, which would then presumably become the chief component of the shifting country's reserve portfolio. So a more disaggregated survey of the likely evolution of exchange-rate arrangements also suggests a likely evolution toward increased multiple currency usage.

The second broad factor influencing such usage is the sense of systemic responsibility borne constantly in mind by most major dollar holders. As far back as the 1960s, most major countries were inhibited from moving out of the dollar because they recognized the implications of their doing so for overall international monetary stability.[30] In 1971, the members of the Group of Ten also agreed not to deposit their dollar holdings in the Eurocurrency markets in order to avoid the "carrousel effect" of creating additional dollar liabilities by so doing.[31] In the recent past, this sense of systemic responsibility has deterred most major dollar holders (including the largest OPEC holders) from dollar conversion -- especially when the dollar was weak. Paradoxically, the likelihood of dollar conversions by these countries is greater when the dollar is strong, which as already noted could explain some of the decline in dollar ratios in 1979 and particularly in 1980. Hence this particular systemic feature cuts against any precipitate shift from the dollar to other currencies, but also suggests that the process is likely to continue even when there is no immediate concern about the outlook for the dollar.

Moreover, under conditions of dollar strength, it is quite likely that the new key currency countries would be running current account deficits and thus continuing to promote international usage of their currencies from the supply side. In fact, supply side considerations, _a la_ 1979-80, are the third major element likely to influence the evolution of the multiple currency system -- and could well be the single most important factor in promoting its continued growth. Balance of payments forecasting is a notoriously difficult business, but there is sufficient reason to expect continued German (and perhaps Japanese) deficits to assign such considerations a major role in promoting multiple currency usage in the immediate future.

More broadly, we have seen that a continuation of surpluses in the oil-exporting countries and deficits in the industrialized countries (excluding the United States) is likely to reduce the global dollar ratio, because the former group maintains a lower dollar ratio than the latter group. Again, the risks seem largely on the downside for the dollar; it is much more likely that the OPEC countries would reduce further their recent dollar ratio (around 67 percent) than that the industrial countries outside the United States would raise their already high ratio (almost 92 percent). However, even a substantial shift in the holdings of total foreign exchange holdings toward oil-exporting countries would reduce the global dollar ratio by only a modest amount.

This conceptual framework suggests a continued slow decline in the share of international currency reserves provided by the dollar, perhaps accelerating in periods of acute pressure on the dollar or if major reserve holders alter their basic exchange arrangements. When the dollar is weak, countries motivated primarily by risk/return considerations will move away from it (as in 1973 and 1978). When the dollar is strong, the new reserve centers are likely to be seeking increased international use of their currencies to finance their current account deficits (as in 1979-80) and those countries which have restrained their diversification proclivities for reasons of systemic stability during periods of dollar weakness may now exercise them; the apparent absence of significant reflows into the dollar after the successful stabilization efforts of November 1978 and October 1979 support this view. On a more secular basis, the likely pattern of payments imbalances and the likely (net) direction of changes in exchange arrangements (and probably in trade shares) also suggest movement away from the dollar.

The DM would appear to be the likely recipient of most of the shift away from dollars, partly because Germany appears likely to run the largest external deficits among the new reserve centers over the next few years, but more fundamentally because Germany best meets the criteria for reserve currency status among the several "new" centers. However, the yen should also experience a growing role as, to a lesser extent, should the Swiss franc and perhaps one or two others. The only scenario under which multiple currency evolution is unlikely would be one of unprecedented systemic stability: no large deficit to be financed by the new reserve centers, continuing dollar stability to obviate desires to move to other currencies (and to mute more general concerns for greater portfolio balance), and an absence of important changes in exchange-rate arrangements. The more likely course would seem to be a continued, albeit moderately paced, growth of the multiple currency nature of the international monetary system.

IV. THE ISSUES RAISED

The development of a multiple currency system would not be without historical precedent. In the decade or so before World War I, France and Germany had become major reserve centers along with the United Kingdom; both their currencies were, in fact, probably more widely held throughout Europe than sterling.[32] Sterling and the dollar co-existed as key currencies during the interwar and early post-World War II periods, with occasional increases in holdings of French francs as well.[33] In the early 1960s, the United States actually initiated several cautious steps in the direction of a multiple currency system.[34] More recently, the use of non-traditional reserve currencies began evolving from the mid-1960s[35] though it has accelerated significantly only since 1978.[36]

The desirability of a multiple currency system must be considered from the standpoint of both the monetary system as a whole and the individual key currency countries. In each case, it is of course necessary to compare such a system with the realistic alternatives.

Several key systemic questions are raised by the advent of multiple reserve currencies. Does increased official use of several national currencies per se expand the likely magnitude of international capital flows, taking into account the effect on private flows as well? Indeed, does increased official use of several currencies tend to expand their international private use by enhancing both their international reputation and their liquidity? Or is there a high degree of substitution between changes in official and private holdings, e.g., as official intervention "takes dollars off the hands of private holders"?

If multiple currency usage does increase the volume of international capital flows, is it likely to do so in a destabilizing direction along the lines of the traditional Gresham's Law problem? Or would a multiplicity of currencies be less unstable than a system based on a single key currency, by providing alternative outlets for diversified investments and thus adding to the prospects for stabilizing speculation? Or is the already substantial flow among national money markets unlikely to be changed very much, in either direction, by gradual increases in reserve currency roles for several more currencies? Answers to these

53

questions are central to analyzing the impact of the evolving multiple reserve currency system on international monetary arrangements.

Second, what is the impact of any such increase of capital flows on the international adjustment process? Do more capital flows increase the amplitude of fluctuations in the exchange markets because the greater availability of additional currencies encourages additional shifting among them -- the traditional Gresham's Law concern?[37] In turn, would such increased fluctuations increase the prospect for periodic -- but perhaps systematic -- over-shooting of exchange rate equilibria?[38] In addition, would asymmetrical overshooting be promoted in the medium run because of a secular (diversification) movement away from the dollar?[39] Would any such additional overshooting in turn either: (1) help the adjustment process by adding to the real impact of external disequilibria and thereby promoting corrective responses; or (2) hinder adjustment by providing incorrect market signals, intensifying the underlying problems in the short run and generating excessive adjustment over the longer run, and perhaps by triggering over-reactions by national authorities? Are there other ways in which the economic impact of greater exchange-rate volatility would affect adjustment?

Third, does the advent of multiple currency usage adversely affect adjustment through permitting more ready financing of key-currency country external deficits? Or do the new reserve centers already feel <u>additional</u> adjustment pressure due to the need to defend the international positions of their currencies, as suggested by Germany in early 1981?[40] Moreover, does the presence of competition among several reserve currencies increase adjustment pressures on the United States -- and perhaps all of the "new" reserve centers as well -- and thus impart added discipline to the system's largest members?[41] More broadly, how is the "proper" mix between adjustment and financing -- the perennial center of much of the debate over international monetary matters -- altered by a multiple currency system?[42]

Fourth, how does the existence of multiple reserve currencies affect the system-wide level of official liquidity? When the debate on international monetary reform began in the early 1960s, some analysts advocated such a system as a way to ensure adequate growth of international reserves.[43] On the other hand, it was immediately observed that the use of <u>multiple</u> reserve currencies might in practice not add much liquidity growth to the system without "explicit or implicit pledges" to that end, because the new reserve currencies might be accumulated primarily by shifts from the old ones and there was little prospect of their attaining much transactions use.[44]

The whole issue of official reserves must, of course, now be considered within the context of a system of flexible exchange rates. Moreover, the liquidity environment itself is greatly different from the early 1960s -- with fluctuating market prices for gold, a very sizable level of dollar holdings and annual SDR creation. The original debate, in both government and academic circles, quickly rejected the multiple currency option, primarily because of the fear of Gresham's Law results and a conclusion that most of the benefits of such diversification could be achieved with much less risk by creating an international asset -- eventually the SDR -- which encompassed the major international currencies in a single basket. That same question must now be answered within the very different context of the 1980s.

Fifth, how is systemic management affected? Do a greater number of countries accept systemic responsibility, and therefore behave more constructively, if their currencies are widely used?[45] Or does anything less than currency hegemony invite both conflict and inefficiency, as Kindleberger has argued for some time? To put the question more neutrally: what modes of conduct and rules of the games are needed to achieve effective operation of such a regime? A related issue is the net impact of a multiple currency system on the developing countries: new privileges would be accorded to the new key currency industrialized countries, but the range of asset choice for LDCs themselves would be broadened.

Several over-arching questions emerge from this set of specific issues. For example, is there an optimal number of key currencies? History has witnessed periods of using

56

none, one, two and three -- and, now, perhaps, four or even more. Does it make a difference how "multiple" the system is? Does the traditional analysis of a "key currency system" have to be altered substantially if there are several key currencies rather than just one?

Another over-arching question is whether the use of multiple national currencies in international finance is more desirable (or less undesirable) under an adjustment regime of fixed parities or one of managed flexibility. The earlier focus on global liquidity levels and reserve shifts must now be augmented, or even supplanted, by a focus on the impact on the stability and adjustment properties of flexible exchange rates.

Most fundamentally, what are the relative costs and benefits of a multiple reserve currency system in the 1980s and beyond? Such a system would permit at least some reserve holders -- those not constrained by systemic concerns -- to "roll their own" baskets of reserves, realizing their portfolio choices with greater specificity than if they were limited to a set basket via, for example, the SDR. It would probably permit the new reserve centers to finance at least some of their external deficits a bit more easily and perhaps a bit more cheaply. Beyond these elements, which from the standpoint of the system as a whole must be regarded as decidedly secondary, a weighing of the several effects outlined here is needed before judgments can be made regarding the desirability of a multiple reserve currency approach.

Finally, is there a substantial difference (in terms of costs and benefits) between: (1) moving to a multiple currency system; and (2) operating such a system once it is in place? Transitional and steady-state considerations need to be distinguished, to the degree possible, since any major systemic change can be disruptive during the adjustment period. On the other hand, it may be hard to anticipate -- or even to know at the time -- when a new equilibrium has been reached so the distinction may not be very significant in practice.

From the standpoint of an individual key currency country, these systemic issues are of course important. Perspectives on these issues may differ between an "old" reserve currency country whose role is declining and an "new" center on the ascendence. Moreover, each key currency country must address certain additional questions.

A key currency role for an individual country adds to that country's ability to finance external deficits. On the other hand, it can both limit to some extent the country's ability to achieve desired adjustment of its position and force it to adopt undesired adjustment measures.[46] Moreover, a country has to meet a number of economic and political criteria to "quality" for key currency status in the first place and maintain it successfully thereafter, a consideration in assessing the prospect for individual currencies to acquire the status and the advantages of doing so.

There is a close relationship between the systemic and more narrowly reserve-country considerations regarding multiple currency usage. The financing capability provided for an individual country by its currency's role relates directly to the impact of that role on total liquidity available to the system. Indeed, it was the very rapid buildup of international dollar holdings in the late 1960s and early 1970s that generated major criticism of the Bretton Woods system, both for creating excesses in international liquidity and for providing "exhorbitant privileges" to the United States.

Those "exhorbitant privileges" finally came to be viewed by the United States as a burden rather than a benefit, however, primarily because the buildup of dollar holdings by others inhibited the exchange-rate adjustment which it needed it terms both of its own economic objectives and the sustainability of the international economic system itself (including avoidance of protectionist trade legislation).[47] The international use of national currencies can thus affect the adjustment process in ways which are of great importance to both the key-currency countries themselves and to the system.

Declining and ascending key-currency countries may view these same factors in somewhat different ways. The inherent dynamics of key-currency development, as evidenced in the cases of both sterling and the dollar, suggests that the center country will tend to view the benefits as outweighing the costs in the early stages of the process but that it will see the balance moving towards the negative end of the scale as its currency's role evolves over the longer run. The early period offers financing advantages at a time when the individual currency comfortably meets the criteria for laying a major international role. As time progresses, however, the very evolution of the role itself jeopardizes the currency's continued position and adjustment constraints begin to set in. Thus the cost-benefit ratio shifts unfavorably over time, certainly from the standpoint of the key currency country itself and probably -- depending on the available alternatives -- to the system as a whole.

From the standpoint of an "old" reserve currency, the main impact of the advent of a "new" reserve currency is likely to be its availability as an alternative asset and thus a source of added pressure in both the liquidity and adjustment senses -- and hence its contribution to hastening the negative evolution of the cost-benefit ratio for the "old" center. At the same time, it is conceivable that the growing acceptance of greater international monetary responsibility by the "new" currency can somewhat limit that negative evolution. This tradeoff is central to whether the United States will welcome the increasingly important role of the DM, yen and other newcomers to international financial prominence.

V. CONCLUSION

Answers to all these questions will require a series of analyses, including reference to the several historical periods when there existed more than one important international monetary asset. Efforts must be made to determine whether multiple currency usage, on balance, expands the level and volatility of international capital flows. Existing models of exchange-rate determination under the current system of managed flexibility need to be modified to incorporate the growth of multiple currency usage. A better understanding will be needed of the impact, under flexible rates, of the additional volume and altered composition of official reserves that could derive from such a system.

If it turns out that significant costs result from the evolution of a multiple reserve currency regime, attention will have to be directed to possible remedies. Can that evolution be stopped, or at least limited, from the demand and/or supply sides? Can its nature be altered, by creating systemic rules or understandings that would limit the adverse impacts? Or should multiple currency usage be permitted to continue to expand with any policy responses aimed directly at its adverse effects, such as overshooting in the exchange markets (e.g., via agreement on target zones) or destabilizing shifts among currencies (e.g., via creation of a Substitution Account)?

All these issues are central to the management of the international monetary system in the 1980s and beyond. They

61

are equally important to the key countries involved --
particularly the United States, as the "old" reserve center,
and to Germany, as the largest "new" reserve center. They
will require an extended period of careful consideration,
both among governments and in conferences such as the one
for which this paper was prepared.

VI. <u>NOTES</u>

[1] Strictly speaking, all monetary authorities for which the IMF has made available its data on the currency composition of national reserves. The Fund's most recently published disaggregated data cover about 90 percent of all foreign exchange holdings for the 1973-80 period. See IMF <u>Annual Report 1981</u>. A series covering about 66 percent of all holdings in 1976, with less currency disaggregation, has been published for the 1970-76 period in H. Robert Heller and Malcolm Knight, <u>Reserve Currency Preferences of Central Banks</u>, Princeton Essays in International Finance, No. 131 (Dec. 1978).

[2] Even after excluding the conversion of dollars into European Currency Units by members of the European Monetary System. Since this transaction is to be reversed at the conclusion of the "first period" of the EMS, the dollars involved are still treated as dollars in this analysis. In 1979, this conversion added a further decline of almost SDR 13 billion to recorded dollar holdings.

[3] Official U.S. data show a decline in foreign official dollar holdings in the United States during the period when the United States ran official settlement surpluses in the late 1960s (1966, 1968, 1969). However, IMF data reveal that global foreign exchange holdings continued to rise during those years and thus imply that the buildup of official holdings outside the United States -- i.e., in the Eurodollar market, which shows up in the U.S. data as liabilities to private foreigners -- was greater than the decline in direct official dollar holdings in the United States. There are substantial differences between the U.S. and IMF data for any given year, as would be expected in light of the different concepts on which they are based, but they tell the same general story over the full period 1973-80.

[4] The only apparent exception was calendar 1973, when the DM absorbed almost 20 percent, for the more limited group of countries published in Heller and Knight, <u>op. cit.</u>, pp. 3-4.

[5] A more general point suggested by the Japanese example is the paradox that a dollar which is strengthening in the foreign exchange markets may serve to <u>reduce</u> the dollar's share in world reserves, at least initially, because other countries intervene to defend their own currencies primarily by selling dollars in light of the continued role of the dollar as chief intervention

currency. Similarly, and often directly related, U.S. balance-of-payments surpluses may actually absorb dollars from the rest of the world and thereby also reduce the global dollar ratio.

[6] It has frequently been noted, of course, that the "official foreign currency holdings" of some OPEC countries are not "reserves" in the usual sense but are more akin to long-term investments of the national patrimony.

[7] George von Furstenberg, "Comment".

[8] As of this writing, the currency breakdown by country groupings had been published only for the first quarter of 1980. See IMF Survey, Jan. 26, 1981, p. 28.

[9] Group of Thirty, Towards a Less Unstable International Monetary System: Reserve Assets and a Substitution Account, 1980, p. 4.

[10] A projection by IMF staff of the demand for non-gold reserves through 1986 suggests that the combined foreign exchange holdings of oil-exporting countries and non-oil developing countries could rise to 59 percent of the global total, from their combined share of 47 percent in early 1980. Assuming unchanged dollar ratios for all groups of countries, such a shift would reduce the global dollar ratio because the former group had a dollar ratio of 67.3 percent in early 1980 while the industrial countries (excluding the United States) had a dollar ratio of 91.8 percent. However, the reduction would be only three percentage points -- from a little over 80 percent to a little over 77 percent. (These numbers exclude the United States. Including the United States produces the lower global dollar ratio shown in Tables 1 and 2, since the United States by definition holds all of its foreign currency reserves in non-dollar form, but could limit further reductions in the global dollar ratio for the reasons indicated in the text.) These projections are in George von Furstenberg, "Estimates of the Demand for Non-Gold Reserves by Groups of Countries, 1982-1986," unpublished paper, 1981, esp. p. 18.

[11] A similar conclusion as to the basic trend was reached in 1980 by the Group of Thirty, which agreed (op. cit., p. 5) "that the pressures making for a greater degree of currency diversification by official and private holders were likely to persist" and (p. 3) "it is unlikely that the dollar can continue indefinitely to provide some 80 percent of the world's foreign exchange reserves."

[12] The Swiss position is articulated in Fritz Leutwiler, "The Swiss Franc as a Subsidiary Reserve Currency: Problems and Prospects," Aussenwirtschaft, Vol 35, No. 1 (March 1980), esp. p. 32: "We have recently modified somewhat our attitude towards a reserve role for the Swiss franc. In principle, we still do not wish to play the role of a reserve center. However, we realize that the franc will be emphasized at least as a minor international medium of exchange, whether we like it or not. If, to some extent, we have to accept the inevitable, it is far better to influence the course of events than to be overrun by them." The German authorities reached a similar conclusion.

[13] One immediate result of this change, particularly in German and Japanese attitudes toward the international use of their currencies, related to the discussion of possible creation of a Substitution Account through which monetary authorities could exchange their existing dollar reserves for SDR-denominated assets created by the IMF. As late as early 1979, these countries supported creating such an Account because they saw it as a way to deflect international use of their own currencies. At that time, they also envisaged placing some of their own dollars into the Account. By early 1980, however, particularly Germany began to see any such Account as a rival to the increased international use of the DM which had become necessary to finance its own deficits. Moreover, the Germans no longer viewed their own dollar holdings as sufficient to permit any conversion into an SDR-denominated asset. The reluctance of the United States to accept open-ended liabilities regarding dollars deposited in an Account was also a major factor in dissolving active discussion of it, but the more central factor was probably the shift of the new reserve centers into deficit positions and the accelerated evolution of the multiple currency system.

[14] Moreover, a detailed recent analysis of the demand for non-gold reserves concludes that there is not likely to be much substitution between gold and non-gold reserves "in providing a buffer for the financing of payments imbalances." See von Furstenberg, op. cit., pp. 11-13.

[15] Rudiger Dornbusch, in one of the most perceptive efforts to date to apply modern portfolio theory to the international financial system, frankly recognizes that "little is known about the dynamics of portfolio adjustment." See his "Exchange Rate Economics: Where Do We Stand?" Brookings Papers on Economic Activity 1980: 1, p. 168.

[16] Avraham Ben-Bassatt, "The Optimal Composition of Foreign Exchange Reserves," Journal of International Economics, Vol. 10, No. 2 (May 1980), p. 288.

[17] BIS, Fiftieth Annual Report, Basle, June 9, 1980, p. 122.

[18] In his paper for this conference, H. Robert Heller argues that the decline in the dollar's share in the private markets may have about ended with a new equilibrium position at roughly current shares. His argument appears to derive mainly from the slowdown in the decline in the dollar's share in recent years and the continued attractiveness of the U.S. financial markets.

[19] Heller and Knight, op. cit., pp. 10-27, and Ben-Bassatt, op. cit., pp. 293-95.

[20] Ben-Bassatt, op. cit, with some modest supporting evidence from Heller and Knight, op. cit., p. 26.

[21] Heller and Knight, op. cit., p. 7, found that the 27 dollar-peggers in their group maintained a dollar ratio of 85 percent in both 1970 and 1976, though exhibiting some decline in the interim when the dollar depreciated from 1971 to 1973. Moreover, on p. 13, they report that the dollar ratios of dollar-peggers clearly became more pronounced as exchange-rate flexibility became increasingly entrenched from 1973-1976, mainly at the expense of sterling.

[22] Ben-Bassatt, p. 239, similarly found a dollar ratio for industrialized countries well beyond (30 percentage points) his calculated optimum, whereas the dollar ratio for developing countries was much less (14 percentage points) "too high."

[23] C. Fred Bergsten, The Dilemmas of the Dollar: The Economics and Politics of United States International Monetary Policy (New York: New York University Press, for the Council on Foreign Relations, 1975), esp. Chapters 4-6 and pp. 386-80.

[24] Ibid., pp. 386-87.

[25] Ibid., pp. 138-52. See especially the table on p. 149.

[26] Valuing gold at the old official price, the ratios for Germany and Switzerland -- which are the lowest of the "new" centers -- stand at the level reached by the United States in the late 1950s.

[27] This definition may be on the liberal side in that it
encompasses only liabilities to official foreigners,
and that it values gold at current market prices
whereas such prices clearly could not be realized by
official holders if there were any substantial liquidation. On the other hand, the non-gold reserves of
these countries are quite likely to continue rising and
a further rise in the market price of gold is by no
means impossible. In any event, data are not available
on the total external liabilities of the new reserve
centers and the calculations are meant to provide very
rough approximations of overall trends only.

[28] IMF, Annual Report 1980, pp. 106-09. By mid-1980,
there were only three major reserve holders (Iraq,
Libya, Venezuela) among the forty countries still
pegging to the dollar. There was only one major
reserve holder (Iran) among the fifteen countries
pegging to the SDR. Fourteen small countries continued
to peg to the French franc, and only one to sterling.
No country is reported as pegging to any of the three
most rapidly growing key currencies -- the DM, yen or
Swiss franc. Saudi Arabia is listed with the floaters,
but in fact maintains an SDR-denominated parity which
is revalued fairly frequently.

[29] Those now in place are wholly backed by gold and
dollars, and are to be subsequently unwound. The
Commission of the EC, European Economy, No. 3 (July
1979), p. 76, concludes that "...the ECU leads a
precarious existence and its legal basis does not
conform to 'full utilization' as a reserve asset and as
a means of settlement...." Throughout this paper, I
have therefore not treated the ECU as an independent
international monetary asset.

[30] The only notable exception was Gaullist France, and to
a much lesser extent French-influenced Spain, which
bought large quantities of U.S. gold -- which was
possible only because the other major dollar holders
refrained from doing so.

[31] Rimmer de Vries, in Domestic and International Implications of the Federal Reserve's New Policy Actions,
Hearings before the Subcommittee on International
Economics of the Joint Economic Committee, November 5,
1979, p. 68, has pointed out that by resisting international use of their own currencies, however, some of
these same countries encouraged a "carrousel effect" in
the non-dollar Euromarkets.

[32] Peter H. Lindert, Key Currencies and Gold 1900-1913,
Princeton Studies in International Finance, No. 24,
1969, esp. pp. 13-19.

67

[33] During 1933, for example, British holdings of francs on occasion exceeded their dollar balances. See Susan Howson, Sterling's Managed Float: The Operation of the Exchange Equalisation Account, 1932-39, Princeton Studies in International Finance, No. 46, 1980, esp. pp. 58-59.

[34] The view was articulated in May 1962 by Robert V. Roosa, "Multilateralizing International Responsibility" reprinted as Chapter 4 of his Dollar and World Liquidity (New York: Random House, 1967), pp. 57-59. In authorizing open-market transactions in foreign currencies in early 1962, the Federal Open Market Committee indicated as one of its aims "in the long-run to provide a means whereby reciprocal holdings of foreign currencies may contribute to meeting needs for international liquidity as required in terms of the expanding world economy." One observer at the time went so far as to say that "it appears that a tentative decision has been reached to adopt the multiple key-currency proposal as a solution to the anticipated future shortage of international liquidity." See John Williamson, "Liquidity and the Multiple Key-Currency Proposal," American Economic Review, Vol. LIII, No. 3 (June 1963), p. 427.

[35] John Williamson, in "Increased Flexibility and International Liquidity," a paper presented to the Williamsburg conference of the Burgenstock Group, May 1974, p. 11, reported that information available to the IMF staff indicated that the proportion of foreign exchange reserves held in the "new" reserve currencies grew from 5-6 percent of the total in 1964 to about double that figure by March 1973. The IMF Annual Report for 1980, p. 64, however, indicates that the latter figure was only 8.3 percent.

[36] The evolution of a multiple currency system was observed in C. Fred Bergsten, "New Urgency for International Monetary Reform," Foreign Policy 19 (Summer 1975), pp. 92-93 and The Dilemmas of the Dollar, pp. 482-88 and 517, and Benjamin J. Cohen, Organizing the World's Money (New York: Basic Books, 1977), esp. p. 246.

[37] As suggested by Leutwiler, op. cit., p. 30: "[A] multicurrency system ... is highly sensitive to speculative shifts between the various reserve currencies...."

[38] None of the exchange-rate models produced to date have satisfactorily accounted for the widely recognized phenomenon of overshooting. The most successful models focus on the effect of real interest rate differentials; see Jeffrey A. Frankel, "On the Mark: A

Theory of Floating Exchange Rates Based on Real Interest Differentials," American Economic Review, Vol. 69, No. 4 (Sept. 1979), pp. 610-22; and Jurg Niehans, "Monetary Policy with Overshooting Exchange Rates," Economic and Social Review, Vol II, No. 4 (July 1980), esp. pp. 287-90. For a summary analysis see Richard M. Levich, Overshooting in the Foreign Exchange Market, Occasional Paper No. 5 (New York: Group of Thirty, 1981).

[39] Such a view for the dollar and DM is expressed by Dornbusch, "Exchange Rate Economics: Where Do We Stand?", p. 165, and in the comment on Dornbusch's presentation by William H. Branson, p. 192: "This official market 'overhang' of an SDR excess supply of 90 billion in dollars and an SDR excess demand of 30 billion in marks presumably puts persistent demand pressure on the dollar and upward pressure on the mark."

[40] There is a striking parallel between the German reaction of 1980-81 and the U.S. reaction of 1960-61 to the first episodes of real external pressure on their currencies. Both sets of authorities raised interest rates when domestic considerations called for lowering them instead, and issued special securities to help finance their deicits. Ex post analysis (Bergsten, The Dilemmas of the Dollar, chapter 8) suggests that the United States feared a collapse of the "dollar overhang" much more than necessary at that time; it is too early in the evolution of the international role of the DM, of course, to judge whether a similar conclusion holds in the German case.

[41] As argued by Pohl, op. cit., p. 45 and F. A. Lutz, The Problem of International Economic Equilibrium (Amsterdam: North Holland Publishing Co., 1962), pp. 63-66.

[42] One of the earliest analysts of multiple currency usage suggested that such a system promoted "the worst of all adjustment worlds": obviation of adjustment pressures when the reserve centers were running small external deficits, excessive adjustment pressures when those deficits are large. See S. Posthuma, "The International Monetary System," Banca Nazionale del Lavoro Quarterly Review, No. 66 (Sept. 1963), p. 246.

[43] Friedrich A. Lutz, The Problem of International Liquidity and the Multiple-Currency Standard, Princeton Essays in International Finance, No. 41 (March 1963); Posthuma, op. cit.; and Roosa, op. cit.

[44] Williamson, "Liquidity and the Multiple Key-Currency Proposal," pp. 429-30.

[45] As suggested by the Group of Thirty, op. cit., p. 16.

[46] There are a number of other effects, but they are secondary to these two major consideratons. The other benefits to the key currency country include political leverage and financial returns for its banks and other citizens. Other costs include the net interest costs of the key currency role and the political leverage made available to others (e.g., de Gaulle). For a comprehensive analysis of the various costs and benefits, see C. Fred Bergsten, The Dilemmas of the Dollar, chapters 7-9.

[47] The postwar record strongly suggests that an overvalued dollar, as in the late 1960s to the early 1970s, and again in 1975-76, is the greatest single threat to maintenance of a liberal U.S. trade policy. See C. Fred Bergsten, "Trade and Money," Chapter 17 in The International Economic Policy of the United States: Selected Papers of C. Fred Bergsten, 1977-1979 (Lexington, Mass: D.C. Heath & Co., 1980), esp. pp. 177-79.

THE MULTIPLE RESERVE CURRENCY SYSTEN IN THE 1980s

C. Fred Bergsten

COMMENT

Robert Pringle

Executive Director, The Group of Thirty[1]

The multiple reserve asset system into which the world economy has stumbled is a far cry from the orderly arrangements dreamed of by those who, from the 1940s to the 1970s, fought the good fight for the "reform" of the international monetary system. They had wanted a system under which not only exchange rate policies but also the supply of international liquidity were subject to a degree of collective, international decision-making. Indeed, in the later years of that period, there was more concern with introducing greater control over the supply of international liquidity (to ensure it was "adequate") than with further increasing the degree of international influence on national exchange rate policies (reformers sought instead to introduce greater exchange rate flexibility).

But the 1970s were bad times for "reformers" everywhere. In international monetary affairs, as in domestic politics, they were on the defensive. The notion that people could, through purposeful, collective action, take their destiny into their own hands -- the dominant theme in political and economic thought, at least in Europe, for nearly a century -- was at a discount. A demand for greater autonomy in decision-making began to make itself felt, both at the individual level and at the national level. In international finance, the decade witnessed a flowering of private-sector financial markets. This private activity united the world's money and capital markets, enabling massive transfers of savings from surplus to deficit regions, just as had happened within nations through the spread of the banking habit in the eighteenth and nineteenth centuries. Reformers saw themselves on the retreat before the all-conquering forces of "the market". The official system -- what was left of it -- began to seem irrelevant.

So now we have a disintegrated "system", with virtually no international supervision of exchange rates, except in the European Monetary System (and the future of that is now in doubt), and no collective influence on the supply of international liquidity. And Dr. Bergsten does not like that at all. He is not a reformer; he is too realistic for that; but he is an "improver".

Yet this ramshackle system has survived the most severe shocks, such as the quintupling of oil prices. The habits of international monetary cooperation, and the basic framework of an open world economy and trading system, have been preserved. Indeed, the number of countries actively participating in what is rightly called "the international financial community" has grown enormously in recent years. That will come to be regarded as the finest achievement of the world-wide commercial banking networks established in the past 20 years.

Dr. Bergsten is eminently fair in presenting differing viewpoints and hypothesis, and it is doubtless partly because his account of our recent experience is so balanced that I came to the conclusions he presented at the Conference with a feeling of ambivalence.

73

He indicted the multiple currency of certain faults. But I wasn't convinced that they were indeed grievous ones, nor was I confident that the improvements he preliminarly suggested would actually make matters much better.

He raised important questions about the connections between exchange rates swings and the adjustment process. But the preliminary evidence adduced for the proposition that a multiple reserve currency system might seriously aggravate exchange rate volatility seems inconclusive.

There are, of course, other possible explanations of recent exchange rate swings, as Dr. Bergsten pointed out. He noted that the development of such a system has on occasion assisted international adjustment -- notably by forcing greater discipline on the United States, as was appropriate, and by making it easier for Germany (by contrast) to avoid sharp deflationary measures to combat its external deficit. Also, even if one grants that some recent exchange rate movements have been excessive, it is not clear what the influence of official portfolio diversification has been.

It is interesting to note that Bergsten does not convict the system of some of the faults alleged by its sterner critics. He does not allege that the system has systematically fueled world inflation. He does not even allege that the system increases global reserves: "the evolution of a multiple currency system probably has had little net impact on the overall level of world reserves".

74

I wish to suggest one or two reasons for taking a somewhat more optimistic view than Bergsten reached. It is clear that the focus of monetary policy today is on domestic credit creation, the supply of domestic liquidity. From this point of view, the advantages and disadvantages of a multiple reserve currency system can be considered by reference to the incentives it creates, if any, for the adoption of appropriate domestic monetary policies. I suggest it creates a more symmetrical set of incentives than the old system, both for reserve centers and for countries at the periphery.

Reserve centers, both old and new, are encouraged to pursue anti-inflationary policies by the need to retain the attractions of their currencies as international currencies. Real benefits are, after all, derived by a country through the process of extending the domain of its currency (the real benefits to its consumers more than compensate for the additional pain inflicted on its central bankers). In turn, countries at the periphery of the system -- smaller OECD countries and developing countries -- will be offered incentives to maintain reasonable standards of economic management by the need to retain their creditworthiness in the markets. By the same token, the system may also be developing a set of sanctions -- loose and imperfect yet adequate -- against the pursuit of inappropriate policies. Meanwhile, the network of reciprocal financial links established between "creditor" and "debtor" countries both at the official level and in the markets, should help to cement the framework of monetary cooperation.

Competition between national currencies for greater acceptance in the market place goes along with competition between borrowers for the available credit from the banking system. There is nothing inherently inflationary about such a system. If one country increases the supply of its currency faster than the internal and external demand for it, the value of that currency will fall and funds will move to another, more stable, currency. Likewise, the total supply of banking credit will be constrained in the short term by bankers' observance of capital and liquidity ratios and in the long run by the profitability of intermediation. Taxes on the process -- e.g., reserve ratios above those banks wish to observe as a matter of prudent management -- will be evaded or passed on to the consumer.

International cooperative action should, in my personal view, focus not on taxing the system (which will be the effect, if not the intent, of most schemes designed to improve it), but on collaborative measures designed to safeguard the system against the very real emergencies to which all financial markets are liable.

NOTES

[1] This comment is based on the preliminary version of the
paper which Dr. Bergsten presented at the Conference.
The comment does not reflect subsequent modifications
in the paper.

THE MULTIPLE RESERVE CURRENCY SYSTEM IN THE 1980s

C. Fred Bergsten

COMMENT

George M. von Furstenberg

Chief, Financial Studies Division
IMF Research Department [1]

CONTENTS

TABLES

I.   INTRODUCTION

Because Dr. Bergsten has subtitled the paper he delivered at the conference as containing "a very preliminary analysis" let me speak first to factual matters. I shall do so without trying to point a finger at specific numbers or sentences that contain Bergsten's views of the record and outlook. In fact, I agree with many of these views. Thereafter some issues relative to the stability and to the possibly inflationary bias of the evolving multiple currency reserve system are taken up briefly in this comment.

II. THE U.S. DOLLAR IN FOREIGN EXCHANGE RESERVES

The currency composition of about 90 percent of total official holdings of foreign exchange is ascertained by the IMF and reported in its Annual Report and elsewhere.[2] The currency denomination of the remaining 10 percent is not known in most cases and could be largely U.S. dollars. For this reason, caution must be exercised in finding trends in reserve diversification from the data published by the Fund. (An example of the available data appears in Table 1.)

Since March 1979 there is the additional complication that 20 percent of the gross dollar holdings of European Monetary System (EMS) members appears as European Currency Units (ECUs) in the official statistics and that 20 percent of the average value of their gold holdings also appears as ECUs and no longer as part of their gold reserves.[3] Since neither the ultimate title nor the yield and risk

81

Table 1. Average level of Foreign Exchange Reserves, First Quarter of 1980

(In million SDRs)

	Industrial Countries		Oil Exporting Countries	Non-Oil Developing Countries	All Countries
	EMS	Other			
U.S. dollar	58,724	36,807	30,517	31,855	157,903
Pound sterling	295	475	1,338	2,566	4,674
Deutsche mark	3,674	3,974	7,575	8,341	23,564
French franc	30	1	1,020	1,074	2,125
Japanese yen	143	2,006	2,234	1,846	6,229
Swiss franc	1,857	1,154	2,320	911	6,242
Netherlands guilder	326	44	454	650	1,474
All currencies	65,049	44,461	45,458	47,243	202,211

characteristics of dollars and gold are surrendered, transformed, or exchanged when these assets are swapped for ECUs
at quarterly intervals, it is useful to treat ECUs issued
against dollars as dollars and ECUs issued against gold as
gold for the purpose of estimating the composition of
foreign exchange reserves identified by currency.

How then has this composition changed?

During the first four years of floating, the U.S.
dollar's share in official holdings rose from 85 percent to
a peak of 87 percent which was reached at the end of 1976.
This share then declined to 80 percent by the middle of 1979
and further to 75 percent by mid-1980. Nevertheless, at the
most recent date, non-oil developing countries held a higher
percentage of their foreign exchange in U.S. dollars than at
the end of the first quarter of 1973: 64 percent compared
with 59 percent. The industrial countries held higher absolute SDR values of U.S. dollars in the middle of 1980 than
at the end of 1976, although the SDR price of the U.S. dol-
dollar declined by 12 percent over this period. Only the
oil exporting countries allowed the SDR value of their dollar holdings to fall absolutely. The 20 percentage point
reduction of the dollar's share in the holdings of oil exporting countries accounted for over half the total diversification out of the dollar. The divergencies that have occurred between oil exporting and non-oil developing countries caution against interpreting the development of a
multiple currency reserve system as a new and universal

movement.

Moreover, changes in the SDR price of the dollar lead automatically to "diversification" or "concentration." The recent rise in the SDR price of the U.S. dollar is currently working in the direction of raising the dollar's share, although sales of U.S. dollars out of official holdings which are designed to stem this rise may be sufficiently large to overcome the revaluation effect. In the past, the intervention purchases of industrial countries have always caused the dollar's share in the total SDR value of foreign exchange reserves identified by currencies to rise when the SDR price of the dollar declined appreciably. Now that the SDR price of the dollar has been increasing, this same process may work in reverse to reduce the dollar's share if the quantity effects (now negative) again exceed the price effects (now positive) on the dollar's share. For industrial countries at least, any diversification out of the dollar is therefore due to and indicative of the current strength of the dollar. Whether or not it also connotes a desire to permanently reduce the share of dollars in total foreign exchange reserves remains to be seen. My hunch is that should the dollar weaken markedly in the future against other major currencies, the foreign authorities involved would again be willing buyers of dollars while their citizens would be net sellers.[4]

III. STABILITY OF THE MULTIPLE CURRENCY RESERVE SYSTEM

Let me now move from the factual record to a question of interpretation dealing with the stability of the multiple currency reserve system. Professor Kenen has pointed out elsewhere that a multiple currency system is not inherently unstable if exchange rates are allowed to adjust continuously between the currencies involved. It could be added that if such a system is nevertheless unstable, shifts in official holdings are unlikely to be the cause.

About half of the foreign exchange reserves not held in U.S. dollars are held in Deutsche mark. It may therefore be useful to concentrate on the latter to assess whether the rise of currencies other than U.S. dollars in official holdings threatens stability.

There has been little increase in the net foreign exchange exposure of Germany to official foreign holders. Almost 70 percent of the growth between year-end 1976 and mid-1980 of DM liabilities to official agencies of other countries (SDR 16 billion) has been matched by the growth of official foreign exchange reserves held by Germany (SDR 11 billion). In fact, Table 2 shows that almost the entire growth in the net reserve liabilities of the principal reserve currency countries (SDR 25 billion out of SDR 26 billion) was accounted for by the United States. Thus, on a net basis, there has been little growth in the exposure of any of the principal reserve countries other than the United States to flights from their currency by official holders.

85

Table 2. The Change in Domestic Currency <u>Liabilities</u>
to Foreign Official Holders Compared with the Change in
Official Foreign Exchange <u>Assets</u>, Year-End 1976 to mid-1980

(<u>In billions of SDRs</u>)

	Change in Domestic Currency Reserve Liabilities (1)	Change in Total Foreign Exchange Reserve Assets (2)	Change in Net Reserve Liabilities (1) - (2)
United States	29	4	25
Germany	16	11	5
Japan	5	2	3
Switzerland	6	3	3
United Kingdom	3	13	-10
TOTAL:	59 1/	33	26

1/ This amount accounts for almost the entire SDR 61 billion change in
official holdings identified by currency.

86

Almost the entire increase in the liabilities to foreign official holders of reserve countries other than the United States has been covered by corresponding increases in their foreign exchange assets.

Another matter to consider when appraising the stability of the multiple reserve currency system is that private holdings of foreign exchange now dwarf official holdings by a substantial margin. Continuing to focus on Deutsche mark as a case in point, the BIS reported that the external DM assets (and liabilities) of reporting European banks amounted to SDR 81 billion at the end of June 1979. At that time, holdings of DM in foreign exchange reserves amounted to SDR 21 billion, or little more than one-fourth of the sum held by private banks. In mid-1979, Germany itself recognized DM liabilities of SDR 40 (32+8) billion in its balance of payments statistics (Table 3), still twice as large as the SDR amount of DM held by foreign official agencies.

A shift of deposits out of DM and into other currencies would tend to be associated with a liquidation of DM assets that would in turn depress their foreign exchange value. The mass that could be mobilized in such private currency substitutions would dwarf any conceivable move out of official DM holdings both quantitatively and qualitatively. Private currency switches are not constrained by the objective of stabilizing exchange rate movements. By contrast, this objective is shared by a number of official holders and is reinforced by international comity. Thus,

Table 3. Germany: Foreign Liabilities (Assets)
by Currency; Balance of Payments Statistics Stock Data

(In billions of DM or SDRs, EOP)

	DM		SDRs	
	June 1979	June 1980	June 1979	June 1980
(1) Foreign liabilities	145 (222)	183 (236)	61 (93)	78 (101)
(1a) Federal Bank	6 (78)	5 (78)	3 (33)	2 (33)
(1b) Deposit Money Banks	110 (140)	135 (154)	46 (58)	58 (66)
of which:				
-- DM liabilities 1/	77 (103)	94 (115)	32 (43)	40 (49)
-- foreign currency liabilities	33 (37)	41 (39)	14 (15)	18 (17)
(1c) Claims of Foreign Banks on Domestic Nonbanks	29 (4)	43 (4)	12 (2)	18 (2)
of which:				
-- DM liabilities	20 (2)	31 (2)	8 (1)	13 (1)
-- foreign currency liabilities	9 (2)	12 (2)	4 (1)	5 (1)

Source: Deutsche Bundesbank via the Fund's Financial Statistics Division
A, Bureau of Statistics.

1/ Belgium-Luxembourg, the United Kingdom, and Switzerland account for
over half this total.

concern about instability produced by currency switching should be directed to diversified private holdings as the principal mass of maneuver in foreign exchange markets and not primarily to official holdings.

IV. DOES THE MULTIPLE CURRENCY RESERVE SYSTEM HAVE AN INFLATIONARY BIAS?

Another question addressed briefly in Bergsten's paper relates to the inflationary effects of the multiple currency reserve (MCR) system. If faster growth in foreign exchange reserves could somehow be attributed to the transition to generalized floating that provided the basis of the development of an MCR system, there might be a prima facie case for attributing an inflationary bias to the system itself. In fact, however, as Table 4 shows, the SDR value of foreign exchange reserves rose almost four times as rapidly from the end of 1968 to the end of 1972 in relation to the growth in the SDR value of imports than in the eight years that have passed since.

To the extent inflationary forces are transmitted through high rates of growth of foreign exchange reserves because of incomplete sterilization (complete sterilization or the maintenance of inflation rates quite different from those in the United States may make little sense if the preservation of fixed exchange rates is the paramount policy objective), such transmission has been greatly reduced by the transition to managed floating. That change in exchange

Table 4. The Percentage Growth of the
SDR Values of Foreign Exchange Reserves and of Imports,
All Countries, Year-Ends 1968-72 and 1972-80

(In per cent or ratio of percentage)

Period	Foreign Exchange Reserves (1)	Merchandise Imports (2)	Ratio (1)/(2)
1968-72	295	74	3.99
1972-80	303	291 1/	1.04

1/ Based on incomplete data.

rate regime, in turn, makes the evolution of a reasonably stable multiple reserve currency system feasible. It also makes any single reserve currency system appear as an anachronism inherited from a different regime.

V.   <u>NOTES</u>

[1] The views expressed are personal and do not reflect those of the International Monetary Fund.

[2] See, for instance, <u>IMF Survey</u>, January 26, 1981, p. 28, Table 3.B., which is shown as Table 1 of this comment.

[3] At the end of 1979, SDR 19.7 billion of ECUs issued against gold and SDR 12.8 billion issued against dollars were contained in the total of SDR 32.5 billion of ECUs outstanding. This total has risen to SDR 47.5 billion by the end of 1980. Because of increases in the ECU price of gold used by the EMS, the gold part advanced to SDR 37.3 billion while the dollar part fell to SDR 10.2 billion.

[4] The extent to which U.S. nationals without significant foreign payments obligations may have been inclined to diversify their liquid asset portfolios by currency is explored in George M. von Furstenberg, "Incentives for International Currency Diversification by U.S. Financial Investors," International Monetary Fund <u>Staff Papers</u>, forthcoming September 1981.

CHAPTER THREE

BALANCING THE SYSTEM IN THE 1980s: PRIVATE BANKS AND THE IMF

Benjamin J. Cohen

William L. Clayton
Professor of International Economic Affairs
Fletcher School of Law and Diplomacy
Tufts University

CONTENTS

TABLES

I. INTRODUCTION

Of all the consequences of the steep increases of world oil prices since 1973, few have been more dramatic than the manner in which balance-of-payments deficits are financed. Rising oil prices have generated severe financing problems for many oil-importing countries (the petro-dollar recycling problem). In lieu of commensurate increases of financing from official sources such as the International Monetary Fund, the task has fallen largely to the private credit markets to recycle surplus earnings of oil-exporting countries onward -- via bond issues and, especially, via bank credits -- to nations in external deficit. As a result, the markets have now come to play a role in "balancing" the system once reserved, in principle, exclusively for multilateral agencies -- in particular, the IMF. As one former central banker has put it, "the private banking system took over the functions proper to an official institution possessed of the power to finance balance-of-payments disequilibria through credit-granting and to create international liquidity... The function of creating international liquidity has been transferred from official institutions to private ones."[1]

Not that the practice of private lending for balance-of-payments purposes is entirely new. Even back in the late 1960s, as much as one-third of all international liquidity creation was occurring through the intermediation of banking institutions between surplus countries (in those days,

96

mainly countries of the Group of Ten) and deficit countries. But up to 1973, the market's role still tended to be relatively modest. It was only with the emergence of the petro-dollar recycling problem that banks came into their own as a major alternative to the IMF as a source of payments financing. A special report to the Organization for Economic Cooperation and Development in 1977 -- the McCracken Group Report -- perhaps best described the development in its historical perspective:

> The shift to increased reliance on private lenders for official financing purposes marked the culmination of a secular transformation of the process of liquidity creation. This transformation had already been going on for some time. Its roots lay in the development of the international financial markets -- in particular, the growth of the Euro-dollar market -- which gradually made it easier for governments to rely on private international financial intermediation rather than on the deficits of reserve centers to obtain new monetary reserves. The international markets act as worldwide financial intermediaries between the lenders and borrowers of loanable funds (including official as well as private lenders and borrowers). Private capital and the accumulated reserves of surplus countries flow into the market and then ultimately are lent on to countries in balance-of-payments difficulties. Increases of demand for credit in borrowing countries are financed by the markets, within the usual institutional and legal constraints, by borrowing or attracting deposits from the banking systems of surplus countries with available loanable funds. The events of 1974-76 simply confirmed and accelerated a trend in the process of liquidity creation that had been evident well before the oil price increases of 1973.[2]

This may be only a change of degree -- but it is a change of degree so profound that it borders on a transformation of kind. It is this transformation of the process of international liquidity creation that is the subject of my paper.

In what follows, I first describe how the transformation came about (Section II), and then review some of the
major changes that have occurred in the relationship between
banking institutions and the IMF since 1973 (Section III).
Then, after Section IV, which attempts to project forward to
the 1980s to give some rough idea of the probable magnitude,
duration, and distribution of the recycling problem, I
discuss the prospective roles to be played by banks (Section
V and VI) and by the IMF (Sections VII, VIII, and IX) in
balancing the system during the coming decade. The paper
concludes with a brief summary and conclusion in Section X.

II. THE TRANSFORMATION OF THE SYSTEM

The story of how the process of international liquidity
creation came to be so dramatically transformed is of course
well known and requires only brief summation here.[3] Once
oil prices began to rise in late 1973, it was clear that
oil-importing countries as a group would for some time face
extremely large current-account deficits in their relations
with oil producers. Some of the largest producers in the
Organization of Petroleum Exporting Countries simply could
not increase their imports of goods and services as quickly
as their revenues: their "absorptive capacity," at least in
the short term, was too low. Accordingly, the balance of
their earnings -- their "investable surplus" -- perforce
would have to be invested in foreign assets or otherwise
lent back to oil-importing nations as a group. But since

reflows of funds from OPEC's "low absorbers" could not be counted upon to match up precisely with the distribution of deficits among oil importers, some of the latter were bound to find themselves in serious payments difficulties. From the standpoint of oil importers as a group, the problem was to insure that nations in overall imbalance would somehow be able to finance their deficits by borrowing sufficient amounts of money at reasonable terms. This in turn would require flows of funds among non-OPEC countries, to channel oil revenues from importers benefitting most from OPEC investments to those who were most in need -- in other words, a recycling of OPEC's investable surplus. Faute de mieux, major responsibility for this task of balancing the system fell to private banking institutions.

The impact of rising oil prices on global payments patterns after 1973 can be seen in Table 1. Prior to 1973, the major oil-exporting countries had tended to run modest surpluses on current account; the industrial group, rather large surpluses; and other non-oil countries, a collective deficit. The effect of OPEC's much larger surpluses after 1973 was to transform the industrial group too into a deficit area (in most years) and to increase enormously the magnitude of the deficits of other oil-importers (including not only the non-oil developing countries but also the East European bloc). In 1975, the industrial countries briefly enjoyed a renewed surplus (as domestic recession cut into the volume of oil imports, offsetting the effect of higher

99

Table 1

Global Payments Balances on Current Account, 1967–80[a]
(billions of dollars)

	1967–72 annual average	1973	1974	1975	1976	1977	1978	1979	1980[e]
Major oil-exporting countries[b]	0.7	6.6	67.8	35.0	40.0	31.9	5.0	68.4	115
Industrial countries[c]	10.2	19.3	-11.6	17.9	-0.5	-4.1	33.4	-9.8	-50
Non-oil developing countries[d]	-9.8	-11.5	-36.9	-45.9	-32.9	-28.6	-35.8	-52.9	-70
Total	1.1	14.4	19.3	7.0	6.6	-0.8	2.6	5.7	-5

Source: International Monetary Fund, Annual Reports.

a. On goods, services, and private transfers.
b. Includes Oman and all members of OPEC except Gabon and Ecuador. This group comprises only those countries whose net oil exports both account for at least two-thirds of the country's total exports and are at least 100 million barrels a year.
c. Includes all members of OECD except Greece, Portugal, and Turkey.
d. Includes all other IMF members (except People's Republic of China).
e. Estimates.

prices), as well as in 1978 (when the OPEC group's absorption of imports was starting to catch up with the growth of its revenues). But with the renewed upsurge of oil prices after the end of 1978, these surpluses once again disappeared. For all oil-importers taken together, over the seven years from 1974 through 1980, combined current-account deficits added up to more than $300 billion.

Of these deficits, it was clear that only a relatively small proportion could be financed by means of direct movements of existing monetary reserve assets from oil consumers to oil producers. In 1973, total reserves of all non-oil countries stood at approximately $140 billion (including gold valued at the former official price of $42.22 per ounce). This total would have been quickly exhausted had countries not had the alternative of borrowing abroad to meet their increased financing requirements. The largest part of the deficits after 1973 had to be financed by running up foreign debts rather than by running down foreign reserves -- "liability financing" rather than "asset financing" of imbalances. The most important source of external financing turned out to be the private sector rather than official lending agencies.

Official lending agencies, it is true, took a variety of steps after 1973 in an attempt to provide sufficient additional financing for deficit countries. But the expansion of such sources simply did not manage to keep pace with increased need.

As might be expected, the broadest effort was undertaken by the IMF. Despite several new initiatives, however,
its contribution to resolution of the petro-dollar recycling
problem, in quantitative terms, was really quite modest.
What was needed from the Fund, plainly, was not just an
increase of members' quotas (which has in fact occurred
twice since 1973) but, even more importantly, an increase of
access to the Fund's resources beyond the strict limits set
by its system of quotas. (Under the quota system established by the Fund's original Articles of Agreement, each
member-country was entitled, when short of reserves, to
"purchase" -- i.e., borrow -- amounts of foreign exchange
from the fund in return for equivalent amounts of its own
currency, with maximum purchases set equal to the member's
initial subscription of reserve assets, representing 25
percent of its quota (its "reserve tranche") plus four
additional amounts each also equal to 25 percent of its
quota (its "credit tranches"). "Repurchases" -- i.e.,
repayments -- were generally expected to be made within 3-5
years.)

Precedent for an expansion of access to Fund resources
already existed in two special facilities that had been
created earlier, during the 1960s, to help members cope with
particular types of payments problems -- the Compensatory
Financing Facility, established in 1963 to assist countries,
particularly producers and exporters of primary products,
experiencing temporary shortfalls of export revenues for

reasons largely beyond their own control; and the Buffer Stock Facility, established in 1969 to assist countries participating in international buffer-stock arrangements designed to stabilize the price of a specific primary product. Each of these two facilities initially permitted a member to borrow an amount equal to 50 percent of its quota over and above its regular credit tranches.[4]

Building on these precedents, the Fund in the 1970s erected several more such special facilities in an effort to cope with its members' increased need for financing, including a temporary one-year Oil Facility (1974), to help countries meet the initial balance-of-payments impact of higher oil prices; a second one-year Oil Facility (in 1975); an Extended Fund Facility (1974), to provide financing for longer periods (up to ten years) and in larger amounts (up to 140 percent of quota) for members experiencing "structural" balance-of-payments problems; a Trust Fund (1976), to provide special assistance to the Fund's poorest members (for up to ten years) out of the proceeds of sales of a portion of the Fund's gold holdings; and a Supplementary Financing Facility (1979), also known as the Witteveen Facility, to provide extra credit to members experiencing very large deficits in relation to their quotas. By the end of 1980, as a result of these and related initiatives, a country could in principle borrow as much as 200 percent of its quota in each of three successive years -- 600 percent in all -- as compared with the 125 percent authorized under

103

the original Articles of Agreement.[5]

But, unfortunately, even this was not enough. The magnitude of deficits after 1973 was simply too great, and much of what the Fund did was really a case of too little and too late. As can be seen in Table 2, even at its peak in the Fund's fiscal year ending April 1976, its net annual lending never exceeded 5.6 billion SDRs (approximately $6-1/2 billion). In fiscal years 1978 and 1979, the Fund actually became a net user of financial resources, as repayments to it of outstanding credits exceeded new loans to members.

Other official initiatives turned out to be equally inadequate. The European Community's special Balance of Payments Financing Program, established after the initial rise of oil prices, never lent more than quite limited amounts of money; and the OECD's proposed $25 billion Financial Support Fund never even got off the ground. Bilateral government-to-government loans were significant only in a few isolated cases (the most prominent being the loans by the German Bundesbank to Italy in 1975-76).

Because official sources failed to keep pace, deficit countries were forced to look to the private sector -- and the markets did not fail to respond. After 1973, the volume of lending through international credit markets, particularly in the form of bank credits, grew enormously, as Table 3 shows. Very quickly private banking institutions came to represent, in quantitative terms, the world's single

Table 2

Net Lending ^a/ by the International Monetary Fund, 1973–80
(millions of SDRs)

Financial Year Ended April 30

	1973	1974	1975	1976	1977	1978	1979	1980
Total loans	1,175	1,058	5,102	6,591	4,942	2,771	4,390	3,897
Reserve tranche	641	607	981	1,324	161	136	2,480	222
Credit tranche	323	239	1,604	461	2,370	1,937	485	1,106
Buffer Stock Facility	5	--	--	5	--	--	48	26
Compensatory Financing Facility	206	212	18	828	1,753	322	465	863
Extended Facility	--	--	--	8	190	109	242	216
Oil Facility	--	--	2,499	3,966	437	--	--	--
Trust Fund	--	--	--	--	32	268	670	962
Supplementary Financing Facility	--	--	--	--	--	--	--	502
Total repayments	540	672	518	960	868	4,485	4,859	3,776
Net lending (+)	+635	+386	+4,584	+5,631	+4,074	-1,714	-469	+121

a. Includes only "purchases" (loans) and "repurchases" (repayments) from the IMF General
Resources Account, plus Trust Fund and Supplementary Financing Facility loans;
excludes SDR allocations, restitution of a portion of the Fund's gold holdings to
members, and distribution of profits from sales of a portion of the Fund's gold holdings.

Source: International Monetary Fund, Annual Reports.

Table 3

Private International Lending, 1973-79
(billions of dollars)

Lenders	1973	1974	1975	1976	1977	1978	1979
Banks in European reporting countries[a]	+62.2	+35.0	+50.5	+55.7	+80.6	+145.2	+164.8
of which in foreign currency (Euro-currency market)	(+56.8)	(+26.8)	(+42.9)	(+47.2)	(+68.5)	(+117.2)	(+137.9)
Banks in Canada and Japan	+5.4	+5.1	-0.3	+4.8	+0.8	+16.2	+15.0
Banks in the United States	+6.0	+19.5	+13.6	+21.3	+11.5	+37.8	+17.1
Branches of U.S. banks in offshore centers[b]	+14.1	+12.6	+15.0	+23.8	+16.2	+15.4	+21.2
Total (all reporting banks)	+87.7	+72.2	+78.8	+105.6	+109.1	+214.6	+218.1
minus: double-counting due to redepositing among the reporting banks	n.a.	n.a.	38.8	35.6	34.1	104.6	88.1
A = Net new international bank lending[c]			40.0	70.0	75.0	110.0	130.0
Euro-bond and foreign issues	9.9	12.3	22.8	34.3	36.1	37.3	37.1
minus: redemptions and repurchases[d]	n.a.	n.a.	3.3	4.3	5.1	8.3	9.6
B = Net new international bond financing			19.5	30.0	31.0	29.0	27.5
A + B = Total new bank and bond financing			59.5	100.0	106.0	139.0	157.5
minus: double-counting[e]			2.5	3.5	4.0	6.0	7.5
Total net new bank and bond financing			57.0	96.5	102.0	133.0	150.0

Source: Bank for International Settlements, Annual Reports.

a. Belgium, Luxembourg, France, Germany, Italy, Netherlands, Sweden, and the United Kingdom, plus Switzerland (from 1975) and Austria, Denmark, and Ireland (from 1978).
b. Bahamas, Cayman Islands, Panama, Hong Kong, and Singapore.
c. In addition to direct claims on end-users, these estimates unavoidably include certain interbank positions.
d. These figures are based on very rough guesses and are inserted mainly for purposes of illustration.
e. Bonds taken up by reporting banks, to the extent that they are included in the banking statistics, and bonds issued by reporting banks for the purpose of underpinning their international lending activity.

106

greatest source of financing for balance-of-payments purposes. This development was in effect the "flip side" of
OPEC's relatively low short-term absorptive capacity.
Insofar as the imports of the largest oil producers could
not keep pace with their rapidly rising revenues, their
investable surplus had to be placed somewhere; and the most
attractive options clearly were to be found in Western
financial markets. This in turn spurred banking institutions to search for new outlets for their greatly enhanced
liquidity. Seemingly among the most attractive of such
outlets were countries in need of supplementary balance-of-
payments financing.

Not all countries were able to avail themselves of such
financing, of course. Poorer LDCs, lacking any standing at
all in international credit markets, still had to rely on
official bilateral or multilateral sources for most of their
foreign borrowing. But for developing nations that were
regarded by the markets as sufficiently creditworthy, as
well as for most members of the OECD, the bulk of payments
financing now came to originate from private sources inter-
mediating between surplus and deficit countries. As a
result, banks found themselves with a dramatic new role to
play in global monetary relations.

III. THE RELATIONSHIP BETWEEN THE BANKS AND THE FUND
Not that all concerned were entirely relaxed about the
banks' new role -- quite the contrary, in fact. The

107

benefits were obvious: had the markets not performed so effectively in recycling petro-dollars, a costly and mutually frustrating scramble among oil importers to pass around their collective deficit might well have ensued. Private lending clearly helped to avert a grave crisis in global monetary relations. But at what price? Risks were evident too, as many observers noted.[6] Unlike the IMF, private banking institutions had neither the legal authority nor (usually) the inclination to make loans to deficit countries subject to policy conditions. Thus, countries that were regarded by the markets as creditworthy were formally unconstrained in their access to financing, so long as they were willing and able to pay the going rate of interest. This created a danger that some countries might be tempted by the availability of such relatively "easy" (i.e., unconditional) financing to postpone painful -- even if necessary -- adjustment measures. Put differently, it suggested that the efficiency of the international adjustment process might be seriously impaired.

The danger was widely acknowledged. Said Wilfried Guth, a prominent German banker, in 1977: "The banks as today's main international creditors are unable to bring about by themselves a better balance between external adjustment and financing."[7] And his sentiment was echoed by Arthur Burns, former chairman of the Federal Reserve Board of Governors, who admitted that "Countries thus find it more attractive to borrow than to adjust their monetary

and fiscal policies."[8]   The problem was best summarized by
the IMF:

>   Access to private sources of balance-of-payments
> finance may ... in some cases permit countries to
> postpone the adoption of adequate domestic stabiliza-
> tion measures.   This can exacerbate the problem of
> correcting payments imbalances, and can lead to adjust-
> ments that are politically and socially disruptive when
> the introduction of stabilization measures becomes
> unavoidable.[9]

Nor was the danger merely hypothetical.   In fact, the
IMF's scenario accurately described what actually occurred
in a number of individual instances.   In Peru, for example,
in 1976, at a time when the country's balance of payments
was under severe pressure owing to plummeting prices for
copper (a major Peruvian export) as well as to a mysterious
disappearance of anchovy stocks from offshore waters (essential for fishmeal, another major Peruvian export), the
government used a new $835 million syndicated bank credit to
avoid painful adjustment measures, such as credit restraints
or cutbacks of fiscal expenditures.   (The government even
announced, shortly after the credit was negotiated, plans to
purchase $250 million worth of fighter bombers from the
Soviet Union.)   The result was further deterioration of
Peru's external balance, domestic social and political
unrest, and eventually even more stringent austerity measures when the government was finally obliged to adopt an
effective stabilization program in 1978.[10]

Similar cases could also be cited elsewhere, e.g.,
Turkey and Zaire after 1975.   In these countries, too,
access to market financing apparently encouraged the

authorities to postpone needed adjustment measures, with consequences ultimately very much like those in Peru.

But this does not mean that all countries yielded to the temptation to postpone needed adjustment measures. In fact, for any example such as the three above, one could cite a variety of counter-examples of countries that at one time or another used their access to market financing to underwrite immediate and effective actions to restore balance-of-payments equilibrium. Particularly impressive was the case of Korea following the rise of oil prices in 1973 and the onset of recession in its principal export markets (the United States and Japan) in 1974. While relying on borrowing in international credit markets to bridge a widening payments gap, the Korean authorities instituted an intensive program of export promotion supplemented by a modest relaxation of monetary and fiscal policy to cushion the domestic impact of recession in foreign markets. In effect, the market financing was used to give the economy a breathing space to reallocate resources to the export sector in a context of continuing real growth. Similar cases could also be cited elsewhere, e.g., Argentina in 1976 and Spain in 1977.

Still, little comfort could be drawn from such "success stories." As the three prior examples demonstrated, the danger inherent in the availability of relatively "easy" financing from the markets was real -- and no one was more aware of it than banking institutions themselves. Certainly

110

the banks recognized that it was not in their interest to make loans to any country which would then do little to ensure its future capacity to service such debt. They, no less than anyone else, had no wish to throw good money after bad. The problem, however, from their point of view, was one of leverage: What, in practice, could they do to ensure that sovereign borrowers would indeed undertake policies that promised a genuine process of adjustment to external deficit?

Variations of terms on offer in the marketplace (e.g., a rise of interest rates or a shortening of maturities) seemed to have little influence on the policies of borrowing governments. As one central banker conceded, it was difficult to "regard this as more than a very marginal contribution to adjustment."[11] Potentially more effective might have been variations of access to the market (whatever the terms on offer) -- i.e., shifts in market sentiment regarding a sovereign borrower's creditworthiness. But the difficulty with that approach was that it might cut off a country's access to financing just when it was most needed. It was certainly not in the banks' interest to force a nation into outright default on its foreign debt.

An alternative approach might have been to exert discipline directly on a borrower through imposition of comprehensive policy conditions. In fact, this was attempted only once -- in the 1976 credit to Peru, which was split into two installments, the first to be drawn immediately, the second in early 1977. Peru's creditors thought that they could ensure adherence to an effective stabilization program by establishing a system for continuous monitoring of the Peruvian economy and by making the second installation of their loan formally contingent upon satisfactory performance. The effort was unique. It was also a failure. In the end, when the loan's second installment came due, no delay was ever seriously mooted despite Peru's plainly evident failure to meet its policy commitments. The banks, as private institutions, simply did not have the legal or political leverage to dictate policy directly to a sovereign government. Since that episode, they have not even tried.

Instead, private lenders have turned increasingly to the IMF, the one lender which, as a multilateral institution backed by formal treaty commitments, does have the requisite legal and political leverage to exercise policy conditionality. In a growing number of instances, where doubts have existed about a country's prospective policy stance, borrowers have been told to go to the IMF first: formally or informally, new financing from the markets has been made contingent upon negotiation of a satisfactory stabilization program with the Fund. As a result, in such cases the Fund has come to play a role as a sort of de facto certifier of creditworthiness in the markets -- the official issuer of an unofficial "Good Housekeeping Seal of Approval."[12] As one banker has said: "Conditional credit from the Fund is increasingly viewed as an 'international certificate of

112

approval' which enhances the ability of a country to borrow in the private marketplace."[13] The procedure has been favored by lenders because of the Fund's high professional standards, its access to confidential information, and -- above all -- its recognized right to exercise policy conditionality. This role has been accepted by the Fund because, in effect, it "gears up" the IMF's own lending while ensuring that new financing in such cases will be used to support a well conceived process of adjustment. And it has been tolerated by borrowers because it has preserved the banks' new role in balancing the system.

IV. RECYCLING IN THE 1980s

A key question for the 1980s is whether banks will be willing and able to continue playing this critical balancing role. For an answer, it is first necessary to determine the magnitude of the problem involved -- that is, (1) how large the OPEC surplus is likely to be; and (2) how the counterpart deficits among oil importers are likely to be distributed.

1. The OPEC Surplus

As is well known, the evolution of OPEC's investable surplus has proved extraordinarily difficult to forecast.[14] Early projections of the financial accumulations of oil producers proved far too pessimistic, primarily because they failed to anticipate the rapid growth of OPEC's import absorption after 1973. Later projections proved far too optimistic, primarily because they failed to anticipate the renewed upsurge of OPEC prices after 1978. Similar difficulties make forecasts for the 1980s equally problematic.

Nonetheless, some idea of the probable order of magnitude of OPEC's surplus can be gained by looking at recent projections by Morgan Guaranty Trust Company (whose early forecasts for the 1970s proved to be among the most accurate published).[15] In the September 1980 issue of its monthly World Financial Markets, Morgan Guaranty outlined three alternative scenarios for the period to 1985, distinguished chiefly by differing assumptions about the future trend of oil prices: (i) a "base case," with the real price of oil (i.e., the nominal price of oil relative to prices of other goods and services) rising by an average of 3 percent per annum; (ii) an "optimistic case," with the real price of oil remaining unchanged; and (iii) a "pessimistic case," with the real price of oil rising by an average of 7 percent per annum. The resulting projections, reproduced in the top line of Table 4, differ considerably:

(i) In the base case, OPEC's surplus declines from 1980 but remains close to $80 billion during 1983-85.

(ii) In the optimistic case, OPEC's surplus rapidly dwindles, in effect replicating the experience of the years 1975-78 (when oil prices were essentially flat in real terms).

114

Current-Account Balances of Selected Countries, 1974-85: Three Scenarios by Morgan Guaranty Trust Company
(billions of dollars, annual averages)

	1974-75	1976-79	1980	1981[e]	Base Case		Optimistic Case		Pessimistic Case	
					1982	1983-85	1982	1983-85	1982	1983-85
OPEC	+51	+36	+118	+90	+87	+76	+68	+33	+91	+130
10 small industrial countries[a]	-12.5	-11.6	-25.3	-26.9	-22	-25	-17	-2	-23	-69
12 major non-oil LDCs[b]	-14.6	-12.0	-38.3	-45.1	-40	-51	-34	-22	-43	-103

Base Case: Real price of oil rises by 3% per annum in 1982-85.

Optimistic Case: Real price of oil remains unchanged after 1981.

Presimistic Case: Real price of oil rises by 7% per annum in 1982-85.

Source: Morgan Guaranty Trust Company, World Financial Markets, September 1980.

a. Australia, Denmark, Finland, Greece, Ireland, New Zealand, Portugal, Spain, Sweden, Yugoslavia.
b. Argentina, Bolivia, Brazil, Chile, Colombia, India, Ivory Coast, Korea, Philippines, Taiwan, Thailand, Turkey.
e. Estimate assuming a 1% rise of the real price of oil in 1981.

(iii) In the pessimistic case, OPEC's surplus, after falling temporarily in 1981-82, rises again to a level of about $130 billion in 1983-85.

Of these three scenarios, which is apt to prove closest to the mark? My own view is that on average oil prices are most likely to continue rising in real terms. Indeed, there seems little question that economic as well as political factors will continue to exert upward pressure on oil prices so long as these prices remain below the level at which substitute fuels could become available in sufficient quantitities.[16] The reasons are clear:

(i) Even quite conservative projections of the growth of global demand for oil suggest continued pressure on current and prospective supply in the medium-term. Conservation efforts in the major consuming countries have proceeded rather more slowly than had been hoped, and cost factors as well as environmental considerations are likely to continue to forestall very rapid expansion of alternative energy sources (e.g., coal, nuclear, synfuels, geothermal, etc.). Short of a major and sustained recession in the industrial world, therefore, growth of global demand can on these grounds alone by expected to leave little or no margin over available supply. Taking account as well of demand for stockpiling purposes, which can certainly be expected to remain strong, the conclusion seems unavoidable. World oil-market conditions will remain tight through at least the middle of the present decade, even if current levels of production in the main exporting countries are maintained.

(ii) Unfortunately, it is also not at all likely that current levels of production in many exporting countries will be maintained. Political pressures within OPEC to conserve petroleum resources and lower production have become stronger in recent years and are still growing. Increasingly, OPEC countries regard their production decisions in portfolio terms, i.e., as a trade-off between one type of asset (oil in the ground) and another (paper in the bank). And with worldwide inflation and exchange-market instabilities threatening the long-term value of paper assets, it is little wonder that most producers have begun to alter their preferences in favor of keeping oil in the ground. The frequency of decisions by individual OPEC countries in recent years to reduce production levels, ostensibly for "technical" reasons, is no accident. Quite the contrary, it is in fact a highly rational response to these countries' central problem of portfolio management. The most likely scenario is that the majority of OPEC's members will continue to adjust the level of their output to exploit the apparent inelasticity of global oil demand. The result should be even greater upward pressure on oil prices.

(iii) In addition, one cannot rule out the risk of political upheavals in or among producer countries. Neither the Iranian revolution nor the Iran-Iraq War was expected. In an area as potentially volatile as the Gulf region, the risk of similar shocks is very high. The 1979 attack on the

117

Grand Mosque of Mecca suggests that the apparent stability of even the Saudi regime must be regarded as questionable; how much more so some of the smaller producer states, with their narrow ruling elites and large foreign labor populations. In a global market where supply and demand are so finely balanced, even a small shortfall of supply can generate a sharp upward movement of prices. And as the experience of the past two years testifies, even very short-term price increases tend to "stick," owing to the continued wide gap between oil prices and the effective cost of alternative energy sources. In effect, there is a "ratchet effect" at work to ratify the economic consequences of political disturbances. This will almost certainly result in a greater increase of the real price of oil over time than might otherwise be expected on the grounds of purely economic analysis.

(iv) Finally, we must acknowledge that the major consuming countries -- in particular, the United States -- are much less able now than before to bring political leverage to bear on developments in the market. In 1973-74, America was on much better terms with both Iran and Saudi Arabia than it is today. At present, the ability and willingness of the United States to protect Western interests in the Gulf region is held in question, and even Saudi Arabia has distanced itself to a certain extent from close alignment with American policy objectives. The evidence can be seen, for instance, in the Saudi Government's admitted reluctance to maintain for long production above its "normal" (i.e., desired) rate of 8.5 million barrels a day, despite repeated pleas from the United States; as well as in its past threats to reduce output should America accelerate purchases for its strategic oil reserve. The effect is to remove a non-economic constraint on economic forces exerting upward pressure on oil prices.

For all these reasons, I see no way of avoiding a continued rise of the real price of oil on average through at least the middle of the present decade. To be sure, at the moment some dampening of upward pressure after the recent run-up of prices has become evident, partly as a result of slackened growth in the industrial world; and partly as a result of the Saudi Arabian Government's declared policy of "engineering" a glut in order to compel other OPEC members to accept a unified, long-term, price-indexation formula. But such softness is hardly likely to persist, unless the setback to growth in oil-importing countries turns out to be much deeper and more prolonged than most experts currently predict, or the effective cost of alternative energy sources turns out to be much lower than most experts currently believe. If the Saudi formula is adopted, oil prices would rise automatically at rates somewhat higher than inflation. But even if it is not, renewed real price increases must be expected in the medium-term.

Assuming this to be the case, OPEC's surplus will

necessarily remain large. By definition, an increase of the surplus can be avoided only if OPEC's absorptive capacity rises pari passu with its income, as it did (albeit with a lag) after the first jump of prices in 1973-74. Some commentators profess themselves to be rather sanguine on this score.[17] But in my view circumstances today differ significantly from those of the 1970s. In the 1980s, many OPEC countries appear neither as willing nor as able to raise their expenditures as rapidly as before. The changes in Iran are, of course, a major difference. In addition, other OPEC countries such as Algeria and Nigeria seem to be running up against real limitations on their ability to absorb foreign imports at faster rates, while Saudi Arabia and some of the smaller Gulf producers are becoming increasingly concerned that faster rates of growth could eventually generate severe internal social and political instabilities. Indeed, one of the main reasons why Saudi Arabia and its allies in the Gulf region (OPEC's price "doves") have tried to hold down price increases is to prevent too rapid growth of their spendable revenues; but so long as the "hawks" in OPEC (led by Libya and Algeria) are able to promote a policy of production cuts to raise prices, the surpluses of the "low absorbers" are bound to rise pari passu. The prospect therefore, in my judgment, is for the collective OPEC surplus to remain sizable through at least the middle of the present decade. Even Morgan Guaranty's base-case scenario could turn out to be overly optimistic.

2. The Distribution of Deficits

If forecasting the size of OPEC's surplus is difficult, forecasting the distribution of the counterpart deficits among oil importers is well nigh impossible. However, if the experience of the 1970s is at all useful as a guide, we may fairly conclude that, as before, the largest share of the burden is likely to be borne by two relatively narrow groups of countries -- (i) the smaller members of the OECD, and (ii) newly industrializing nations of the Third World. From 1974 through 1980, these two groups accounted for as much as two-thirds to three-quarters of the combined current deficits of all oil importers, and were among the largest of all borrowers in international credit markets.

As a companion to its projections of OPEC's surplus to 1985, Morgan Guaranty also estimated the probable deficits of ten small industrial countries and twelve major non-oil LDCs that have been particularly heavy borrowers in recent years. Reproduced in the second and third lines of Table 4, these estimates suggest that the more oil prices rise, the greater will be the proportionate burden borne by these 22 countries. Indeed, in Morgan Guaranty's pessimistic case, their combined deficits would actually exceed OPEC's surplus; and even if the real price of oil were to remain unchanged through 1985, they would account for more than two-thirds of the total.

Much the same conclusion may also be drawn from recent projections by the World Bank in its 1980 World Development

121

Report, reproduced in Table 5. Of all oil-importing developing countries, "middle-income" countries (i.e., LDCs with a GNP per person above $360) are expected to account for three-quarters or more of combined current-account deficits in the present decade -- a situation essentially unchanged from the decade of the 1970s. The category of middle-income countries includes virtually all of the LDCs that have been significant borrowers from the markets in recent years.

V.   NEW CAUTION AMONG PRIVATE BANKS

Thus, it appears likely that the OPEC surplus will continue to be relatively large over the next few years at least, and that the counterpart deficits among oil importers will continue to be concentrated in roughly the same comparatively small group of countries. Whether private banking institutions will be willing or able to continue taking major responsibility for financing these deficits, however, is another question entirely.

In earlier years, private lenders practically fell over themselves in their haste to satisfy the demands of sovereign borrowers. Flush with funds, they were anything but hard-pressed to accommodate new or existing customers. Particularly from 1976 onward, owing to the relative ease of monetary conditions in major financial centers, terms of international loan business eased sharply: spreads narrowed, maturities lengthened, and the range of borrowers finding access to the market widened considerably. By the end of

Table 5

Current-Account Deficits of Oil-Importing Developing Countries, 1970-90: World Bank Estimates
(billions of dollars)

	1970	1973	1975	1978	1980[e]	1985[p]	1990[p]
Total	8.3	6.7	39.6	27.1	61.0	78.4	102.4
"Low-income" countries	1.2	2.3	5.4	5.7	10.0	18.6	32.0
"Middle-income" countries	7.1	4.4	34.2	21.4	51.0	59.7	72.2

Source: International Bank for Reconstruction and Development, World Development Report, 1980. For country
classifications, see source.

e. Estimates
p. Projections based on the World Bank's "High Case", which makes the following assumptions about real growth
rates of GNP in 1980-85 and 1985-90:

	1980-85	1985-90	(1970-80, actual)
Low-income developing countries	4.1	4.6	(3.3)
Middle-income developing countries	4.9	5.7	(5.5)
Oil exporters	6.3	5.9	(6.1)
Industrialized countries	3.3	4.0	(3.1)

123

1978, it was clear that an outright borrowers' market had developed in international lending.

Not surprisingly, concern concurrently began to grow about the prudence of such a hectic pace of activity. Even as early as 1977, some of the larger American banks were questioning whether lenders might not be seriously overextending themselves. By 1979, such fears had become widespread in the international financial community. Indeed, the change of attitude in more recent years has been striking. Today lenders are a good deal more cautious about doing business with oil importing countries than they used to be.

This caution is reflected in the leveling off of such lending in 1979-80, despite rising oil deficits. In 1979, according to World Bank figures, lending to non-oil LDCs grew by only some 12 percent, one-eighth the rate attained in 1978; and in the first half of 1980, bank credits and bond issues to these countries were actually down nearly 15 percent over the same period in the preceding year.[18] In part, the slowdown was a direct result of the heated pace of borrowing in earlier years. Precisely because of the borrowers' market that had prevailed in 1976-78 (when deficits were contracting), oil importers could now meet at least a part of the initial impact of higher OPEC prices by drawing down reserves that had previously been stored up, or by activating credits that had previously been contracted but not yet disbursed. Of non-oil LDC bank loans outstanding at the end of 1979, 20.8 percent had not yet been disbursed, as compared with 22.8 percent a year earlier.[19] Of at least equal importance, however, was the conspicuous change in the attitude of lenders.

Looking forward to the next few years, the key issue is whether this change of attitude is likely to persist. Can banking institutions be expected to return to doing business with oil-importing countries in the future in amounts and at terms comparable to those of the recent past? Few observers doubt that in the near term at least (i.e., 1981-82), most oil importers should have little trouble in financing the bulk of their increased deficits at reasonable cost (although some individual countries may encounter rising market resistance because of heightened risk perceptions). But beyond the near term "the picture," as the IMF has warned, "is cloudier ... uncertainties are great."[20] In fact, an increasing number of the more important borrowers of recent years may well soon find their access to the markets circumscribed as well as their costs raised owing to the changed attitude of lenders. Several considerations all point toward this same conclusion:

(i) First is the apparent decline in the profitability of overseas lending in recent years. As the Bank for International Settlements pointed out in its 1979 Annual Report, competition among lenders in 1977-78 resulted in a "compression of the banks" earning margins to levels that seemed to be based on the assumption of a future without problems or losses.... It is not easy to see how these spreads can leave scope for building up adequate provisions against future losses."[21] Most banks now agree. The impact of low spreads was particularly strong on U.S. banks, whose capital ratios tend to be higher than those of their European or Japanese counterparts. Although to some extent the effect of narrow margins can be offset by larger income from negotiation and management fees or from collateral business, the fact remains that rates of return in general seem to have declined, and lending institutions have already begun to strive for some widening of spreads and shortening of maturities. Indeed, in the opinion of the IMF, a major explanation of the slowdown of lending in 1979-80 was precisely that lenders "were insisting that a hardening of terms was inevitable," resulting in "a standoff between borrowers and banks."[22]

(ii) Second is the heightened perception of risk inherent in lending to oil-importing countries -- not just economic risk (stemming from higher oil prices and the already strained capacity of some countries to meet debt-service requirements), but, increasingly, also political risk (reflecting the political volatility of many parts of the Third World). This too suggests a widening of spreads and shortening of maturities on financing in the years to come. More importantly, it suggests a greater selectivity and market differentiation according to the creditworthiness of borrowers than has tended to be the case in the past.

126

For many countries, the relative cost of borrowing may be expected to rise significantly. For some, access to the markets may be curtailed in absolute terms (since many risks -- in particular, political risks -- cannot be captured merely by a hardening of loan terms).

(iii) This consideration is also likely to be rein-forced by a third consideration -- the marked concentration of loan portfolios that has occurred since 1973. With the bulk of foreign business going to a quite small number of countries, many banking institutions have found themselves running up against internal (self-imposed) exposure limits; and while such limits themselves are apt to prove quite flexible over time, the fact is that lenders increasingly express a need to diversify their portfolios more in the future than they have done in the past. This can only add to the constraints on access and costs of financing in selected cases.

(iv) A fourth consideration is the relationship between external and domestic assets in the portfolios of banking institutions. Between 1973 and 1979, the ratio of net international claims to net domestic assets of banks in major credit-market countries rose by more than two-thirds (from 10.2 percent to 17.2 percent)[23]; and although this relationship also is apt to prove flexible over time, its rise too suggests a likelihood of greater selectivity in lending to sovereign borrowers in the future. Many banks now seem to feel that they have already built up too much foreign paper on their books and that, over the next few years, a greater proportion of their business should go to domestic customers.

(v) A fifth consideration is capital adequacy. For many banks, capital base (shareholders equity plus reserves) deteriorated badly in recent years as a result of efforts to maintain or increase profit margins through intensified leverage. Future growth of earning assets, therefore, may be constrained unless banking institutions can raise new equity capital. But new equity capital is notoriously difficult to obtain in conditions of high inflation and low profitability -- i.e., the kinds of conditions that are most likely to prevail over the next few years. Some limitations on the overall expansion of lending, therefore -- including inter alia lending to oil importers -- ought prudently to be anticipated.

(vi) Finally, it is necessary to take note of changes in the regulatory environment bearing on the international activities of banking institutions. Regulatory authorities have for some time been expressing concern about certain potentially imprudent features of lender behavior -- e.g., the relative narrowness of spreads and length of maturities for even quite high-risk borrowers; concentration of loan portfolios; possible over-exposure to oil-importing coun- tries in general or to selected individual oil importers in particular; and under-capitalization. In the future, authorities can be expected to insist on more caution and selectivity in lending to sovereign borrowers. As is well known, major central banks are moving toward a requirement that banks consolidate all of their lending activities -- foreign as well as domestic -- for the purpose of satisfying capital requirements. This could well limit leverage and restrict overall lending activity. Central banks are also likely to enforce exposure limits more strictly and to urge more market differentiation according to creditworthiness. Such changes cannot help but add to the difficulties of many borrowing countries.

For all these reasons, I would argue that a return to a borrowers' market in international lending over the next few years may be regarded as highly unlikely. As Rimmer de Vries of Morgan Guaranty has pointed out, even if the real price of oil were to rise by only 3 percent per annum between now and 1985 (Morgan Guaranty's base case), banks would have to increase their lending to oil importers by some 30 percent or more each year in order to provide the same fraction of financing requirements as in the recent past.[24] This would be twice the growth rate of their capital base recently and would greatly increase the concentration of risk in their balance sheets. Not that this means that major borrowers among the smaller OECD countries and industrializing LDCs are likely to be shut out of the markets altogether. But it does mean that such borrowers are going to have to take their place in the queue, like everyone else, and settle for whatever amounts and terms

129

they can get; and that in the absence of new techniques or channels for market financing, these amounts and terms are likely to be less satisfactory, from their point of view, in the future than they have been in the past.

VI. NEW APPROACHES TO PRIVATE FINANCING

This raises the question whether any new techniques or channels for financing might be found to enable banks to continue playing their intermediation role, between surplus and deficit countries, on the same scale as before. Two major possibilities suggest themselves.

1. Greater Direct Participation.

Until now, the great bulk of payments financing for deficit countries has been provided by a quite narrow circle of large institutions with headquarters in Europe, North America, and Japan. Over the next few years, the private sector's pre-eminent role in balancing the system could be preserved if other, new participants were attracted into the business, e.g., Arab or OPEC banks, or "second-tier" banks in industrialized countries. Prospects for such a development, however, do not appear exceptionally bright.

Direct participation in syndicated credits to deficit countries by Arab banks or banks from other OPEC countries has to date been relatively limited -- certainly in relation to capital -- primarily because of an apparent aversion to the risks associated with such lending. Moreover, of the loans that have been extended to oil importers by such

130

institutions, the greatest share has been skewed toward Islamic or Arab borrowers. Room for expanded financing by these institutions certainly exists. The question is whether they can evolve either the administrative ability or the commercial inclination to increase and broaden significantly the scope of their international activity. Much will depend on political developments in major oil-producing countries.

Second-tier banks (e.g., U.S. "regional" banks) have done relatively little direct lending internationally during the boom years since 1973, chiefly because of the small size of their overall portfolios and their lack of technical skill in assessing risks. Most such institutions lack the resources to go into the business on a large scale on their own; and even if some do (either individually or via consortia), they are unlikely to risk it without at least some hardening of terms as compared with the recent past. In the United States specifically, wider participation might perhaps be encouraged by the accelerating trend toward multi-state banking (which might also increase the placement power of first-tier banks insofar as they are able to acquire smaller regional or local banks). But in major credit-market countries generally, wider participation is unlikely without development of new and more attractive financing instruments.

2. Broader Placement Activity.

As an alternative to greater direct participation by

131

new banks, older participants might achieve the same result by widening the placement of loans that they themselves continue to negotiate and manage. From their point of view, this option would have the advantage of preserving for them profitable negotiation and management fees or collateral business even while relieving them of a greater share of the asset burden of credits. The problem lies in making foreign paper sufficiently attractive to institutions that have not traditionally shown much interest in such "esoteric" investments, e.g., second and even third-tier commercial banks, savings institutions, insurance companies, and pension funds. Although to some extent the historic resistance of such institutions to international assets in their portfolios has been eroded in recent years[25], here too no significant change is likely without the development of new and more attractive financing instruments.

Thus, the real question is how innovative the markets can be in their techniques of lending. The 1970s demonstrated that banks do not lack for imagination and ingenuity. Can they show similar skills in adapting to the prospective circumstances of the 1980s? The possibilities are numerous, e.g., commodity-option bonds (tying the capital value of securities to the price of some key commodity such as gold or oil); project loans (tying loans to particular projects whose future cash flow is judged high enough to ensure successful debt service); equity-conversion options (offering conversion options in specific projects at

132

pre-arranged prices); indexing or exchange guarantees
(promising constant purchasing power at maturity); or
insurance schemes (protecting investors against the risk of
default by sovereign borrowers). But no one can say for
sure what specific trends are likely to emerge. Only one
thing seems certain -- that the 1980s will demand at least
as much creativity in financing techniques as did the 1970s,
if the private sector is to continue to play an important
role in balancing the system.

VII. RELATIONS BETWEEN THE FUND AND THE PRIVATE BANKS

What about the public sector -- specifically, the IMF?
The challenges to the Fund in the coming decade will be
three-fold. First, insofar as the markets seem likely to
continue to play an important role in the provision of
payments financing, the Fund must continue to address itself
to the possibly detrimental effect of the availability of
unconditional financing on the efficiency of the international adjustment process. Second, insofar as it also seems
likely that the markets will be unable to play their balancing role on quite the same scale as before, the Fund must
additionally address itself more than in the past to the
needs of some of the largest and most persistent borrowing
countries, if a costly scramble among oil importers to pass
around their collective deficit is to be averted. And
third, insofar as it seems likely that market financing will
have a significant impact on the overall supply and rate of

growth of monetary reserves in the world, the Fund must address itself to the new complications entailed for the task of controlling international liquidity. Each of these three issues will be considered in turn.

With respect to the first issue[26], numerous sources have called for a closer relationship between the IMF and private lenders in order to minimize the danger that individual deficit countries might be tempted to postpone painful adjustment measures because of their access to market financing "without strings." In the words of Wilfried Guth: "It is increasingly recognized by both authorities and banks that a better coordination of private and official lending is desirable."[27] In the words of Federal Reserve Board Governor Henry Wallich: "The principle is to get the private sector to continue its lending, subject to having the country's policies disciplined by the Fund."[28]

The question is: What shape might the relationship take? In practice, an unofficial sort of working relationship already exists in the informal "certificate of creditworthiness" procedure described earlier. The advantage of the procedure is that it gives some assurance that troubled countries will in fact undertake the policy measures required to restore external balance. The disadvantage is that it accentuates the discontinuities to which, frequently, the adjustment process is prone as a result of shifts in market sentiment regarding the creditworthiness of individual countries. As former U.S. Treasury Secretary Michael

Blumenthal pointed out in 1977:

> Countries ... may avoid recourse to the IMF -- and adoption of needed adjustment policies -- as long as access to private financing is more or less readily available. When the situation deteriorates to a critical point, it becomes evident to all, and there is sudden, discontinuous change.[29]

From a systemic point of view, it would seem desirable to avoid such abrupt discontinuities by involving the Fund at an earlier stage of the adjustment process -- before the critical point is reached. The issue, as Secretary Blumenthal went on to indicate, "is whether there is legal and practical scope for earlier involvement by the IMF."[30]

Proposals for earlier involvement by the IMF generally follow one of two alternative approaches. One approach would formalize the presently informal "certificate of creditworthiness" procedure. A number of sources have argued that the IMF should become, de jure and not just de facto, an international credit-rating agency.[31] The Fund would be empowered to play an overt role in assessing the policies and performance of prospective borrowers, perhaps by publishing its presently confidential reports based on its annual economic consultations with member-countries. Precedent for this exists inter alia in publication by the OECD of annual reviews of its members' economic situations. Moreover, the Fund is already authorized by its amended Articles of Agreement to exercise "surveillance" over the policies and performance of its members. In effect, therefore, the approach would be no more than an extension of existing practice. The advantage, according to proponents, is that it would retain the present arms-length relationship of the Fund with private lenders. Banks, and not the Fund, would still make the ultimate decisions about to whom to lend and how much to lend.

The alternative approach would formalize the presently informal links between private and official lending through some kind of cooperative financing arrangements. This idea was first raised by Gabriel Hauge of Manufacturers Hanover Trust Company in 1977,[32] and has since been supported by a variety of public officials and private observers.[33] Two principal variants are mentioned -- (1) parallel financing, which would involve separate negotiations and loan contracts but would make eligibility for private credit contingent formally (and not just informally, as at present) on meeting IMF lending conditions; and (2) co-financing, which would directly link joint private and IMF loans through cross-default clauses. For private lenders, cooperative financing would offer the advantage of utilizing the Fund's expertise in determining a country's borrowing capacity and the Fund's clout in ensuring appropriate policy conditionality; yet lenders could continue to select which loans they would be willing to make. For the Fund, the advantage would be the limit set on access to unconditional market financing by countries that might otherwise be tempted to postpone needed adjustment measures.

Significantly, neither of these approaches has found much favor among any of the parties directly involved --

namely the IMF, the private banks and the borrowing governments. At the IMF, proposals to transform the Fund into an official credit-rating agency or to formalize cooperative financing arrangements with private banking institutions have been greeted with caution, if not dismay. Fund officials have always been reluctant to share with private lenders all the information contained in IMF consultation reports on economic conditions in particular countries, not least because this might undermine the confidential basis on which such information is obtained in the first place. (The precedent of the OECD's annual economic reviews is dismissed on the grounds that these are negotiated documents, differing only infrequently from the opinions of member-governments, rather than truly independent analyses based on information not otherwise publicly available.) They are even more reluctant to take on, in the words of one, "the twin roles of loan manager and bailiff."[34] To do so, they argue, would severely threaten the Fund's independence and greatly complicate its role as adviser to member-governments. In principle, the Fund is supposed to maintain a posture of neutrality between debtor and creditor countries. In practice, any of these proposals would give the appearance of placing it squarely on the side of creditors, and thus might seriously compromise is objectivity in the eyes of debtors.

Fund official stress that the IMF is a multilateral agency with broad public-policy responsibilities. Whereas a private lender can always choose to terminate business in an individual country if the outlook there seems unprofitable, the Fund is obliged to maintain good relations with all of its member-governments. The Fund cannot appear to be subservient to the interests of private lenders (or to the lenders' home governments). Above all, the Fund cannot appear to be "bailing out" private lenders that have become overextended in specific instances.

The "bail out" issue has been one of the thorniest aspects of the relationship between the IMF and banks. Even with nothing more formal than the present "certificate of creditworthiness" procedure, the Fund occasionally has been accused of lending, in effect, to refinance private loans on the verge of default. Fund officials fear that any more formal arrangement would appear to imply IMF responsibility for risky loans, "in effect affording the private banking community the full faith and credit of the constituent treasuries of the various member nations."[35] Nothing could more severely threaten the Fund's independence than to appear to be the guarantor and collector of private credits to sovereign borrowers. Furthermore, nothing could more severely threaten the Fund's discipline over borrowers -- presumably the whole point of the exercise -- if banking institutions, feeling protected by an implicit IMF guarantee, were to be tempted to lend without caution in dubious cases.

Fund officials also note a variety of legal and

138

practical difficulties in the way of a more formal relationship with private lenders. For example, if cooperative
financing arrangements are to be pursued, what criteria
would the Fund use to decide which banks may or may not
participate in individual credit packages? And in the event
of debt default or restructuring, how would the Fund choose
among the competing claims of different creditors? A
further complication is created by the existence of clauses
in IMF-country agreements that are confidential between the
two parties. Private lenders would find it difficult to
participate in financing arangements where the terms and
conditions are not all publicly known. Yet if such terms
and conditions were all to be revealed, once again the
tradition of confidentiality that presently exists between
the Fund and its member-goverments would be undermined.

Clearly, the only way to preserve the Fund's independence in such circumstances would be to make private lenders
formally subservient to the IMF, rather than the reverse.
The Fund would have to be legally empowered not only to rate
the creditworthiness of individual countries and/or participate in cooperative financing arrangements with private
lenders, but also to prohibit private lending in specific
instances and to require it in others. In effect, the Fund
would have to be granted authority to allocate credit on a
global scale -- which, not suprisingly, is the main reason
why such proposals have failed to find much favor among
lenders.

Private lenders stress their distinctive responsibilities. In the words of Rimmer de Vries: "While the Fund is responsible to its member governments, banks have important responsibilities to their depositors and shareholders. Both should remain independent in their lending decisions."[36] As profit-seeking institutions, they should not be compelled to subordinate their objectives or modify their lending criteria. If markets are to work efficiently, banks must be able to form their own judgments which loans they may or may not be willing to make. As one observer has argued:

> Were this not so, banks could justifiably be considered as segments of a banking structure dominated at the core by an official institution, which would be very hard to reconcile with the principles of autonomous judgment, individual responsibility and freedom to choose between alternative circuits of financing, all of which are well entrenched in the traditions of Western market economies and pluralistic societies.[37]

Thus, a conundrum is evident. A mutuality of interest clearly exists between the Fund and the private banks. Both are interested in assisting countries through periods of balance-of-payments difficulties, and both want to ensure that the financing they provide will be used in such a manner that in time the resulting debt can be satisfactorily serviced. Yet it is equally clear that the interests of the Fund and the private sector do not entirely coincide; and where they do not, any formal relationship linking the two would have to make explicit whose mandate will predominate in what circumstances. One way or another, one or the other would have to sacrifice a certain amount of its traditional selectivity and autonomy. No wonder, then, that IMF

140

officials and private lenders alike have been less than enthusiastic about such proposals.

No wonder also that borrowing countries have been unenthusiastic. For them, one of the great attractions of market financing of deficits is the maneuverability it gives them vis-à-vis creditors -- the option to play of one source of financing against another and, above all, to use their access to the markets to evade IMF conditionality. By definition, proposals to formalize links between the IMF and privare lenders are designed to reduce that degree of maneuverability. As one observer has commented, this is "hardly calculated to appeal to politically sensitive governments."[38] For political leaders in deficit coun- tries, the only possible benefit of such proposals is that they might strengthen the network of outside pressures available to offset domestic forces that are opposed to the adoption of adequate adjustment measures. Otherwise, as another source has argued, there is little to recommend such arrangements from the borrower's point of view:

> Once the public and private lenders join forces, deficit countries will be left with no alternative sources of financial assistance; there will be no escaping IMF conditionality, little choice but to accept whatever terms the IMF and private banks choose to lay down. Thus, countries with large external debts and payments deficits which require external financing can expect to have less autonomy over their interna- tional economic affairs if these proposals are adopted.[39]

Given such negative attitudes on the part of all three parties involved, there seems little likelihood that any proposal for earlier formal involvement by the Fund could be

141

successfully implemented. Quite the contrary. In fact, there seems no way to influence directly the lending practices of banking institutions that would not encroach on the accepted responsibilities or privileges of at least one of the parties concerned. "The dice are loaded," one observer has noted: "If something isn't a breach of confidentiality, then it's a breach of sovereign rights, and vice versa."[40] Realistically, therefore, we cannot expect much support to develop for either of the approaches mentioned. All three parties want to preserve their traditional freedom of judgment and action. None is likely to back a formal restructuring of the relationship between the IMF and private lenders.

Not that this rules out more informal approaches, such as those that exist in the "certificate of creditworthiness" procedure. Unofficial coordination of private and official lending in critical situations has clearly demonstrated its worth and can be expected to evolve further in the future. Private lenders have learned to pay more heed to the overall situation in borrowing countries, borrowers have learned to pay more heed to the advice of the IMF, and the IMF has learned to pay more heed to the role played by market financing in the process of payments adjustment. Moreover, on an informal and unwritten basis, innumerable lines of communication have been opened up affording banks access to selected pieces of information contained in Fund consultation reports from IMF staff, their own national authorities, or even from borrowing countries themselves. The Fund is still developing the principles and procedures it will use in implementing its responsibility for surveillance of members. Over the course of the next decade we can probably anticipate that, as these principles and procedures evolve, more scope will be provided for involvement by the Fund at an earlier stage of the adjustment process through voluntary cooperation based on the enlightened self-interest of all parties.

But at the same time it must be acknowledged that such limited approaches fall quite short of the ideal insofar as discontinuities characterize the adjustment process. Discontinuities may well be lessened as a by-product of informal contacts among the IMF, banks, and borrowers. But it is hardly likely that they will be eliminated altogether, so long as payments imbalances continue to be handled pragmatically on a case-by-case basis. This is not an argument against private financing of deficits per se. It does suggest, however, that the risk of discontinuities in the adjustment process must be regarded as part of the price paid for the benefits of financing by the private markets.

VIII. THE RESOURCES OF THE FUND

The second challenge to the Fund over the next decade will be to provide more resources for the legitimate needs of those members that encounter rising resistance from the private markets. Can the Fund increase significantly the

143

scale of its own lending to such countries?

In fact, there are two questions here: (1) Can the Fund acquire sufficient loanable resources to meet the potential needs of deficit countries?; and (2) Can deficit countries be persuaded to meet their needs by turning more to the Fund? The answer to neither of these questions is prime facie obvious.

1.   Loan Resources.

One reason why the Fund's quantitative contribution to the resolution of the petro-dollar recycling problem in the 1970s was so modest was that the Fund did not have a great deal of money to lend. In the first year after oil prices started to rise, as Table 6 shows, IMF loanable resourcs amounted to barely SDR 7 billion (approximately $8.5 billion); and even at their peak over the decade (1978), at a time when IMF net lending was negative, those resources never topped SDR 12-1/2 billion ($16 billion) -- still quite small in relation to the renewed oil deficits of 1979 and 1980.   More recently, the Fund's financing capacity has grown substantially, as a result of the recent 50-percent increase of members' quotas (finally ratified by the requisite majority of member-governments in late 1980).[41]   But even so, quotas now correspond to only 4 percent of world imports, as compared with 12 percent in 1965.[42]   The Fund's own resources still remain rather small in relation to potential need in the 1980s.

To supplement its loanable resources the Fund basically

144

Table 6

Loanable Resources of the International Monetary Fund, 1973-80
(millions of SDRs)

	Financial Year Ended April 30							
	1973	1974	1975	1976	1977	1978	1979	1980
Usable currencies[a]	5,200	6,500	10,100	7,800	5,300	11,200	8,800	10,600
SDRs[b]	617	499	510	461	771	1,371	1,290	1,407
Total	5,817	6,999	10,610	8,261	6,071	12,571	10,090	12,007

a. "Usable currencies" are those that are available to the Fund for net sales through its operational budget, except for those currencies held by the Fund in excess of quota.
b. In the Fund's General Resources Account only.

Source: International Monetary Fund, Annual Reports.

has two options. One is to borrow directly from countries in balance-of-payments surplus -- which means, of course, mainly OPEC countries, in particular Saudi Arabia and other "low absorbers" around the Persian Gulf. The other option is to borrow from the markets. To a considerable extent, the first option has already been employed, e.g., in the funding of the two Oil Facilities and the Supplementary Financing Facility, roughly half of which came from OPEC countries; and more recently in the well publicized agreement with Saudi Arabia to borrow 4 billion SDRs ($5 billion) in each of two, and possibly three, successive years.[43] Such deals, however, require difficult and protracted negotiations, and are frequently hampered by political considerations (e.g., the issue whether to seat the Palestine Liberation Organization as an observer at IMF annual meetings). Accordingly, in coming years attention will also have to be paid to the second of the Fund's two options -- namely, borrowing from the markets, either through direct loans or through issuance of its own bonds or notes.

On the face of it, this option seems attractive. There are no legal barriers to such operations (the Fund's Articles of Agreement authorize it to borrow a member-country's currency, as long as the member agrees, from any source) and it certainly would enable the Fund to augment its capacity to meet the needs of deficit countries. But problems exist. Some of these are only technical, for example, the question of exchange risk. Since the IMF's claims are denominated in

SDRs, if it were to borrow a currency in the market and that currency were to appreciate relative to the SDR before the loan for which it was used came to maturity, the Fund could suffer a serious foreign-exchange loss. Technical problems are usually amendable to technical solutions. For example, the Fund could borrow a package of currencies more or less in proportion of their importance in determining the value of the SDR. But some problems could turn out to be more serious, especially the question of potential market reception.[44] Unlike the World Bank, the IMF has no callable capital commitments (i.e., guarantee provisions). Therefore, an assessment by private lenders of the creditworthiness of the Fund would have to be based largely on its holdings of currencies, gold, and SDRs. Since many of the currencies held by the Fund are not very useful, and since any sales of its gold require an 85-percent majority vote of member-countries, private ratings of the Fund's creditworthiness may not in fact be very favorable.

Ultimately, market assessments are bound to be shaped by judgments about the political attitude of the Fund's major members and the extent to which they may -- or may not -- be prepared to back Fund commitments. No doubt the necessary assurances will be given, formally or informlly, and some amount of borrowing from private sources will indeed take place. But it would probably be unrealistic to expect such borrowings to represent anything more than a modest supplement to traditional sources of IMF financing.

Over the course of the next decade, we can most probably
anticipate that the Fund's loanable resources will be
augmented -- but not dramatically.

2. Fund Conditionality.

Apart from its limited resources, there was also a
second reason why the IMF contributed so little quantitatively to resolution of the petro-dollar problem in the
1970s -- its tradition of policy conditionality. As already
indicated, one of the great attractions of market financing
for deficit countries is precisely the opportunity it gives
those countries to evade Fund conditionality. Many governments simply do not like to borrow from the IMF unless they
have to -- which, as mentioned above, helps to account for
the discontinuities in the international adjustment process
that have recurred since 1973. For the future, the question
is whether the Fund's concept of conditionality ought to be
altered in some fundamental way.

Whether the concept can be changed is not at issue.
The Fund's conventional interpretation of conditionality is
the product of a process of gradual adaption to changing
historical circumstances and is by no means "set in stone."
As the former general counsel of the IMF has written: "There
is no absolute standard of conditionality."[45] Indeed, as
such, the word "conditionality" does not even appear in the
Fund's Articles of Agreement; and in the organization's
early years, there was some question whether it even had the
right to make borrowing subject to conditions. It was only

over time that, as a result of accumulating experience and precedent, a recognized interpretation of the Fund's pre-rogatives emerged to govern members' access to credit. Two landmark decisions of the Fund's Board of Executive Directors stand out in this connection. In the first, in 1948, the Board agreed that the IMF could challenge a member's request for finance on the grounds that inter alia it would not be "consistent with the provisions of the Agreement," and indeed that the Fund could "postpone or reject the request, or accept it subject to conditions."[46] In the second, in 1952, "conditions" were defined to encompass "policies the member will pursue ... to overcome the [bal-ance-of-payments] problem"[47] -- in other words, policies that promise a genuine process of adjustment to external deficit. Since 1952, this has been the accepted meaning of the term "conditionality."[48]

The 1952 decision was also important for establishing a practical distinction between a member's reserve tranche (in those days, called its gold tranche) and its four credit tranches, by ruling that borrowing in the reserve tranche would receive "the overwhelming benefit of any doubt."[49] Subsequent practice also created a distinction between a member's first credit tranche and its remaining ("upper") credit tranches, as summarized in the Fund's 1959 Annual Report:

> The Fund's attitude to requests for transactions within the first credit tranche ... is a liberal one, provided that the member itself is also making reason-able efforts to solve its problems. Request for

transactions beyond these limits requre substantial justification.[50]

Over the course of the 1950s and 1960s, the Fund evolved a practical expression of policy conditionality in the form of its stabilization programs, which members have come to be obliged to submit when applying for financing in their credit tranches. In the case of a request in the first credit tranche, members may express their policy intentions at a relatively high level of generality. But for upper credit tranches, programs have to be correspondingly more precise and rigorous in design. Stabilization programs vary considerably in detail, but almost all have come to cover, in some degree, a country's monetary, fiscal, credit, and exchange-rate policies, as well as its trade and payment practices.

With the evolution of stabilization programs came a parallel evolution of Fund thinking on balance-of-payments problems. In time, an institutional approach was developed that stressed most centrally the monetary nature of external disequilibrium. In the words of one authoritative Fund publication: "The central element of this approach was the estimation of the prospective demand for money.... By controlling domestic credit creation during the period under review so as to equal the estimated change in the demand for money, the authorities could keep the external accounts in balance."[51] Thus most payment problems were reduced essentially to a matter of excess domestic demand, and solutions essentially to a matter of curbing monetary

growth, balancing the government's budget, and setting a
"realistic" exchange rate -- whether a country's deficit
could be attributed solely to defects of its own internal
policies or not.[52]

It is this approach that has encouraged countries to
evade Fund conditionality whenever possible by recourse to
marketing financing. According to IMF data covering the
period 1967-1976, the proportion of net loans to members in
their upper credit tranches dropped from 58 percent prior to
1974 to only 19 percent in 1974-76 (despite a sharp rise in
total borrowing from the Fund)[53], and this decline appears
to have persisted in more recent years as well.[54] To some
extent, this development may simply reflect the increased
availability of financing from the Fund's growing spectrum
of special facilities, as well as from private sources. But
even more importantly, it reflects profound dissatisfaction
with the Fund's traditional interpretation of conditionality.

That dissatifaction seems justified. In an era of
persistent OPEC surpluses, it may fairly be argued that
deficits can no longer be treated as if they were a transitory phenomenon resulting from incompetence or carelessness
on the part of domestic policymakers, and amenable to
traditional policy prescriptions for domestic demand restraint. Oil-induced deficits perforce must be expected to
continue until oil importers can make the necessary "structural" adjustments to the altered relative cost of energy.

151

This may take a long period, and in the meantime, it would seem reasonable for the Fund to make a greater effort to supplement private lending by reforming its own lending policies. For example, the Fund could make more money available for longer-term, structural measures to narrow net dependence on oil imports or to broaden the foreign-exchange earning capacity of deficit countries. If the Fund is able to play a greater role in balancing the system in the 1980s, it will almost certainly need to yield, in some measure, to calls for a more flexible interpretation of conditionality.[55]

To a certain extent the Fund has already yielded to such calls, by issuing (in 1979) a new set of guidelines on conditionality explicitly acknowledging that adjustment in many cases might require a longer period of time than traditionally assumed in Fund stabilization programs, and pledging to "pay due regard to ... the circumstances of members, including the causes of their balance of payments problems."[56] Also, an increasing proportion of Fund lending is now being directed through the Extended Fund Facility, thus, making available more financing for longer periods than had generally been true in the past. More such adaptations can be expected in coming years.

Interestingly, as these changes are being carried out, the Fund is finding itself moving closer to the traditional province of the World Bank -- just as, simultaneously, the Bank seems to have begun moving the other way. Also under

152

pressure to do more for countries hard hit by the increased relative cost of energy, the Bank in 1979 started to shift from its usual emphasis on long-term project lending to relatively short-term program lending for so-called "structural adjustment" purposes. The object of such lending, in the words of a senior Bank official, is "to provide support for member countries already in serious [balance-of-payments] difficulties, or unmanageable deficits arising from external factors which are not likely to be easily or quickly reversed."[57] This sounds remarkably similar to how the IMF explains its own lending policies.

In fact, what we are witnessing is a partial convergence of the roles of the Fund and Bank under the impact of persistently rising oil prices. Just as the traditional division of labor between private banking institutions and the Fund has been blurred by the petro-dollar recycling problem, so too has the division between the Fund and the Bank. In the 1980s, it will be increasingly difficult to maintain clear distinctions among these three key sources of financing.

IX. THE FUND AND WORLD LIQUIDITY

The third challenge to the IMF concerns the impact of private market financing on the overall world supply and rate of growth of monetary reserves. There is no question that the changes of the last decade have greatly complicated the task of controlling international liquidity. Some

153

sources deny the importance of aggregate liquidity control in today's world of exchange-rate flexibility.[58]   But insofar as a quick and efficient adjustment process cannot be assured through Fund surveillance or other means, liquidity considerations are by no means irrelevant.[59]   Indeed, in the absence of really effective multilateral surveillance of adjustment policies, and in the presence of inevitable differences of opinion about what these policies should be, access to external financing can permit countries to run larger and longer deficits than might be appropriate from a systemic point of view.   In turn, this can lead to an unduly rapid growth of international liquidity.   Despite the advent of flexible exchange rates, most observers agree that there is still a need for strengthened control of the supply and rate of growth of reserves in accordance with multilateral evaluation of global requirements.[60]   Since most governments still insist on managing their exchange rates, their decisions in turn still collectively determine the stability or otherwise of international monetary relations.   The task of liquidity management was never easy.   But in today's altered circumstances it is even more difficult than ever, for at least two reasons.

First, the increased role of private lending in balance-of-payments financing has blurred the conventional analytical distinctions between official and private liquidity and between international and domestic liquidity -- a point stressed, in particular, by the McCracken Group

Report. These distinctions, the Report argued, now "have largely lost their operational meaning."[61] Since deficit countries today can borrow so freely from private banking institutions, official reserve stocks have become a comparatively minor element of international liquidity and official liquidity can no longer be measured (if it ever could be) simply by the outstanding stock of monetary reserves held by central banks. Nor, since deposits in domestic banking systems are the reserve base of the international credit markets, can international liquidity now be measured simply by the outstanding stock of foreign assets held by banks. The result is that today even a qualitative assessment of the magnitude and adequacy of international liquidity is an extremely difficult operation.

Beyond this analytical problem is a second, institutional problem: the lack of any formal mechanism to ensure that private lending in the aggregate will in practice accord with cosmopolitan criteria. As the function of liquidity creation has been transferred in part from official to private channels, so the task of supervision has passed in part from international to national agencies. The surveillance of the latter, however, does not usually extend beyond the perspective of national interest. Consequently, no recognized arrangement presently exists to ensure that the overall level and rate of growth of private lending to sovereign borrowers will remain consistent with sound objectives for the system as a whole. As one source has argued: "The possibility thus exists of lending booms outside the control of the international community which could well worsen the problems of some future inflation. Equally serious is the possibility that a destruction of reserves would exacerbate a world recession."[62]   In the words of the McCracken Group Report:

> The limits of reserve-creation have become ill-defined and fluid, being set now by the private market's judgement of the creditworthiness of individual countries rather than by official multilateral evaluation of the needs of the system as a whole.[63]

In effect, the world monetary system has taken on some of the characteristics of a domestic credit system without a central bank. Few observers doubt that, if domestic credit creation were left entirely in the hands of private institutions, prolonged periods of excessive or deficient lending might occur. "Money does not manage itself" is the old adage. The same argument applies at the international level as well. As one observer has noted: "If liquidity control is to be effectively pursued, new mechanisms [will] be needed."[64]

Once again, the problem is a practical one: What shape might these mechanisms take? The object is to gain some form of leverage over the aggregate volume of international financial intermediation by private banks. Unfortunately, the IMF as presently constituted is simply incapable of exercising any such influence.

Historically, the Fund has always dealt solely with official financial institutions, and hence has been able to

156

influence the scale of private intermediation only indirectly, through its leverage on national monetary policies. In the future, it would be only with its projected program of borrowing from the markets that the Fund might gain some direct means of leverage over private international lending. By absorbing some part of the effective supply of loanable funds, Fund borrowing would limit the total of financial resources available to banking institutions for lending onward to deficit countries. By varying its operations in the markets at its own discretion -- now borrowing more when the growth rate of reserves seems excessive, now borrowing less (or perhaps even buying debt) when growth seems deficient -- the Fund could exercise direct control over private creation of international liquidity.

But there, of course, is the rub. Authority to borrow on the open market at its own discretion would give the Fund enormous influence over the stance of monetary policy in the system as a whole -- in effect, transforming it into a kind of world central bank. Monetary policy is still regarded as an essential element of national sovereignty. Most governments are loath to transfer their formal money-making powers to a supranational institution. Consequently, most governments can be expected to turn thumbs down on any but the most limited extension of the Fund's role in controlling private liquidity creation.

As with the adjustment process, so here too expectations about the Fund's prospective role must be realistically tempered. Formally or informally, the Fund can be expected to preserve some role for itself in the management of liquidity creation from official sources; certainly, it can be expected to promote greater use of the SDR as an alternative to national currencies in interational reserves (e.g., by further periodic allocations of SDRs as well as, perhaps, by establishment of an IMF substitution account). But any direct powers over the creation of liquidity from private sources will most likely by constricted by the collective decisions of Fund members. Ultimately, the main locus of control over the availability of resources for private international lending must be expected to remain where it always has -- with national governments.

Can governments, then, establish more effective control over private creation of international liquidity? Market observers have frequently noted the key role played by domestic monetary policy in the major financial centers in determining the overall pace of liquidity creation through international lending.[65] The symbiotic relationship between internal and external credit markets means that if domestic monetary variables are genuinely under the control of the central banks in these countries, so too will the total volume of credit (offshore as well as onshore) created in their currencies be under their control. With international liquidity available on market terms in national currencies, the supply and rate of growth of reserves in the world as a whole now ultimately depends on monetary developments and policies in a handful of issuing countries. As the McCracken Group Report has described it:

> What we have today is something that is moving toward what can perhaps best be described as a market-oriented or "federative" international system. Under this system the availability and terms on which official international liquidity can be obtained are determined in individual cases by private institutions. For the system as a whole, however, they are determined by the joint product of the monetary policies being followed in half a dozen or more major financial centres closely interconnected through the international financial markets....
>
> The overall level of lending activity in the international markets will depend on developments in each of the major national markets to which they are closely related. If developments in these national markets are under the control of monetary authorities acting in consultation with each other, the level of activity in the international markets will be brought under control as well.[66]

This suggests that central banks in the major financial centers already have it within their power to assure effective control of international liquidity through appropriate coordination of their individual monetary policies. Collectively, they can limit the availability of financial resources to private lenders if each central bank takes more explicit account of external considerations in formulating its internal policy objectives. In the words of the IMF: "it [is] necessary to consider the offshore and traditional lending components as an aggregate."[67] Provided this is done, deficit countries regarded by the markets as creditworthy would no longer be able to count on such easy access to payments financing, and the scale of international liquidity creation in the aggregate would be more likely to remain consistent with sound objectives for the system as a whole. Most probably, this is the direction in which events will move in the 1980s.

In practical terms, this means that traditional definitions of money supply are likely to be widened to include offshore as well as onshore currency deposits[68]; credit expansion targets are likely to be broadened to encompass foreign as well as domestic lending[69]; and interest rates are likely to be managed with an eye to influencing external as well as internal loan demand. Institutionally, this may be handled through existing channels for central-bank cooperation, such as the Bank for Interantional Settlements, or else through some new international equivalent of a Federal Open Market Committee. Either way, the important point is that monetary authorities in the major financial centers increasingly are going to find it necessary to look beyond the perspective of national interest, narrowly defined, in their surveillance of private lending institutions. In the words of the McCracken Group Report: "Monetary authorities must act increasingly in terms of the broader interests of the world community as a whole."[70] To the extent that they do, multilateral control of global liquidity will be considerably improved. The interational monetary system would no longer lack for the equivalent of a central bank.

X. CONCLUSION

The changes wrought in the process of international liquidity creation over the last decade have been substantial. Private banking institutions, the IMF, national central banks, and even the World Bank have found their roles significantly altered under the impact of the petro-dollar recycling problem. In the 1970s, banks came to represent, in quantitative terms, the world's single greatest source of financing for balance-of-payments purposes; the IMF, in turn, found itself the official issuer of an unofficial "certificate of creditworthiness" through its legal and political authority to exercise policy conditionality. In the 1980s, further changes in the system are likely, given the prospect of a persistently large OPEC surplus and potentially serious borrowing problems for a number of oil-importing countries. From the private markets, further innovations in financing techniques may be expected, to encourage greater direct participation in international lending and to broaden the placement of foreign debt. From the IMF, further efforts to coordinate official and private lending on an informal basis may be anticipated, as well as periodic borrowing to supplement its own loanable resources and more flexible interpretation of its concept of conditionality. From central banks, closer coordination of national monetary policies may be expected, in an attempt to re-exert control over the aggregate supply and rate of growth of world monetary reserves.

161

Increasingly, traditional distinctions separating the roles of private banking institutions, the IMF, central banks, and the World Bank will be blurred. This may not be the neatest way to balance a monetary system, but, with luck, it might just work.

XI. NOTES

1. Guido Carli, Why Banks are Unpopular, The 1976 Per
    Jacobsson Lecture (Washington: International Monetary
    Fund, 1976), pp. 6, 8.

2. Towards Full Employment and Price Stability, A Report
    to the OECD by a Group of Independent Experts, chaired
    by Paul McCracken (Paris: OECD, 1977), para. 159. In a
    still longer historical perspective, Charles Kindle-
    berger has pointed out that -- on an intermittant basis
    -- private bankers at least since the Medici have made
    a practice of last-resort lending to governments at
    times of financial crisis. See his Manias, Panics, and
    Crashes: A History of Financial Crises (New York:
    Basic Books, 1978), ch. 10. The difference today is
    that only with the growth of Euro-currency market has
    balance-of-payments lending from private sources tended
    to become a regular practice.

3. For more detail on the story, see Benjamin J. Cohen,
    Banks and the Balance of Payments, in collaboration
    with Fabio Basagni (Montclair, New Jersey: Allenheld,
    Osmun, 1981), ch. 1.

4. More recently, the Compensatory Financing Facility has
    been liberalized to permit borrowing up to 100 percent
    of quota.

5. See IMF Survey, October 13, 1980, p. 297, and January
    26, 1981, p. 17. For more detail on the Fund's various
    special facilities, see Joseph Gold, Financial
    Assistance by the International Monetary Fund: Law and
    Practice, IMF Pamphlet Series No. 27 (Washington: IMF,
    1979); and IMF Survey, September 30, 1980, "Supplement
    on the Fund," pp. 5-8. It should be noted that of
    these facilities, only three -- the Compensatory
    Financing Facility, the Buffer Stock Facility, and the
    Extended Fund Facility -- represent permanent additions
    to the IMF's lending authority. See note 41, below.

6. See e.g., David O. Beim, "Rescuing the LDC's," Foreign
    Affairs, Vol. 55, No. 4 (July 1977), pp. 717-731;
    Harold v. B. Cleveland and W.H. Bruce Brittain, "Are
    the LDC's in over their Heads?", Foreign Affairs, Vol.
    55, No. 4 (July 1977), pp. 732-750; W.H. Bruce
    Brittain, "Developing Countries' External Debt and the
    Private Banks," Banca Nazionale del Lavoro Quarterly
    Review, December 1977, pp. 479-501; U.S. Senate Commit-
    tee on Foreign Relations, International Debt, the
    Banks, and U.S. Foreign Policy, A Staff Report (Wash-
    ington: 1977); Frances Stewart, "International Debt
    Prospects," Ditchley Journal, Spring 1978, pp. 57-73;
    Lawrence G. Franko and Marilyn J. Seiber (eds.),

163

Developing Country Debt (New York: Pergamon Press, 1979); Christopher Davis, Financing Third World Debt, Chatham House Papers, No. 4 (London: Royal Institute of International Affairs, 1979); and Jonathan D. Aronson (ed.), Debt and the Less Developed Countries (Boulder, Colorado: Westview Press, 1979).

7. Wilfried Guth, in Wilfried Guth and Sir Arthur Lewis, The International Monetary System in Operation, The 1977 Per Jacobsson Lecture (Washington: International Monetary Fund, 1977), p. 25.

8. Arthur F. Burns, "The Need for Order in International Finance," in International Banking Operations, Hearings Before the Subcommittee on Financial Institutions Supervision, Regulation, and Insurance of the House Committee on Banking, Finance and Urban Affairs (Washington: March-April, 1977), p. 860.

9. International Monetary Fund, Annual Report, 1977, p. 41.

10. For more detail on the Peruvian case and other examples cited in this section, see Cohen, op. cit., ch. 4 and appendix.

11. J. A. Kirbyshire, "Should Developments in the Euro-Markets be a Source of Concern to Regulatory Authorities?," Bank of England Quarterly Bulletin, Vol. 17, No. 1 (March 1977), p. 44.

12. See e.g., Giovanni Magnifico, "The Real Role of the IMF," Euromoney, October 1977, pp. 141-144; Charles Lipson, "The IMF, Commercial Banks, and Third World Debts," in Aronson, Debt and the Less Developed Countries, ch. 12; and Carl. R. Neu, "The International Monetary Fund and LDC Debt," in Franko and Seiber, op. cit., ch. 11.

13. Richard D. Hill, in International Debt, Hearings before the Subcommittee on International Finance of the House Committee on Banking, Housing and Urban Affairs (Washington: 1977), p. 127.

14. In 1974-75, a number of estimates were published projecting the trend of OPEC's surplus forward to 1980. For more detail and discussion, see e.g., Benjamin J. Cohen, "Mixing Oil and Money," in J.C. Hurewitz (ed.), Oil, the Arab-Israel Dispute, and the Industrial World (Boulder, Colo.: Westview Press, 1976), pp. 197-198; and Thomas D. Willett, The Oil-Transfer Problem and International Economic Stability, Essays in International Finance, No. 113 (Princeton, New Jersey: International Finance Section, 1975), pp. 5-7.

15. See David Marsh, "Absorbing the OPEC Surplus," _The Banker_, September 1980, p. 49.

16. See e.g., Exxon Corporation's "World Energy Outlook," Reported in _The New York Times_, December 19, 1980, p. D4; and "Can OPEC Stanch the Overflow?," _Citibank Monthly Economic Letter_, April 1981, pp. 5-6.

17. See e.g., Marsh, _op. cit._

18. International Bank for Reconstruction and Development, _Borrowing in International Capital Markets_ (EC-181/-801), November 1980.

19. International Bank for Reconstruction and Development, _World Debt Tables_ (EC-167-80), November 1980.

20. International Monetary Fund, _International Capital Markets: Recent Developments and Short-Term Prospects_ (Washington: September 1980), p. 5.

21. Bank for International Settlements, _Annual Report, 1979_, pp. 103, 106.

22. International Monetary Fund, _International Capital Markets_, p. 3.

23. _Ibid._, p. 9.

24. Rimmer de Vries, "I.M.F. Reform Now Needed," _The New York Times_, August 8, 1980, p. D2.

25. See e.g., "A Growing Commitment to Foreign Securities," _International Investor_, April 1980, pp. 109-113.

26. The discussion in this section, as well as in Section IX, borrows from Cohen, _Banks and the Balance of Payments_, ch. 6.

27. Guth, _op. cit._, p. 26.

28. Henry C. Wallich, as quoted in an interview with James Srodes, "Governor Wallich Wants the IMF to Advise LDC Lenders," _Euromoney_, April 1977, p. 24.

29. W. Michael Blumenthal, "Toward International Equilibrium: A Strategy for the Longer Pull," Remarks at the International Monetary Conference, Tokyo, Japan, May 25, 1977 (typescript).

30. _Ibid._

31. For discussions, see e.g., Harry Taylor, "It'll Take More Than the Fund to Solve the LDCs' Problem," Euromoney, May 1977, p. 64; and Cary Reich, "Why the IMF Shuns a 'Super' Role," Institutional Investor, September 1977, p. 182.

32. Hauge first broached his idea at the International Monetary Conference in May 1977. For elaboration, see Gabriel Hauge, "How the Banks Should Work With the Fund," Euromoney, October 1977, pp. 59-60; and Gabriel Hauge, in Gabriel Hauge and Erik Hoffmeyer, The International Capital Market and the International Monetary System, The 1978 Per Jacobsson Lecture (Washington: International Monetary Fund 1978), pp. 16-17.

33. See e.g., J. A. Kirbyshire, "Should Developments in the Euro-Markets be a Source of Concern to Regulatory Authorities?," Bank of England Quarterly Bulletin, Vol. 17, No. 1 (March 1977), p. 45; H. O. Ruding, "Lenders Ought to Consult the IMF," Euromoney, February 1980, pp. 34-38; Taylor, op. cit; David Levine, "The Poor Borrowers Could Do Better if the Risks Were Shifted," Euromoney, November 1977, p. 77; and Jessica P. Einhorn, "Cooperaton Between Public and Private Lenders to the Third World," The World Economy, Vol. 2, No. 2 (May 1979), pp. 229-241.

34. Quoted in Srodes, op. cit., note 28, p. 24.

35. Srodes, op. cit., p. 24.

36. Rimmer de Vries, "The International Debt Situation," World Financial Markets, June 1977, p. 12.

37. Magnifico, op. cit., p. 142.

38. Einhorn, op. cit., p. 235.

39. U.S. Senate Committee on Foreign Relations, op. cit., p. 66.

40 Reich, op. cit., p. 816.

41. See IMF Survey, December 15, 1980, p. 377. It should be noted that, in fact, the net impact of the quota increase is less than it appears, since, with the ratification of the quota increase, the Fund's Supplementary Financing Facility (which was established only to provide temporary "bridge" financing) was formally terminated.

42. The Economist, January 24, 1981, p. 15.

43. *IMF Survey*, April 6, 1981, pp. 97-101. As a quid pro quo, Saudi Arabia received an immediate doubling of its quota in the Fund placing it sixth among member-nations in voting strength. Promises of additional loan commitments have also been reported from Kuwait and the United Arab Emirates, as well as from Japan and several West European countries. See *The New York Times*, May 8, 1981. p. D1.

44. See e.g., "LDC Prospects and the Role of the IMF," *World Financial Markets*, September 1980.

45. Joseph Gold, *Conditionality*, IMF Pamphlet Series, No. 31 (Washington: IMF, 1979), p. 2.

46. Decision No. 284-4, March 10, 1948, reprinted in J. Keith Horsefield (ed.), *The International Monetary Fund, 1945-1965*, Vol. III: *Documents*, p. 227. Italics supplied.

47. Decision No. 102-(52/11), February 13, 1952, reprinted in Horsefield, *op. cit.*, p. 228.

48. For some discussion of the evolution of the Fund's concept of conditionality, see Horsefield, *op. cit.*, Vol. II: *Analysis*, ch. 18, 20, 21, 23; Gold, *Conditionality*; Manuel Guitian, "Fund Conditionality and the International Adjustment Process: The Early Period, 1950-70," *Finance and Development*, December 1980, pp. 23-27; and Frank A. Southard, Jr., *The Evolution of the International Monetary Fund*, Essays in International Finance, No. 135 (Princeton: International Finance Section, 1979), pp. 15-21.

49. See note 47.

50. International Monetary Fund, *Annual Report, 1969*, p. 22.

51. Rudolf R. Rhomberg and H. Robert Heller, "Introductory Survey," in *The Monetary Approach to the Balance of Payments*, A Collection of Research Papers by Members of the Staff of the International Monetary Fund (Washington: IMF, 1977), pp. 7-8.

52. The only explicit exceptions to this approach, prior to emergence of the petro-dollar recycling problem, came with creation of the Compensatory Financing and Buffer Stock Facilities, both of which were premised on the possibility of deficits attributable to factors beyond a country's immediate control. The two temporary Oil Facilities also accepted that deficits could be due chiefly to external rather than internal causes.

53. "A Profile of 1967-76: Role Played by Resources of Fund in Financing Payments Needs," IMF Survey, June 5, 1978, p. 164.

54. See International Monetary Fund, Annual Reports. But cf. IMF Survey, February 9, 1981, p. 33.

55. See e.g., Group of 24, Outline for a Program of Action on International Monetary Reform, reprinted in IMF Survey, October 15, 1979, pp. 319-323; North-South: A Programme for Survival, Report of the Independent Commission on International Development Issues (Brandt Commission) Cambridge, Mass.: MIT Press, 1980), Ch. 13; Sidney Dell and Roger Lawrence, The Balance of Payments Adjustment Process in Developing Countries (New York: Pergamon Press, 1980), Ch. 3-4; and Rimmer de Vries, "Urgent Tasks on the International Scene," Challence, March-April 1981, p. 49.

56. See IMF Survey, March 19, 1979, pp. 82-83; and Gold, Conditionality, pp. 14-37.

57. E. Peter Wright, "World Bank Lending for Structural Adjustment," Finance and Development, September 1980, p. 21.

58. See e.g., John Williamson, "The Growth of Official Reserves and the Issue of World Monetary Control," Paper prepared for the American Enterprise Institute Conference on the International Monetary System Under Stress, February 28-29, 1980 (typescript).

59. See e.g., Thomas D. Willett, "International Liquidity Issues and the Evolution of the International Monetary System," Paper prepared for the American Enterprise Institute and the Joint Economic Committee's Special Study on Economic Change, January 1980 (typescript), Ch. 2, pp. 91-95, and Ch. 3, pp. 3-6.

60. For a discussion, see Andrew D. Crockett, "Control Over International Reserves," International Monetary Fund Staff Papers, Vol. 25, No. 1 (March 1978), pp. 1-24.

61. Towards Full Employment and Price Stability, para. 160. See also International Monetary Fund, Annual Report, 1978, p. 48, and Willett, "International Liquidity Issues," Ch. 1.

62. Vijay Joshi, "Exchange Rates, International Liquidity and Economic Development," The World Economy, Vol. 2, No. 2 (May 1979), p. 262.

63. Towards Full Employment Price Stability, para. 161.

64. Crockett, op. cit., p. 15.

65. See e.g., ibid., p. 20; Towards Full Employment and
     Price Stability, paras. 466-470; and Geldoph A.
     Kessler, "The Need to Control International Bank
     Lending," Banca Nazionale del Lavoro Quarterly Review,
     No. 132 (March 1980), pp. 57-81.

66. Towards Full Employment and Price Stability, paras.
     466-477.

67. IMF Survey, September 3, 1979, Supplement:
     "International Lending," p. 283.

68. In most industrialized countries, foreign bank deposits
     held at domestic banks are not presently included in
     the definition of domestic money supply. See e.g., H.
     Robert Heller, "Why the Market is Demand-Determined,"
     Euromoney, February 1979, p. 44.

69. See e.g., Williamson, op. cit.; and Kessler, op. cit.,
     pp. 79-80.

70. Towards Full Employment and Price Stability, para. 468.

BALANCING THE SYSTEM IN THE 1980s: PRIVATE BANKS AND THE IMF

Benjamin J. Cohen

COMMENT

Sir Joseph Gold
Senior Consultant, International Monetary Fund[1]

CONTENTS

I.   INTRODUCTION

Professor Cohen's paper is admirable in its sweep and scholarship. I am tempted to paraphrase Oscar Wilde and say: "I wish I had written that." I hope that nobody will make the retort that was made to Wilde.

As someone called a "discussant," however, I assume that my function today is to provoke discussion, which means that I should express some doubts or differences or raise some further questions, even if I agree with much that Professor Cohen has written.

I begin, therefore, with some doubt about the introductory pages of the paper in which the assumption is expressed that the function, to quote Professor Cohen, of "balancing" the system, "once reserved in principle, exclusively" for the Fund and other multilateral agencies, came to be taken over by the banks. He implies that it would be preferable if the major part of this task were in fact undertaken by the Fund rather than by private banks.

I am doubtful about this view if it is meant to reflect the intention of the Fund's original Articles. There is ample evidence in the original Articles that the Fund was meant to supplement and not replace resources that member countries could recruit elsewhere.

I suggest that it is not undesirable for the banks to undertake a massive share of balance of payments financing. The problem is how the task of this form of financing should be shared between banks and the Fund. Two fundamental, and

172

I think uncontroversial, limits should be observed on balance of payments financing by banks: they should not lend beyond the limits of their own safety and their lending should not have the effect of obstructing adjustment. It is a weakness of the international monetary system that there are no criteria for the observance of these limits and no central authority for establishing or administering criteria. Obviously, the limits are closely related to each other. If there are improvements in adjustment and in the procedures for achieving it, banks may find it prudent to lend more.

The issue of the optimal distribution of balance of payments financing between the banks and the Fund leads me to pose three questions that are intimately related to Professor Cohen's paper:

First, is it preferable that financing by the Fund should be undertaken with subscribed resources or with borrowed resources?

Second, why have the Fund's subscribed resources been inadequate according to almost any reasonable test throughout most of the Fund's history and at the present time?

Third, if the Fund must borrow, is it preferable that it should borrow from official sources or from banks?

These are complicated questions, and I offer only a few reactions to them.

173

II. SUBSCRIBED VERSUS BORROWED RESOURCES

It seems to me that a major advantage of increasing subscribed resources and reducing the need for borrowing by the Fund is that the sense of responsibility of governments for the international monetary system is more likely to be sustained. In addition, something of the original spirit of mutual assistance among members can be preserved, although it is more difficult to make this assertion in a world of persistent deficits by many countries and persistent surpluses by others.

One expression of the spirit of mutual assistance is that, with ample subscribed resources, the Fund is in a better position to provide more assistance on concessional terms, and under less pressure to arrange subsidies to help its poorer members to pay charges to it.

The Fund is less able to act in the spirit of mutual assistance if it has to borrow on a substantial scale. Loans to the Fund tend to encourage the impression that they represent a special favor to the Fund or a special sacrifice by lenders. This impression has its effect on the financial and nonfinancial terms proposed by lenders when a loan agreement is being negotiated. Unfortunately, a similar impression has developed in some countries when increases in quotas are proposed. The U.S. Congress, for example, attaches a lengthening list of instructions to the U.S. Executive Director on aspects of the Fund's policies. Many of these instructions would be more appropriate for

174

organizations like the Red Cross. The technique, it is true, is to give instructions to the U.S. Executive Director and not to the Fund itself, which would be legally unacceptable, but if he does not prevail in a reasonable number of his enforced pursuits, one wonders what the reaction of Congress will be to further support for the Fund.

Major emphasis on borrowing by the Fund can lead to a situation in which members encourage it to look to borrowing as the primary or sole process for increasing its resources. There may be circumstances, however, in which borrowing becomes difficult. Even if resources were not scarce, it might be difficult for the Fund to borrow if lenders were to regard the Fund's usable resources as an inadequate guarantee of repayment.

Borrowing has been justified on the principle that it is appropriate when necessary to meet the abnormal needs of members, while subscriptions should be sufficient to satisfy normal needs. The distinction is sometimes expressed as the difference between the Fund's need for temporary or bridging resources and its need for permanent resources. An advantage of borrowing when justified according to this principle is that the rearrangement of quotas and voting power for transitory reasons can be avoided. Negotiations on the size and distribution of increases in quota are labyrinthine in difficulty. Moreover, legislation is necessary for a change in the U.S. quota or for lending by the United States to the Fund, but not if the Fund proposes to borrow dollars in the market, although the concurrence of the Administration is then required.

Although borrowing has these advantages, it would not be justifiable, in my opinion, if borrowing were preferred simply as a means of avoiding the agony of negotiating increases in quotas, or of avoiding the difficulties of getting legislation through Congress.

III. INADEQUACY OF SUBSCRIBED RESOURCES

Why have quotas limped so far behind needs, according to any reasonable test, even though members constantly emphasize that subscriptions should be the main source of financing the Fund? The present guidelines on the use of the Fund's resources are evidence of this inadequacy. They provide for annual use equivalent to 150 percent of quota for each of three years, apart from transactions under two policies with light conditionality. A limit of 600 per cent of quota is placed on total outstanding use, apart from outstanding use under the same policies and the oil facilities, and with allowances made for programmed repurchases (i.e., repayments). Even these multiples of quota can be exceeded if the Fund finds that it should meet a greater need. The amounts I have mentioned can be compared with the provision of the Articles that authorizes the Executive Board to grant a waiver whenever the Fund's total holdings of a member's currency would exceed 200 percent of quota, which means whenever outstanding transactions would total

176

100 percent of quota or a little more.

There are no authoritative statements on the reasons for resistance to substantial increases in the size of the Fund. One reason may be a disinclination to give more extensive authority to the Fund to determine the composition of the reserves of members whose currencies would be used by the Fund in its transactions. Members have not wanted a supranational organization in any sense of that word. Reserve positions in the Fund are assets with desirable characteristics, but members seem always to think that the characteristics could be improved when compared with some other reserve assets.

The inadequacy of quotas has provided an argument for keeping them inadequate. Members used to be reluctant to accept the Fund's conditionality in the higher credit tranches in return for the modest assistance they could get on the basis of quotas. Proposals to increase quotas substantially have been met in the past with the response that members were not using the Fund's resources in the higher credit tranches.

Although in the past the Fund made the larger part of its assistance available to developed members, it is now often perceived as predominantly an institution for the succor of developing members. This perception may be reinforced if the huge amount of assistance available to participants in the European Monetary System makes it unnecessary for them to approach the Fund. The effect could be a reluctance by developed members to increase quotas adequately because they would see no realistic prospect of direct benefits for them in such increases. Another reason for reluctance on their part might be the unrelenting pressure of developing countries to reduce the Fund's conditionality, with no apparent level at which the process would stop, together with pressure by these members to increase their relative voting power.

Two further reasons for reluctance to increase quotas may be, first, the difficulty of a radical, even though justified, rearrangement of quotas, and, second, a disinclination to increase the amounts available under those policies of the Fund that call for only light conditionality, coupled with the fact that each member's eligibility to use resources under these policies is defined in terms of the member's quota.

IV. OFFICIAL LENDERS VERSUS BANKS AS LENDERS

When the Fund's subscribed resources have seemed inadequate to meet needs, the Fund has preferred hitherto to borrow from official lenders. The Interim Committee of the Board of Governors has shared this preference and has declared that its support for borrowing did not exclude "a possible recourse to the private markets if this were indispensable." As support for borrowing from private sources, this formulation cannot be called half-hearted; it represents a much smaller fraction of cordiality.

A major argument, once again, for borrowing from official sources is that it emphasizes the sense of responsibility that governments should have for the international monetary system. Moreover, the prospect exists, perhaps for the same reason, that the terms of borrowing from official sources will be better than those offered by banks. For example, even if there were to be no difference in the rate of interest, would banks be willing to forgo charges and commissions? The terms of borrowing might not be the only relevant consideration. Official lenders to which a market-like rate of interest was being paid might be disposed to make contributions in order to subsidize the payment of charges by poorer members on transactions financed by the Fund with borrowed resources. Banks would have no such inclination.

Nevertheless, we may see something of a convergence between the terms on which the Fund will be able to borrow from official lenders and the terms that banks may offer. This convergence may become necessary in order to induce official lending to the Fund on a massive scale.

The reluctance of some officials, at least in the past, to see the Fund resort to the market has been based on a variety of considerations. These officials have not wanted the Fund to become a competitor in the capital markets. They have been concerned about the Fund's inexpertness as a borrower in the market. They have not wanted the Fund to put itself in a position in which private lenders might pass

179

adverse judgments on the Fund as a potential borrower or suggest modifications in the Fund's policies. They have thought that it was derogatory for the Fund to waive its immunity from suit as a condition of loan agreements with banks. The Fund's own preference for borrowing from official sources might create the impression that it did not have the support or confidence of its members if it turned to the market.

Professor Cohen suggests that extensive borrowing by the Fund from private banks in order to give it authority over the resources that banks could use to create official liquidity would be an advantage of this form of borrowing by the Fund. I agree with Professor Cohen that support by members for such a project would not be forthcoming, even if the legal condition that borrowing must be for the purpose of enabling the Fund to conduct its financial transactions were met.

Much has been made of technical difficulties of a legal or regulatory character if the Fund were to consider borrowing from private banks. The U.S. Treasury has sent to a Congressional committee, I think on two occasions, a staff memorandum explaining some of these difficulties. I agree with Professor Cohen that technical solutions can be found for technical problems. It becomes progressively more obvious that some of the difficulties foreseen at one time are disappearing. For example, the repeal by Congress of the Gold Clause Joint Resolution has disposed of concern that courts in the United States might not sustain the validity of the SDR as a unit of account. The spread of that unit of account is phenomenal.

V.   PROSPECTS

Experience suggests that the Fund's subscribed resources will not be increased on the massive scale that could be justified. Furthermore, given the present and perhaps future concentration of surpluses, it might be impossible to reach agreement on a redistribution of quotas that would make borrowing unnecessary. The Managing Director has made it clear in public speeches that the Fund would attempt to satisfy its needs by borrowing from official sources but that the idea of borrowing in the market is still being entertained. That borrowing might be a pilot project at the outset. Its success, however, might depend on some assurance of a continuous resort to the market.

The Fund might want to borrow from banks in order to keep all sources of finance open to it. This form of borrowing might spur members to lend or to lend larger amounts. If the asset offered by the Fund to lenders in return for loans is a desirable one, why should members concur in the holding of it by banks rather than themselves?

The choice for the Fund when borrowing need not be between official and private lenders. It could borrow concurrently from both. Its capacity to borrow from official lenders might give greater confidence of repayment to private lenders. Furthermore, borrowing from private lenders might contribute to the growth of a secondary market in which official lenders could transfer or acquire obligations of the Fund more readily. A similar effect might be achieved by borrowing from official lenders on terms that would enable them to transfer their claims to private as well as public entities.

I am led by this last possibility to suggest that, in the short run, innovation might be more likely in debtor-creditor relationships negotiated between the Fund and members than between the Fund and private banks. One could foresee, for example, placements of Fund paper with many central banks or deposits by them of their reserves with the Fund.

Borrowing by the Fund in the market could be part of some form of conjoint operation by the Fund and private banks. Professor Cohen points out, quite rightly, that the traditional attitudes of the Fund, the banks, and members seeking assistance from the Fund have not been helpful to such an operation. The Fund has wanted to preserve the fact and appearance of its independence, and to take no responsibility for the judgments of other lenders. Banks have wanted to preserve their own freedom of judgment. Members have not wanted collaborative arrangements between the Fund and banks, or even close contacts between them as a recognized policy, for fear that the Fund might have a deterrent influence on lending by banks.

Yet, if members face a persistent stringency, new traditions may have to be developed. It would be fair if all three parties were to relax their present attitudes. A thought that has crossed my mind is that, if the Fund were to consider borrowing from banks, it should do so on terms that the banks would provide some measure of direct assistance to the member. I would not be overcome with gratitude if banks offered to lend to the Fund because they wanted to maintain their business while allowing the Fund to assume all the risk. An arrangement of the kind that I have mentioned would meet a number of the problems noted by Professor Cohen, including the objection often heard in Congress and elsewhere that use of the Fund's resources enables the banks to be bailed out. An amendment of the Articles would not be necessary for the arrangements that I have mentioned.

It should be noted that an amendment to the U.S. Bretton Woods Agreements Act last year calls on the Secretary of the Treasury to report to Congress on the adequacy of the Fund's resources, the feasibility of borrowing in the market, and methods to enhance cooperation between the Fund and the banks.

I am aware that my comments have been confined almost wholly to the financing of the Fund's activities and not to the contribution these activities should make to adjustment, to the protection of the international monetary system, or to its evolution. It is not desirable to separate these aspects of the Fund from each other, or to think that the volume of the Fund's financial activities is the sole measure of its worth. You will recall Ben Jonson's lines:

"It is not growing like a tree
In bulk, doth make man better be."

It is equally true that growing like a tree in bulk doth not, in itself, make the Fund better be.

VI. <u>NOTES</u>

[1] These comments are the personal views of the author and are not to be attributed to the IMF.

BALANCING THE SYSTEM IN THE 1980s: PRIVATE BANKS AND THE IMF

Benjamin J. Cohen

COMMENT

Thierry Aulagnon

Alternate Executive Director for France
to the International Monetary Fund

CONTENTS

I.   INTRODUCTION

My task is considerably simplified, thanks to a comprehensive and at the same time extremely well-documented report circulated by Professor Cohen. His report provides us with an excellent overview of the dramatic changes that have occurred in the respective functions of the IMF and the commercial banks since the first oil shock.

That is not to say that I fully subscribe to all the conclusions of the introductory paper. I would, therefore, like to offer some personal remarks, presented from the point of view of an insider (if I may say so), on the evolution of the approach followed by the IMF in assisting members to meet their financing requirements and to adjust to the new conditions of the world economy.

I would like first to outline the present response by the Fund to the challenge of recycling which stems from the second oil shock. I will then try to outline the various implications of this new approach for the Fund itself as well as for the relations between the Fund and the Commercial banks.

II.   THE RESPONSE BY THE FUND TO THE SECOND OIL SHOCK

Professor Cohen has recalled how, following the first oil shock of 1973-74 and the profound alteration of the international pattern of current account balances, the private banking institutions came to represent, in quantitative terms, the world's single greatest source of financing

188

for balance of payments purposes. I consider such a development as fully appropriate: the banking system has shown a remarkable ability to undertake recycling on the required scale, in spite of the concerns that had been voiced at the beginning of the period. This response helped avert a serious crisis in global monetary relations and limited the deflationary impact of the oil shock. Further, the experience for the banks involved has been largely positive, in the sense that losses on this international lending have been as low or even lower than on domestic lending.

The key question for the 1980s is whether the marked swing in payments imbalances resulting from the second major round of oil price increases can or will be handled as before in the same flexible and effective manner by the international banking community.

Professor Cohen has provided us with a lucid analysis of the various considerations which could lead to a change of attitude on the part of private lenders: the decline in the profitability of overseas lending, the growing perception of economic and political risk inherent in lending to oil-importing countries, the concentration of loan portfolios, the adequacy of capital, the regulatory environment. To these considerations I would add the question of mismatching between assets and liabilities.

I think, however, that the market mechanism is basically sound and that in the 1980s banks will continue to play the same effective role they have played in the past, the

last two years included. But it is very likely that considerations of prudence will pay an increasing role. This
might lead to some hardening in the conditions of international lending, to a higher degree of selectivity and
perhaps to a level of financial flows not entirely commensurate with the actual needs of developing countries for
rapid and sustained economic growth.

In this context, commercial banks will continue to play
the major role in the current phase of recycling. But it is
clear that the Fund, in discharging its responsibilities as
guardian of the adjustment process, will have to supplement
commercial banks by providing deficit member countries with
additional resources. In my view, the necessity of an
increasing role of the Fund in the recycling process does
not exclusively -- or even principally -- result from the
uncertainties affecting the prospects for private financing,
but stems from four more fundamental considerations:

-- First, I do not think that the Fund should become
   a credit-rating institution, since this would not
   be consistent with its cooperative nature.
   Nevertheless, the involvement of the Fund often
   acts as a catalyst both to the flow of external
   private capital, through the enhancement of
   member's basic creditworthiness, and to the flow
   of assistance from donor or creditor countries.

-- Secondly, we may assume that the oil surpluses
   will not decline as rapidly as after the first oil

190

shock and that profound imbalances faced by oil-consumer countries will prevail over a long period of time. Accordingly, the assistance of the Fund both in financing and in setting up adjustment programs will be more indispensable than ever, if the non-oil developing countries are to muster a level of financing flows consistent with reasonable import levels and growth rates.

-- Thirdly, we should not lose sight of the fact that there are a number of countries in the group of low-income developing countries that do not have access to the private markets and for which, in addition to large flows of concessional loans as well as of public aid, the assistance of international institutions -- and of the Fund particularly -- is indispensable.

-- Finally, it is beyond doubt that in a number of instances, bank financing has served mainly to give temporary support to consumption expenditures at levels that were not sustainable, or has flowed to countries whose capacity to service and manage debt on commercial terms was quite limited, or to countries that have departed from sound policy management to the detriment of their growth and balance of payments prospects. A timely intervention of the Fund in such countries is, therefore, needed to promote the necessary adjustment conducive to a sustainable level of balance of payments deficit.

For these reasons, the Fund has recently taken measures to increase its role in the recycling process. I would like to mention the most important of them:

-- First, recognizing the structural nature of the non-oil developing countries difficulties, the Fund has developed a new approach to the concept of conditionality. According to the Fund's new policy, the adjustment programs supported by the institution's resources contain not only tradi- tional demand management measures to reduce excessive budget deficits and monetary expansion, but also policies geared to increasing the supply of resources and broadening the productive base. The stabilization program devised by the Fund, with the cooperation of the World Bank is, there- fore more and more an integral part of a longer- term strategy to encourage domestic savings, investment and growth.

-- Secondly, the Fund has recognized that its ability to advocate adjustment policies would be enhanced by its capacity to make larger amounts of financ- ing available to its member countries. It has, therefore, decided that countries that were ready to pursue sound demand and supply policies could draw the equivalent of 450 percent of their quotas over a 3-year period of time. This represents a dramatic increase from the previous practice of only a year ago when drawings in excess of, say, 300 percent, were quite exceptional, and a few years prior to that when drawings were strictly limited, under the Fund's Articles, to 100 percent of quotas.

-- Finally, in order to meet the financing requirements resulting from this new policy of enlarged access, the Fund has decided to borrow in 1981 between 6 and 7 billion SDRs which will supplement its ordinary resources which were increased by 50 percent at the end of last year.

Two comparisons with earlier periods give an indication of the scale and nature of the new approach followed by the Fund after the second oil shock. First, the Fund's lending operations during 1981 might well exceed 12 billion SDRs, whereas they had never exceeded 4 billion SDRs in the period 1974 to 1979. Secondly, the response to the second oil shock has not been, contrary to what happened between 1974 and 1978, to establish new facilities with a low degree of conditionality. This reflects the Fund's strong belief that financing on a larger scale has to go hand in hand with structural adjustment.

It is clear however, that while much has already been accomplished, further progress is warranted to meet the financing needs of the non-oil developing countries. I would like to try to indicate the various implications of this new approach, for the Fund itself, as well as for the commercial banks.

III. IMPLICATIONS OF THE NEW APPROACH FOR THE FUND AND THE COMMERCIAL BANKS

The Fund's new approach has two very important implications for the Fund.

The first is that, if the Fund is to lend larger amounts for longer periods, it will need to have additional resources. The Fund increased its regular resources from SDR 40 billion to 60 billion SDRs late last year, through the seventh general review of quotas. But clearly, as pointed out by Professor Cohen, the total of Fund quotas has been steadily declining as a proportion of world imports (from 12 percent in 1965 to about 7 percent at the present time). As a result, our capital still has to catch up to the level required by the present pace of our lending policy. The Fund's quotas, which are the fundamental source of financing in a cooperative and intergovernmental institution have, therefore, to be further increased. The eighth general review of quotas should provide the Fund, in due time, with a substantial amount of additional resources.

It is clear, however, that reaching an agreement on an increase in our capital will be time-consuming. This will be all the more so because it has already been agreed that this increase will include a selective adjustment in members' quotas, aimed at reflecting the new realities of our world more accurately than does the present capital structure of the Fund. In the meantime, our more active lending policy will require substantial and immediate supplementary borrowings. In this regard, it is particularly gratifying that the Managing Director could reach an agreement with the Saudi Arabian Monetary Agency under which the Fund will be able to borrow up to 4 billion SDRs a year in each of the next two years, with the possibility of some additional borrowings in the third year. I can also confirm to you that the central banks of a number of industrialized countries are actively contemplating the possibility of lending 1 billion SDRs to the Fund in 1981. There is, thus, a good chance that the financial needs of the Fund will be largely covered, in advance of the eighth general review of quotas, through official bilateral borrowing, but the possibility of approaching the private markets has not been ruled out by the Interim Committee.

The second implication concerns the relations between the Fund and the World Bank. Insofar as the Fund develops new kinds of financial programs that cover a longer period of time and include supply-side policy recommendations, it is in effect getting closer to the borderline that divides its activities from those of the Bank. It is only fair to add, however, that at the same time the World Bank has embarked on an ambitious program of structural adjustment lending which represents an important departure from its past policy of project-oriented lending, and this program also narrows the gap between Bank and Fund operations. The convergence of policies of the Fund and the Bank will require a higher and more sophisticated degree of cooperation between the two institutions than in the past, in order to ensure that the stabilization policies advocated by the Fund will remain compatible with the investment programs supported by the Bank. Some important progress has already been made in the field of cooperation, through the setting up of joint or parallel missions and a better distribution of information between the two institutions. But more should be done. Such cooperations is not intended to establish some sort of cross-conditionality -- the agreement with one institution being subject to an agreement with the other -- since this would not be consistent with the principle of independence of each. Rather, cooperation is designed to better serve the institutions' common purpose of promoting the structural adjustment of the deficit countries' economies.

I would like now to turn to another set of implications of the increasing role of the Fund in the recycling process, namely, the consequences in terms of relations between the Fund and the commercial banks.

First, there is the question of cooperation under normal circumstances. I am among those who call for a closer relationship between the IMF and private lenders, for they have common interests in spite of their distinct responsibilities and types of approaches. I do think that the present situation -- a situation in which the banks call on the Fund only as a last-resort lender, while the Fund avoids giving help to banks in assessing country risks -- is not satisfactory. I agree with Professor Cohen that we should further reflect on the relation that ought to develop between commercial banks and the Fund in assessing the needs of developing countries and the ways of financing them. This is, of course, a very sensitive issue since it touches on the very nature of the Fund which should not, in my view, become a credit-rating agency but should remain a cooperative and intergovernmental institution. At the same time, we must ensure that banks' lending decisions are made against the most comprehensive information available on the debtors' economies. To that end, without violating the principle of confidentiality on which discussions between the Fund staff missions and the national authorities are based, we should increase the scope of economic and financial data published by the Fund, subject to the agreement of the members concerned. We should also urge debtor countries themselves to publish timely data on their economies, including comprehensive data on the level and structure of their external debt and debt service ratios.

In other words, I do not think that any kind of formal link between the Fund and private lenders -- for example through granting the Fund the necessary legal power to prohibit private lending in specific instances and to require it in other cases -- would be appropriate. On the contrary, a formal link would undermine the credibility of the Fund and alter the quality of its relationship with its members. But an increased flow of information between the Fund and private bankers would help ensure a better coordination of their mutual initiatives.

This cooperation between the Fund and the private lenders is particularly warranted in cases where there is a risk that the resources made available on a large scale by the Fund might be utilized to finance repayments to the banks.

The relationship between the Fund and the commercial banks should be improved not only under normal circumstances but also in crisis situations. While any debt restructuring by the commercial banks should be regarded as exceptional, once a decision to restructure is reached, the terms need to be tailored carefully to assure the eventual normalization of debt payments. This implies that the conditions of restructuring should be consistent with the adjustment program which the Fund considers feasible in terms of the country's economic and social realities. Given this necessary interdependence, the Fund has a useful role to play, by meeting with creditor and debtor representatives to clarify the country's economic policies and prospects.

IV. CONCLUSION

On the whole, it seems to me that the Fund is presently in a better position than it was after the first oil shock to supplement effectively the role of commercial banks in the recycling process, but it also seems that more should be done to improve cooperation between the Fund and the private lenders.

I would like to conclude by pointing out that the challenge of recycling in the 1980s will not be met only through the combined action of the Fund and of commercial banks. Successful recycling requires the appropriate combination of private financing, the resources of the Fund and of the World Bank, and official flows. Taking into account the difficulties that the low-income developing countries will face, for a long time to come, in securing access to private markets, in my view it is essential that the flows of international development assistance be substantially increased.

BALANCING THE SYSTEM IN THE 1980s: PRIVATE BANKS AND THE IMF

Benjamin J. Cohen

COMMENT

Kevin Pakenham

Amex Bank Ltd., United Kingdom

Professor Cohen's paper covers a great deal of ground, interestingly and well. With much of it, I agree. Although it would be impossible to summarize, the central issue it addresses is clear: what will be the roles of the IMF and the private banks in the 1980s? He concludes that the roles will become somewhat more blurred than at present. The main reason he sees for this is the need for the IMF, and other official lenders, to be more prominent as providers of finance to deficit countries.

In my few comments, I want to point out some of the dangers in a blurring of roles and to suggest that the role of the private banks should be kept as distinct as possible. I want to suggest that the current assignment of roles is reasonably appropriate and we disturb the current arrangement at our peril.

In considering the outlook for the 1980s, we should distinguish the macro from the micro: it will help us bring into focus the roles of different parties to the international adjustment process.

With Professor Cohen's macro view, I have few quarrels. First, the non-oil developing countries (non-oil LDCs), will continue to run large deficits as a counterpart to the OPEC surplus. We forecast a non-oil LDC deficit of $132 billion by 1984.

Secondly, it is likely that banks will be less willing lenders to non-oil LDCs; though I note that the reasons evidenced are not markedly different than those in the mid 1970s, which subsequent events disproved. It is most difficult to quantify banks' willingness to lend. On the one hand, I am more optimistic than Professor Cohen on the future role of the Arab banks. Our studies show that their risk aversion is not different from the commercial banks in the Group of 10 countries, and their lending capacity is very considerable. On the other hand, I am less optimistic about opening bond markets to non-oil LDCs. Outside the banking system, the resistance to new issuers is considerable.

Thirdly, I agree that the IMF and other official lenders will play a greater role, but as I will argue later, I have reservations on this. Reductions in IMF conditionality I view with concern.

Lastly, it appears that the IMF will find it hard to influence the rate of growth of international liquidity, its traditional role. This is a consequence of the changed international monetary system with floating exchange rates and liquidity creation by the private markets. I am not hopeful that the IMF will act as a coordinator of Group of 10 central bank interest rates and international credit policy. Central bank cooperation still seems on the decrease. In any case, attempts to control international credit are going to be most difficult to implement.

I now want to move from the macro environment to the micro: the individual country situation. It is in this context I want to consider more closely the role of private banks.

Professor Cohen examines in a number of pages the
question of whether the adjustment process for each country
can work properly when the private banks are a major credit
source to sovereign borrowers. His doubts arise from three
sources: first banks do not make their lending conditional;
secondly, in consequence, banks are inclined to encourage
overexpansion; and thirdly banks are not able to force
changes in policy.

I think these doubts and worries are excessive.
Furthermore, I think there is no satisfactory alternative to
the current arrangement in its broad outline.

Let me cite five arguments suggesting the current
system works well and is unlikely to be much improved on.

First, as Professor Cohen grudgingly admits, there are
plenty of examples of successful adjustment without the
discontinuities attendant on a crisis. In the period
1975-1977, a number of countries. (Korea is the best example) tightened their domestic policies as foreign credit
became harder to come by. Other examples are Argentina,
Brazil, and the Philippines. We are seeing the same process
now. Tighter conditions make LDC governments reconsider
their policies and put greater emphasis on improving the
current account position. Professor Cohen suggests the
ratio of success to crisis is one to one. I think it is
more likely twenty successes to one crisis.

Secondly, even in countries that have run into foreign

exchange crisises, where they have not been able to adjust
quickly enough to avoid a restructuring of debt (e.g.,
Zaire, Turkey, Peru), eventually adjustment has taken place.
Peru is a good example. Perhaps, one could say the banks
should have taken a tougher line sooner; if they had, you
could argue adjustment would have been easier. But it is
always easy to criticize banks along this line -- no doubt
similar criticism can be made of bankers to any domestic
corporation hit by debt crisis. In any case, luck plays a
significant role. In Peru, it is hard to say how far the
country suffered from bad management and how far from bad
risk. I doubt whether the risk of debt crises can be
avoided if rapid economic development is to be attempted.
Debt crises are a sign of risk taking, not necessarily bad
management. I would remind you of the history of the United
States: 1870 to 1900, the industrial transition, was a
period of frequent financial crisis.

Thirdly, I think private banks are effective in influencing government policies despite the absence of formal
conditionality. LDC officials have become very expert in
judging their country's ability to raise finance and how
close to the wind they can steer to generate maximum growth
without a debt crisis. Bargains are struck between banks
and governments on the basis of mutual advantage. The
private markets place their own conditionality on borrowers.

Fourthly, the process of adjustment is a more complete
one when it operates through private financial markets.

Adjustment should not just apply to crisis situations but should be continuous. It should involve both additional inflows of capital when an economy is operating below an equilibrium current account deficit, and restrictions on availability of foreign credit when overextension is evident. Such a two-way street operates more easily with a free market. It should be noted that under the Bretton Woods system, surplus countries could never be forced to expand by the IMF, and in this failure lay seeds of its collapse.

Lastly, the current role assignment provides a method of resolving those occasional crisis situations without excessive conflict. The IMF and foreign governments can act as arbitrators, rather than participants pari passu with the banks. In this respect, I am nervous of IMF reducing its conditionality and becoming a major lender.

Can governments or the IMF be any more effective as lenders in the case of serious debt crisis? The record of the Paris Club in the 1950s and 1960s is not encouraging. I suspect that, if anything, governments find it easier to default to other governments than to private sector banks. I would suggest that as soon as the IMF becomes a major lender, it will lose its role as, dare I say, an honest broker.

Let me conclude: The problem of individual country adjustment is a problem of economic development. The problem will have to be continually resolved, it will not go

away.   There   is   no   one   correct   development   policy,   no
riskless   lending   policy.   Development   depends   on   entrepre-
neurs and risk takers.   The private sector is better fitted
for this role than official institutions.   Private banks
should be a stimulus, a way of bringing growth and development.   I think banks will play an increasing role in this
task.   I very much hope so.

CHAPTER FOUR

THE EUROPEAN MONETARY SYSTEM:

PAST EXPERIENCE AND FUTURE PROSPECTS

Jacques van Ypersele

Chef de Cabinet of the Belgian Finance Minister and
former Chairman of the EEC Monetary Committee

CONTENTS

208

I.   INTRODUCTION

It is a great pleasure for me to attend this conference on the international framework for money and banking in the 1980s. I would like to share with you a few thoughts on the European Monetary System (EMS).

Almost exactly two years ago, in fact, when the EMS had just been born, I was also in this city to participate in a conference at Brookings on the subject: "The EMS: Its Promise and Prospects". With the benefit of two years of experience with the EMS behind us, it might be interesting today to look back upon this promise and upon the expectations we had then, and to see to what extent they have been fulfilled. This brief survey of the EMS experience which I would like to conduct for you should also allow us to take a new look at the objections that were raised against the EMS when it started and which I tried to refute (inevitably in a rather abstract way) at the Brookings conference.

The international environment has changed noticeably during the past two years, thus making our short experience with the EMS diversified enough to bear a retrospective look and to yield lessons for the future.

At the time of the European Council Meetings in Bremen and Brussels that resolved to set up the EMS, the economic outlook for the Community during the 1980s was undoubtedly brighter than it is now: the European Community as a whole had eliminated the current deficit caused by the 1973-1974 oil price increase, and was indeed running a combined current account surplus of some $17 billion, while the current surplus of the OPEC countries had virtually disappeared; the terms of trade of industrialized countries as a whole, and of the European Community within that group, had registered a considerable improvement since 1974 and were fairly stable; rates of inflation in member countries, though still much too high in some cases, had fallen from the 1974-1975 peaks; finally, there had been some narrowing of inflation differentials between member countries, and the sharp divergence in balance-of-payments performances among them, which characterized the early 1970s, had been substantially reduced.

In brief, the external position of the European Community as a whole was quite strong, and conditions for exchange rate stability among member countries were more favorable than they had been for a number of years. As many observers have remarked, the good performance of the EMS during its first year was partly due to the favorable circumstances under which it was launched.

There is now a rather different set of circumstances. The doubling of crude oil prices during 1979 pushed the OPEC current surplus to about $70 billion in 1979, and $110 billion in 1980. This year it is likely to be reduced only slightly to $100 billion and next year to about $90 billion according to the IMF.

The implications for the EMS are twofold: on the one

hand, the European Community's terms of trade have once again sharply deteriorated; most of its member countries have been thrown into current deficits, and inflationary pressures have been rekindled. The balance-of-payments impact of this new oil price increase has been unevenly distributed, since some member countries are more dependent on imported oil than others. Furthermore, because of differences between countries regarding their capacity or resolve to control inflationary pressures, national inflation rates are diverging once again within the Community. On the other hand, OPEC countries once again have to dispose of vast surpluses, which they will seek to invest partly in short-term assets within the European Community, but with a tendency to direct their capital to those countries with the strongest financial performance, thus possibly aggravating exchange rate strains within the Community.

In this swiftly changing international environment, the performance of the EMS to date has to be appraised in relation to the fixed set of goals that its creators envisioned for it. So I will first review those goals before examining the results achieved by the EMS so far, and then outline proposals for the future.

II. OBJECTIVE: A ZONE OF MONETARY STABILITY IN EUROPE

The Bremen communique of 1978 referred to the creation of "a zone of monetary stability in Europe". By this was meant a zone wherein stable exchange rates between national currencies would be maintained, preferably not in a superficial and artificially constraining way, but above all though a convergence of the member countries' internal economic performances toward internal stability. Western Germany's Minister of Finance, Hans Matthoffer, clearly expressed the purpose when he said that the stability of exchange relationships within the EMS was not to be pursued for itself but rather as "the point of crystallization of a community of stability".[1] Furthermore, the enhancement of monetary stability within such a zone was viewed as a positive contribution to the stability of the international montary environment, and in particular to the relationship with the dollar.

This move toward a greater degree of exchange rate fixity among European currencies came about largely as a result of a growing dissatisfaction with exchange rate flexibility and with the great measure of instability it seemed to impart to foreign exchange markets. Such instability was felt to be harmful to investment and growth prospects in European economies. European business executives often complained that, because of every-present exchange risks and uncertainty about inflation rates, they were unable to give their companies a full European dimension and to reap the potential benefits of a market as large as Western Europe. But monetary instability is not necessarily an underlying feature of exchange rate flexibility. A number of influential voices, including some prominent

212

economists, who had long campaigned for flexible exchange rates, still continue to extol the virtues of flexible rates and to hail their near-generalization in the spring of 1973 as a great step forward in international economic relations. Since the arguments they use still underlie most of the criticisms directed at exchange rate fixity in general and at the EMS in particular, they deserve careful consideration.

In a world of independent nations but interdependent national economies, flexible exchange rates could in principle perform two irreplaceable functions: adjustment on the one hand, insulation on the other. Whenever a balance-of-payments disequilibrium develops in a country and throws the demand for foreign exchanges out of balance with the supply, exchange rate flexibility should allow a quick and automatic variation in the price of foreign exchange to restore external equilibrium swiftly and painlessly.

Since the demand for and supply of foreign exchange, within a country, are much influenced by the country's macroeconomic policy relative to the policies of other countries, both through the effect of aggregate demand on imports and through the response of short-term capital movements to intercountry interest-rate differentials, exchange rate flexibility makes compatible, to some extent, national economic policies that are pursued in uncoordinated fashion. Exchange rate fixity on the other hand implies that some other mechanism of accomodation -- running down reserves, deflating aggregate demand, or controlling imports and capital outflows -- has to be found whenever a shortage of foreign exchange develops. These alternative mechanisms place obvious constraints on the ability of a country that is open to trade and capital movements to pursue certain domestic policy objectives.

As to the insulation function performed by flexible exchange rates, it is obviously related to their capacity to restore equilibrium in the foreign exchange market. A country can afford to ignore external constraints and to pursue national economic objectives in a relatively autonomous manner only to the extent that the exchange rate mechanism takes care of external imbalances engendered by its own actions. Thus, for instance, under fixed exchange rates, a country that pursued a more expansionary policy than its trading partners would rapidly bring about growing trade deficits, deplete the country's reserves, and possible lead to the erection of protective barriers. Under flexible exchange rates, by contrast, the more rapid expansion can simply translate into a continuous depreciation of the country's currency vis-a-vis the less inflationary countries. By the same token, countries that are more oriented toward internal price stability can be insulated by an appreciating currency from the inflationary tendencies that develop outside of them, tendencies which would surely contaminate them under exchange rate fixity. Thus, exchange rate flexibility was said to "bottle up" inflation in the countries where it originated. According to Milton Friedman's classic essay, flexible exchange rates "are a means of permitting each country to seek for monetary stability according to its own lights, without either imposing its mistakes on its neighbors or having their mistakes imposed on it".[2]

In a world where rates of inflation have a tendency to diverge wildly, as in the 1973 boom and subsequent episode of stagflation-recession, in which balance of payments were thrown sharply into disequilibrium by the oil price increases, exchange rate flexibility played the role of a safety valve. Thus wrote Marina v.N. Whitman: "There can be little doubt that the avoidance of a wholesale retreat into competitive protectionism in the face of accelerating and divergent rates of inflation, the oil crisis, and the subsequent widespread recession, was made possible by the shift from pegged rates to managed floating".[3]

More recently, prominent critics of the EMS and of the relative exchange rate fixity built into it have deplored the fact that countries with relatively stable prices, such as Germany, might have to accept a certain amount of imported inflation from the more inflationary ones. Thus Dr. Otmar Emminger, former president of the Deutsche Bundesbank, recently remarked at an American Enterprise Institute Conference in Washington: "Our experience in Germany has clearly shown that in the past free floating, far from having an inflationary effect, shielded us from imported inflation. Germany and Switzerland went over to floating in early 1973 not primarily with the aim of adjusting their payments balances but mainly in order to shield their monetary systems from destablising inflows of foreign exchange".[4]

Why is it then that the practical experience with generalized floating among the major currencies has not been satisfactory enough to give this sytem permanent credibility and acceptability? Contrary to what its advocates expected, flexibility has been accompanied by much instability in exchange markets and exchange rates have fluctuated much more widely than underlying economic conditions and inflation differentials would seem to warrant, while payments imbalances between industrial countries, far from being swiftly eliminated, remained on the average very large after 1973.

The first difficulty with the flexible rate system is that adjustments apparently do not take place in the manner predicted by simple theoretical models that focus on the trade balance. Flows of international trade appear to be influenced only slowly by exchange rate variations, but react quite rapidly to variations in aggregate demand. There is a new mood of "elasticity pessimism" which is borne out by a number of empirical studies. For instance, a recent econometric analyses by Miles[5] finds that in almost all of the sixteen cases studied in the period 1962 to 1967, the trade balance was not affected by a devaluation; indeed it worsened initially, and the small improvement in the year following the devaluation was not large enough to recoup the initial worsening. There is a temporary improvement in the balance-of-payments, which appears to be a stock adjustment phenomenon lasting about two years and which is explained in the Miles study by the devaluing country's desire to rebuild its real balances. Real balances are initially reduced by a devaluation and are rebuilt by an exchange of bonds for money resulting in a net capital inflow. One may add that, in today's conditions, where trade deficits are mostly due to oil-price increases, exchange rate variations are even less effective for adjustment, given the low price-elasticity of demand for oil in the short run. Hence, even more emphasis should be laid on adjustment by means of internal economic policies.

Of course, such evidence is not sufficient to invalidate the case for flexible exchange rates. One can still claim that exchange rate variations will work for adjustment if they are accompanied by the right supporting measures aimed at aggregate demand. In the case of countries with a chronic deficit and a high rate of inflation, a currency depreciation can presumably be effective if it is accompanied by measures to control aggregate demand and the money supply. On the other hand, currency appreciation can reduce a balance-of-payments surplus if it goes hand in hand with expansionary measures at home.

The question becomes then whether such supporting

217

measures, which are necessary in any case, are more likely to be taken with a variation in the exchange rate than without. The record of recent experience with flexible exchange rates among major currencies leaves one skeptical on that score. As Henry Wallich puts it concisely: "The promise of speedy adjustment of payment imbalances through exchange rate movements has reamined unfulfilled, perhaps because the very ease with which exchange rates could move has diminished political pressure to adopt appropriate fiscal and monetary policies".[6]

Along the same lines, it has been argued that exchange rate variations will be effective for adjustment provided they lead to "real" changes in exchange rates and are not offset by an increase in the inflation differential. But, as we shall see, such offsetting movements in the form of "vicious" or "virtuous" circles tend to emerge under exchange rate flexibility, especially in the more open and smaller economies.

A crucial factor in altering the nature of the exchange rate adjustment mechanism, by comparison with the expections of the proponents of exchange rate flexibility, has been the importance of short-term capital movements. As Fritz Machlup commented: "Few of us realized before the 1960s that capital movements would swamp the foreign-exchange market to such an extent that transactions associated with the flows of merchandise could become relatively insignificant".[7]

The fact that asset markets react much more rapidly than the flows of trade, so that exchange rates are more and more often determined by portfolio adjustments is undoubtedly behind the prevalence of the phenomenon of "overshooting".

Under flexible exchange rates, a country whose currency appreciates because of, say, a favorable trade balance, will not necessarily see its trade surplus being corrected very fast by the exchange rate appreciation. But that country is likely to attract in the meantime, short-term foreign capital which speculates on the chances of a further appreciation; and the surplus which appears in the balance of capital flows will in effect cause a new appreciation, thus justifying ex post the speculators' expectations. The reverse phenomenon will of course occur in a country whose currency initially depreciates because of a deficit on current account.

This capital mobility, coupled with the tendency of asset markets to adjust more rapidly than goods markets, is what causes "overshooting" and also reduces the effectiveness of the insulation that exchange rate flexibility was supposed to provide. Imagine a country that takes advantage of the "license to inflate" which exchange rate flexibility supposedly gives and lets its currency depreciate accordingly. If overshooting occurs, the exchange rate depreciation will exceed the inflation differential. But the rising prices of imported goods will feed the inflationary process, and a vicious circle of depreciation-inflation is likely to get started. Excessive movements in the exchange rate thus tend to be accomodated ex post by price movements.

Thus, under flexible exchange rates, capital movements make it difficult for a counry to keep under control an inflationary process which, under fixed exchange rates, would at least be disciplined by the external constraint. The freedm to inflate under the false protection of a flexible exchange rate may rapidly turn into an uncontrollable addiction[The fear of being thrown in such vicious circles, coupled with a growing recognition of the short-run ineffectiveness of exchange rate variations in correcting fundamental disequilibria, helps to explain the very strong resistance to devaluation shown by all member countries of the EMS when their currencies come under pressure.

This reason for dissatisfaction with floating -- the fear of vicious circles associated with overshooting movements -- is of course much greater for more open and smaller economies. It applies with less force for more closed and large economies such as the American one.

The reasoning behind this statement is that changes in exchange rates result in greater changes in import prices for smaller economies. Secondly, the changes in import prices have a greater influence on domestic prices in more open and smaller economies that heavily depend on imported goods.

Let us take these two factors again. First, changes in exchange rates result in greater changes in import prices in smaller economies. These economies are apt to face a highly elastic supply of imports and may also have a lower demand elasticity because they can less easily substitute domestic for foreign goods.

Second, import price changes have a greater influence on domestic prices in more open and smaller economies that depend heavily on imported goods. In such economies imports of final goods enter to a greater extent directly into domestic consumption, and as imported inputs to make domestic goods.[8]

In the EEC, the degree of openness as expressed in the imports of goods and services as a share of total domestic demand is the following: Ireland (54%), Belgium (49%), Netherlands (47%), Denmark and United Kingdom (each 30%), Italy (25%), Germany (23%), and France (20%). Comparable figures for the United States and Japan are about 10%.

Not only are the reasons for dissatisfaction with floating rates less forceful for large countries, but it is clear that at the present there is no viable alternative to floating on a world wide basis between large economic entities such as the United States, Europe and Japan.

At the regional level, such as the EEC, where the economies are closely integrated, where on the average intra-EEC trade represents more than 50% of the trade of all member countries, the disadvantages of floating are greater, and a system of stable but adjustable rates is feasible as the EMS experience proves.

III. THE EMS PERFORMANCE DURING ITS FIRST TWO YEARS

Has the EMS succeeded so far in fostering closer monetary coopration and creating a zone of monetary stability in Europe? I propose to answer this complex question in three steps:

-- First I will claim that the EMS was quite successful in promoting greater nominal exchange rate stability among member countries;

-- Next I will admit that unfortunately this greater exchange rate stability was not accompanied by a greater convergence of member countries' economic results, although this criticism has to be qualified because of the second oil shock.

-- Finally I argue that the EMS' relatively unsatisfactory performance with regard to convergence, and in particular the persisting divergence of inflation rates among member countries, has not so far inconvenienced the more price-stable countries in the way that its detractors like to stress.

For the sake of brevity I will not describe here the specific mechanisms of the EMS, which by now have been amply covered, analyzed and illustrated in many official documents and financial publications. I will concentrate instead on

222

the results achieved by the operation of those mechanisms. The interested reader can consult another article in which the mechanisms are described in some detail.[9]

1. Greater Exchange Rate Stability

First of all it appears that the EMS has succeeded in eliminating the phenomenon of "overshooting" among member countries' currencies and has thereby contributed to much greater exchange rate stability, without at the same time making the system and the parity-grid as rigid as some had feared. The exchange mechanism, which specifies the authorized limits of fluctuations between currencies, has performed well.

Since the EMS came into force on 13 March 1979, the fluctuations in the exchange rates of the currencies participating in the system have been the most moderate recorded for eight years, notwithstanding the realignments of 23 September and 30 November 1979 and the recent devaluation of the lira. For the Community currencies taken together, the annual average fluctuation against the ECU in 1979 was 1.9% compared with 2.7% in 1978 and an average of 5.2% over the period 1973-1978. One must reach back to 1972 to find a lower figure (1.2%).

This relative stability was achieved without making the exchange mechanism and the parity grid as rigid as many had feared. Indeed this was the most important fear expressed at the start of the system and it underlaid most of the

223

objections made to the EMS. Nevertheless, three realignments of central rates within the EMS have taken place so far -- the September 23, 1979 realignment, the devaluation of the Danish krone in November 1979, and the devaluation of the lira recently -- and these realignments were accomplished swiftly and quietly. On the recent devaluation of the lira, the _Financial Times_ commented that "the devaluation itself showed how EEC politicians and central bankers have mastered the technical details of carrying out exchange rate adjustments without causing undue flutters on the currency markets".

Second, one has to underline the amount of flexibility which is provided by the authorized 2.25% margins of fluctuation between EMS currencies (6% in the case of the lira).

Finally, one has to remark that the system floats vis-a-vis third currencies, and that this property gives each EMS currency some additional flexibility.

These elements of flexibility, coupled with diverging national price movements, explain the fact that some real exchange rate movements occurred for the EMS currencies in this period. At one extreme, the largest competitive gains were recorded by Denmark and Ireland, with "real" depreciation in the order of 15%. In the former case the competitive gain was largely due to exchange rate depreciation. In the latter case, the competitive gain was due to the appreciation of Sterling, which plays an important role in the effective exchange rate of Ireland. Belgium, too, has achieved an improvement in its competitive position, as a result of a good price performance, and has made up part of the loss of competitiveness experienced in the years 1973-1976. At the other extreme, Italy is the only country within the EMS to have shown an appreciation in its real exchange rate. Prior to the recent devaluation of the lira, Italy's loss of competitiveness since March 1979 may have amounted to some 10% against all her major trading partners, but to nearly 15% vis-à-vis EC member countries.[10] The devaluation of the lira can thus be seen, in retrospect, as a necessry adjustment of real parities that had gone far out of line. It also indicates that an increasing divergence of inflation rates cannot be sustained for too long among trading countries without endangering external stability.

2.   Insufficient Convergence Toward Internal Stability

Although normal exchange rate stability is a desirable goal and although it has possibly helped sustain business and trade among the EMS members, it was not envisioned by the EMS creators that stability was as an objective in itself.   Rather, exchange rate stability is a means toward, and a result of, the convergence of the member countries' national economic performances.

On this score, the EMS has visibly not produced very satisfactory results.   The weighted average inflation rate in the European Community, coming down from the 1975 peak, reached a low 6.8% in 1978, but climbed again to 8.7% in

225

1979 and 11.8% in 1980. In addition the divergence among member countries' inflation rates went up: the weighted standard deviation of the inflation rates went up from 1.31% in 1978 to 1.65% in 1979 and to 2.29% in 1980. Excluding sterling, the weighted standard deviation was 1.52% in 1978, 1.74% in 1979 and 2.47% in 1980.

One should nevertheless qualify the negative impression left by these raw numbers. In fact, one should not compare the period since the beginning of 1979 with the immediately preceding years in view of the strong inflationary impulse of the second round of oil-price increases, the start of which roughly coincided with the launching of the EMS. As Niels Thygesen stressed recently, a fairer basis of comparision would be with the two or three years following the first wave of oil-price increases in late 1973. The surge in both the average inflation rate and the dispersion around it inside the EEC, has been smaller over the past two years than in 1973-1975. A preliminary verdict, therefore, is that the second oil-price increase has generated less violent and less persistent inflation in the EEC countries than the first. This is all the more remarkable when account is taken of the fact that most EEC currencies appreciated during 1973-1975, whereas -- with the exception of Sterling -- they have remained relatively stable on the average in effective-rate terms since the start of the EMS.

Thygesen concludes that "though it would be naive to attribute this difference to the reinforcement of European monetary cooperation between the 1973-1975 period of the snake/mini-snake and the EMS of 1979-1980 -- the higher priority in most countries to anti-inflationary policies being no doubt the basic explanatory factor -- the relative improvement in inflationary performance is too often over-looked by critics of the EMS".[11]

This qualification being made, the fact remains that inflation rates have increasingly diverged during the first two years of the EMS. The fact that this divergence of inflation rates could increasingly develop within a system of relatively stable exchange rates without creating great tensions is surprising and it contradicts previous expecta-tions. In such a system one could expect a country whose costs and prices would start diverging upwards from its partners' average to gradually lose its competitiveness and therefore to see downward pressure building up on its currency. The EMS mechanisms would then lead this country to adopt a stricter monetary policy in order to defend its exchange rate, which would at the same time help stabilize its costs and prices. Thus, under normal circumstances, the EMS exchange mechanisms and the instruments associated with it -- in particular the divergence indicator -- would have helped bring about a lesser divergence of inflation rates. The increasing divergence that was observed instead was not due to improper functioning of the mechanisms, but to a peculiar set of circumstances.

The divergence indicator played a useful role,

especially in the cases of Belgium and Denmark. The authorities of both countries played by the rules when their
currencies crossed their respective divergence thresholds.

Tensions within the EMS, whenever they occurred, seem
to have been provoked less by inflation differentials than
by balance-of-payments considerations. For instance, in the
episode of weakness of the DM against the French franc a few
months ago, which was reflected in the behavior of their
respective divergence indicators, the paradox was that the
strong-currency country, France, had a rate of inflation
which is -- and has been for a number of years -- more than
double the rate of the weak-currency country, Germany.
Similarly, when the Belgian franc came under attack in 1979,
in the spring of 1980 and recently again, the Belgian rate
of inflation was among the lowest in the European Community.
By contrast, in 1979, France and Italy remained strong
within the EMS, thanks to their favorable balance-of-payments situations, though with much higher rates of inflation. This pattern seems to have continued in 1980, with
the French franc remaining at the top of the EMS most of the
time, the Belgian franc being rather weak, the Italian lira
weakening as Italy's external account deteriorated sharply,
and the German mark following the same pattern for essentially the same reason, despite Germany's remarkable performance on the front of internal price stability. In recent
months however, this situation began to change with the DM
firming up.

228

To a large extent, the same kind of pattern could be observed in the exchange relationships between EMS countries and third countries in the period under review: a recent IMF memorandum observes that "the sharp deterioration of the current account positions of the EMS countries relative to other major industrial countries seems to account primarily for the downward movement in the exchange rates of the EMS currencies since early 1980. Particularly important in that context was a gradual realization that the factors behind the change in the pattern of relative external positions against the EMS countries are likely to persist over the next few years. The sharp appreciation of the pound sterling in real terms over the past three years -- in excess of 50 pecent -- is clearly attributable in large degree to current account developments and prospects related to North Sea oil and the deep U.K recession".

3. Were More Stability-Oriented Countries Forced to "Import" Inflation Under EMS Rules?

According to many prominent critics of the EMS, the pursuit of exchange rate stability and the resulting commitment on the part of member countries to intervene in order to preserve the agreed-upon parity grid leads those among them that are more attracted toward internal price stability and more successful in attaining that goal to give it up partially by "importing" the inflation which originates within laxer partners. This can occur both as an effect of the tendency toward uniformity of price displayed by internationally traded goods and because the strong-currency countries, through their interventions on foreign exchange markets, may be induced to expand their money supplies beyond what they deem appropriate for internal stability.

In response to that argument, which is of course perfectly respectable on a theoretical plane, I think it is appropriate to make the following points:

(1) The three realignments of central rates that occurred proved that the EMS was not as rigid as was feared by many initially. A major concern in Germany had been that it would be impossible under EMS rules to achieve in time the unavoidable parity readjustments;

(2) While it is true that speculative flows of capital lead strong-currency countries to intervene in order to prevent appreciations of their currencies beyond the authorized limits, as happened several times during the first year of EMS, the volume of those interventions was never so large as to prevent the objectives of internal monetary growth from being achieved in the intervening countries. For there are ways to neutralize the effects of such interventions on the monetary base, and the Bundesbank in Germany, among others, used them. During the third trimester of 1979, the tensions within the EMS were strongest, because of the renewed weakness of the dollar, and during that period the Bundesbank had to purchase foreign exchange worth 20

billion Deutsche mark. But the effect of these speculative capital inflows on the monetary base in Germany
was largely offset by internal credit restrictions.[12]
And data on the growth of the monetary stock in Germany
do not indicate that it accelerated during that period;
on the contrary, it decelerated.

(3)   Finally, the turnaround in the current account of
      Germany's balance-of-payments, with a 10 billion
      Deutsche mark deficit in 1979 and a deficit of 28
      billion Deutsche mark in 1980, as well as the outflow
      of German short-term capital toward the dollar in 1980
      have pushed the Deutsche mark toward a median or lower
      position within the EMS until recently. Therefore one
      could no longer claim that the exchange mechanism
      prevented an appreciation of the Deutsche mark.

When the movement of short-term capital between dollar
and the DM reversed its course and when the DM showed some
weakness within the EMS, the EMS rules forced the Bundesbank
to sell foreign exchange in order to support the mark and to
follow a generally restrictive monetary policy. Then some
German observers complained that such behavior was forced
upon their monetary authorities at a time when internal
conditions would possibly call for a more expansionary
policy. But surely the EMS could not be blamed for the
strength of the dollar vis-à-vis the DM. And it is doubtful
whether, if the EMS did not exist, German authorities would

have let the DM depreciate further against the dollar and run the risk of a vicious circle of depreciation-inflation.

One could sum up the debate by saying that German commentators tend to accuse the EMS of being inflationary when the DM is strong against the dollar and of being deflationary when the DM is weak against the dollar. But it seems to me that the fluctuations between the dollar and the DM are more responsible for these events than the EMS.

IV.   SOME PRACTICAL PROPOSALS FOR THE FUTURE
1.   Improving Policy Coordination Toward the Dollar

In the present state of affairs, it is to a large extent the Bundesbank -- jointly with the Federal Reserve -- that determines the common EMS policy toward the dollar. This is one aspects of the key currency position enjoyed (or endured) by the DM within the EMS, and it reflects the great financial stability which Germany offers in the eyes of international investors. If other EMS currencies were equally attractive from the view point of financial stability, no doubt international investors would more equally spread their short-term assets over the European Community, and occasional flights from or to the dollar would not be so massively concentrated on the DM. Thus, in the long run, a better convergence of economic performances within the Community might be conducive to a more balanced common policy toward the dollar.

Meanwhile, the current state of affairs has obvious

232

drawbacks. When the dollar weakens, the flight toward the mark creates tensions within the EMS. The Federal Reserve can help relax those tensions by using its SWAP-credit line with the Bundesbank to sell DMs on the market. However, when the dollar has regained some strength, the U.S. authorities have to purchase DMs on the market in order to extinguish their debt toward the Bundesbank, and sometimes they do it without much regard for the state of exchange relationships within the EMS. A new upsurge of the DM and new tensions can thus arise, which may not bear any objective relationship with underlying economic conditions in the European Community.

At other times, when the weakness of the dollar does not push the DM upward, the use of the DM as the favorite intervention currency by the Federal Reserve may again create tensions within the EMS. Thus in the first weeks of April 1980, interest rates in the U.S. dropped, and so did the dollar; but at the same time the DM was weak within the EMS due to the magnitude of Germany's current account deficit. Nevertheless the Fed started selling DMs in order to sustain the dollar, thus pushing the DM down to its floor in the EMS, and forcing the Banque de France to buy DMs. The Fed realized this after a while and used French francs in limited amounts to intervene in support of the dollar.

But European central banks, by using the dollar too exclusively for their interventions without coordination, can be guilty of the same kind of sin toward the U.S.

233

currency. Americans have often complained of the dominant use of the dollar for market interventions. This use can create strong -- even though unintended -- upward or downward pressures on the market rates of the dollar, irrespective of any development in the underlying balance of payments of the United States, simply because European countries' surpluses or deficits caused them to switch from eager to reluctant dollar holders, or vice versa. Therefore the Americans found a particular feature of the EMS attractive: the replacement, in principle at least, of the dollar by Community currencies for market interventions and by the ECU in the settlement of mutual credits.

According to the present EMS rules, when a country intervenes at the margins to sustain its currency, it can use the VSTC (very short-term credit) facilities provided by the system, in which case its debt will be denominated in ECUs but can be repaid at any time before maturity in the creditor's currency. However, the bulk of market interventions in the EMS so far have been "intra-marginal", involving therefore no FECOM (Fond European pour la Cooperation Monetaire) financing and presumably continuing, as before the EMS, to be carried out mostly in dollars.

The current system of bilateral SWAP-credits between the Federal Reserve and European central banks totals more than $15 billion, out of which $6 billion is between the Fed and the Bundesbank. But in practice it has been only the credit line with the Bundesbank (and to a modest extent, in

1980, with the Banque de France) that is activated.

I would thus present the following proposal, which was formally introduced by the Belgian Prime Minister at the most recent European Council in Maastricht. One feasible step toward a better coordination of policies toward the dollar would be to replace part or all of the existing bilateral SWAP agreements by a FECOM-Federal Reserve SWAP-credit line. This credit line could be used in such a way as to stabilize the exchange market within the EMS instead of creating tensions, to the extent that the currency used by the Fed for reimbursing the FECOM would not need to be the same as the one borrowed for intervention. Suppose, for instance the Fed draws on its credit line with the FECOM and borrows a certain amount of ECUs; it then requests the FECOM to convert those ECUs into DMs in order to intervene on the market, and the FECOM borrows those DMs from Bundesbank. At this stage then, the FECOM would be a creditor of the Fed (in ECUs) and a debtor of the Bundesbank (in DMs).[13]

In a second stage, at the time of reimbursing the FECOM, the Fed would consult with its European partners, and would notice, for instance, the strength of the DM and the relative weakness of the Belgian Franc. It would then buy Belgian Francs to reimburse FECOM. The FECOM would end up being creditor of the Belgian National Bank and debtor of the Bundesbank, a situation analogous to the one that might result from activating the VSTC mechanism in the EMS.

235

2. Securing a Better Convergence Among Member Countries' National Economic Performance

Another immediate goal worth striving for is better convergence among member countries' national economic performances. This is indeed essential for a successful continuation of the EMS experience. Though there are, as I pointed out earlier, external circumstances that explain why an increasing divergence of inflation rates could develop within the EMS without so far creating tensions and endangering the stability of exchange rate relationships, this state of affairs should not be taken for granted. The increasing weakness of the Italian lira last year, and its recent devaluation, were no doubt a reflection of Italy's persistent inflation at a rate much above its EMS parters.

Thus, among the urgent tasks facing the EMS, it must secure a greater degree of convergence toward internal stability among member countries' national economic performances, and possibly set up new mechanisms for achieving convergence.

One area in which greater convergence should be strived for is the sensitive field of wage formation. One could at least aim at a greater harmonization of policies affecting incomes development.

A second area of convergence is greater harmonization of fiscal policies which at present are much too divergent and contribute to divergences in balance-of-payments positions and inflation rates.

3.   Enlarging the Role of the ECU

As announced in the December 1978 agreement, the final consolidation of the EMS' mechanisms and procedures should entail "full utilization of the ECU as a reserve asset and a means of settlement". Once again, I believe that immediate steps can be taken to enlarge the role of the ECU, without having to wait for the final stage of the EMS to come about. These immediate steps could, moreover, make the transition to the final stage easier.

If the ECU is to be fully used one day as a reserve asset and a means of settlement within the EMS, one could start by removing, totally or by steps, existing limits on its acceptability for settlement between central banks. Under the present arrangements, when a member country intervenes at the margins and uses the VSTC facilities for that purpose, its debt will be denominated in ECU. If the debt is repaid before maturity, the creditor's currency can be used for that purpose. ECUs will normally be used for paying the debt at maturity, but the creditor has no obligation to accept a settlement in ECUs for more than 50% of his claim. For intra-marginal interventions, the debtor has no automatic access to the VSTC facilities, but can be granted such access with the creditor's agreement, in which case the rules for settlement which I just mentioned will apply.

In the EMS' final stage, it is clear that all the claims and debts between EMS central banks should be denominated and settled in ECUs. Meanwhile, one could already

237

change the 50% acceptability limit which now exists, either by dropping it entirely, or by specifiying a less restrictive limit such as, for instance, total acceptability up to the point where a central bank holds a certain proportion of its reserves in ECUs.

Another direction in which the role of the ECU can be enlarged is in its private use. There are obvious steps that could be taken in this direction. EMS governments and European institutions could issue ECU-denominated bonds or short-term notes, or bonds with an ECU guarantee; and private banks could issue and trade certificates of deposit denominated in ECUs, in the same way as such CDs denominated in SDRs have very recently been issued on the London market by a group of banks.

Making the ECU more acceptable would also imply that national regulations regarding its use should be scrutinized so as to eliminate any discrimination which presently exists against this unit as compared to other denominations such as the dollar.

Such promotion of the ECU for private use would not only enhance its potential status as a reserve asset; it might also usefully complement the pursuit of other goals by the EMS. By offering the ECU as a suitable alternative to the DM or another national currency for the purpose of reserve diversification by dollar-holders, it would help reduce potential tensions that exist in the EMS whenever there is a massive conversion of dollars into one national

238

currency or vice-versa.

4. Bringing the United Kingdom Within the EMS

Finally, I believe it has now become feasible and desirable to make the United Kingdom a full-fledged member of the EMS by having the pound sterling participate in the exchange mechanism, though preferably with the 6% authorized margins of fluctuation that also apply to the lira. This larger margin would simply recognize the petro-currency character of sterling and the corresponding likelihood that sterling will remain more volatile on foreign exchange markets and therefore need more flexibility than other European currencies.

This goal is now feasible because inflation seems to be coming down fast in the UK, while the country's balance of payments position is firm. Therefore the objective of stabilizing the country's exchange rate becomes more important, as the advantage of allowing a continued appreciation of the exchange rate in order to fight inflation recedes in importance, while the consequences of a burst of monetary expansion that would follow from upward pressure on the exchange rate are less to be feared.

Opponents to this move in the UK often use the argument that UK membership in the EMS would have caused considerable strains to the system, in view of the fact that sterling has appreciated by more than 20% vis-à-vis the ECU since the fall of 1978. (One must remember, though, that initially sterling was kept out of the EMS because it was thought that membership would maintain the pound at too high a rate.) This statement is probably true, but it is no longer a valid argument for opposing membership, unless one believes that another 20% appreciation of the pound is both likely and desirable.

Of course the rate at which the pound would enter the parity-grid would need to be carefully chosen, but the difficulty in finding an appropriate rate is no proof that continued floating and the dangers of overshooting provide a better solution to the UK's exchange rate problem.

The obvious advantage to the UK would be to become a member of a larger zone of stability which could improve the trade prospects for the UK. A firm commitment to EMS would help stabilize exchange market expectations, and avoid the negative effects of overshooting.

Apart from the benefit for the UK, one definite advantage of bringing the pound in the exchange mechanism of the EMS would be related to the setting up of the Fed-FECOM swap which I proposed earlier as a desirable alternative to the present system of bilateral swaps. Such an arrangement, and the methods of intervention it would entail for the Fed, would become more attractive to Americans if a third great currency, in addition to the DM and the French franc, became available for intervention purposes.

5. Preparing the EMS Final Stage

I have made four practical proposals, namely:

-- To improve the policy coordination toward the dollar by setting up a FECOM-Fed swap credit line;

-- To secure a better convergence among member countries' economic performances;

-- To enlarge the role of the ECU by dropping the existing acceptability limits on its use between central banks and by encouraging its private use;

-- And finally, to bring the pound sterling into the EMS with 6% authorized margins.

I believe these proposals should be acted upon in the short run, and that their implementation would improve both the day-to-day functioning of the EMS and its capability to meet its final objectives. They should not be seen as a way to keep the system alive through minor adjustments while its final stage would remain in limbo for an indefinite future. Nor, should they be seen as a substitute for consolidation into a final stage which one has temporarily given up.

Quite the contrary. These proposals aim at keeping the EMS moving and at making the transition to its final stage easier. Thus their intent is to accelerate the coming of the final stage.

The final stage of the EMS will involve the creation of the European Monetary Fund to replace the existing FECOM. This should represent not merely a minor adjustment of the

241

FECOM, but an important qualitative step forward on the road toward European monetary integration. The ultimate goal should be the creation of a sort of European central bank that could effectively contribute to the harmonization of monetary policies in Europe and stimulate a greater degree of monetary stability.

Transfers in dollars and gold by European central banks to the future EMS will need to be permanent and not simply 3-month renewable swaps as is the case now with the FECOM. This will be necessary for a genuine pooling and joint management of reserves to take place, and will thus lay the ground for a full coordination of monetary and exchange rate policies.

In addition, a real transfer of ownership of gold and dollars to the EMF will allow this institution to regulate the process of ECU-creation according to member countries' needs, instead of making it simply the automatic result of the appreciation of the market value of gold, as is the case under present conditions.

Finally, the existing short-term credit mechanisms will have to be consolidated within the EMF: central banks would transfer to the Fund their competence in the areas of very short term financing and short term monetary support. This consolidation of various mechanisms that were set up at various periods would not only simplify the procedures and multilateralise credit relationships; it would also promote the role of the ECU.

As it is now, the EMS has already achieved positive results, not only in promoting greater exchange rate stability among European currencies, but also in bringing out in the open the necessary conditions of convergence for sustaining exchange rate stability. It has thus reinforced the case for a deeper monetary and economic integration in Europe.

To conclude, I would like to comment briefly on the present stance of economic and monetary policies in the industrial world.

I am convinced that we should keep as a primary objective the fight against inflation, and continue to make the structural adjustments that are needed after the second oil shock. We have to continue to resist the temptation that we could somehow better combat unemployment by putting less emphasis on the struggle with inflation. On the other hand, the structural adjustments we have to make are necessary to decrease the constraints which are imposed on the industrial world by the energy crisis.

Nevertheless we have to pay special care, it seems to me, to the relative weights we give to the various policy instruments we use in our fight against inflation. We can ask ourselves if, after the second oil crisis, we have not relied too much on monetary policy to reduce inflation. Faced with inflationary expectations which were fueled by the second oil shock, monetary policies on the whole have been restrictive and have been accompanied by very high interest rates with occasional sharp fluctuations.

Such policies not only carry the danger of inducing or unduly prolonging a recession; they may also negatively affect the longer-term outlook for growth and productivity. The structural adjustments and the corresponding investment efforts required of Western economies may not materialize rapidly enough in view of the high level of interest rates and the uncertainty that their ample fluctuations create, with the resulting uncertainty concerning exchange rate relationships. Attempts to modify the structure of aggregate demand away from consumption and toward investment may, in a climate where private investment is discouraged, produce instead an absolute decline in the level of aggregate demand and engineer a cumulative depression.

It seems very important -- and this was stressed by many European leaders at the last Summit of the EEC in Maastricht -- that both sides of the Atlantic Ocean should pursue less restrictive monetary policies and use other instruments more actively, such as fiscal and incomes policies, in waging the necessary fight against inflation. Putting emphasis only on monetary policies and neglecting the other instruments implies in my mind, a too simplistic view of present economic realities.

This being said, I want to stress that my comments are not only directed to policies in the United States, but also to Europe. As a matter of fact they apply to my own country, where to bring about the necessary adjustments we

have relied, since the first oil crisis, too much on monetary policy and not enough on budgetary and policies incomes
policies.

V. NOTES

[1] Hans Matthoffer, "Reden in der Feierstunde anlasslich des Wechsels in der Leitung der Deutschen Bundesbank," Frankfort-am-Main, 20 December 1979. Deutsche Bundesbank - Auszuge aus Presseartikeln n. 2, 4 January 1980.

[2] Milton Friedman, Essays in Positive Economics, University of Chicago Press, 1980.

[3] Marina v.N. Whitman, "Sustaining the International Economic System," Princeton Essays in International Finance, June 1977.

[4] Otmar Emminger, "Remarks" at a Conference of the American Enterprise Institute in Washington on 28 February 1980. Deutsche Bundesbank - Auszuge aus Presseartikeln n. 28, 27 March 1980.

[5] Marc A. Miles, "The Effects of Devaluation on the Trade Balance and the Balance of Payments," Journal of Political Economy V. 87, n. 3, June 1979.

[6] Henry C. Wallich, "Exchange rates, Inflation and the Dollar," Impact, n. 30, February 1980.

[7] Fritz Machlup, "Comment" at a Conference on the Emerging European Monetary System, Bulletin de la Banque Nationale de Belgique, n. 4, April 1979.

[8] Peter Kenen, and Clare Pack, , "Exchange Rates, Domestic Prices and the Adjustment Process," Group of Thirty, New York, 1980.

[9] Jacques van Ypersele, "Operating Principles and Procedures of the European Monetary System," in Philip H. Trezise, editor, The European Monetary System: Its Promise and Prospects, Washington, D.C., The Brookings Institution, 1979.

[10] Rainer Masera, "The first two years of the EMS: the exchange rate experience," Seminar on European Monetary Integration, Copenhagen, 13-14 March 1981.

[11] Niels Thygesen, "Are monetary policies and performances converging?," Seminar on European Monetary Integration, Copenhagen, 13-14 March 1981.

[12] Jacques van Ypersele, "Bilanz und Zukunftperspektiven des Europaischen Wahrungssystems," Integration, Institut fur Europaische Politik, February 1980.

[13] Jacques van Ypersele, "The future of the European Monetary System," Institut fur Europaische Politik, 1981.

CHAPTER FIVE

THE MULTICURRENCY MARKET: A REGULATORY AGENDA

Frederick R. Dahl

Associate Director,
Division of Banking Supervision and Regulation,
Board of Governors of the Federal Reserve System[1]

CONTENTS

I. INTRODUCTION

In offering comments on this pertinent and challenging topic, I find it especially daunting to attempt to replace the broad perspectives of John Heimann and Henry Wallich -- the one possessing the verve of the market maker and the other the reflectiveness of the scholar. The perspective that I shall bring to the subject matter this afternoon is the more prosaic one of the supervisory practitioner. As such, I shall restrict my remarks to the prudential aspects of the topic and avoid comments on macro-issues such as multinational reserve requirements or regulatory controls aimed at curbing exchange rate fluctuations. Mr. Forsyth has agreed to offer some comments on those aspects.

I have interpreted our topic to be concerned with the operations and regulation of the international capital and credit markets and not with purely national markets. Of course, since rules are formulated and administered at the national level, and since the institutional participants in international markets are rooted in national banking systems, one has to be concerned with the interactions of various national regulatory systems on international markets. Indeed, that will be a continuing thread throughout my remarks.

II. THE REGULATORY AGENDA

The regulatory agenda for international banking in the 1980s will be crowded. This cannot be doubted. One can

250

already observe that the national regulatory agendas are already full or quickly filling. In the United States, one had thought that the extensive legislation of the past few years would be followed by a period of digestion and respite. This has not proved to be the case. The number of new issues on the legislative and regulatory plate is steadily growing.

Abroad, too, national agendas are swelling. To cite only a few examples: In Switzerland, issues abound in attempting to apply national prudential rules to the totality, domestic and international, of the operations of the Swiss banks. In Germany, the future character of the commercial banks is being reviewed in the light of the report of the Gessler Commission. At the other end of the globe, the Campbell Commission is undertaking a comprehensive review of the banking and financial system in Australia. Others could well be mentioned.

These indications promise change. They also carry with them a great deal of uncertainty. It is not at all clear that the right issue will be identified and addressed, much less resolved.

What, then, should be on the international agenda? Since none of us can lay claim to a great deal of prescience, I suggest we might start by asking some broader questions. Those that come to my mind are the following:

1. What role should commercial banks play in the 1980s in the functioning of the international

financial system?

2. What should be the treatment of banks operating across national frontiers?

3. What are the implications of changing functions of other financial institutions for a framework that has been constructed and is attuned to commercial banks?

I note that these broader questions and their economic implications are being explored in other sessions of this conference. Here I should like to examine some of the prudential or regulatory issues that proceed from them.

III. THE ROLE OF COMMERCIAL BANKS IN THE 1980s

Whatever shifts occur in the relative roles of governments, international institutions, and banks in the financing of the world economy, and whatever other financial institutions emerge as significant players on the international financial scene, the role of commercial banks will be central and crucial. Governments and international institutions are still moving slowly in deciding how they should supplement the private markets. Meanwhile, commercial banking organizations are already equipped with experienced personnel and established procedures to continue their pivotal intermediary function.

That being said, a primary heading on the regulatory agenda has to be the promotion of a healthy and efficient multinational banking system. If we are going to rely on the world's major banks as the principal conduits for world payments and the principal allocators of savings and credit among the world's economies, the condition of those banks and the terms on which they operate have to be matters of public concern. A healthy multinational banking system means not only that risk decisions are taken prudently but also that general confidence is maintained.

During the 1980s, there will be many instances of countries getting into external financial difficulties. Short of revolutionary takeovers and outright repudiation of external debts, these cases are not worrisome to me as a bank supervisor. The system is pretty well equipped to handle them through renegotiations and restructuring of external obligations. A number of these renegotiations have recently taken place.

With such situations arising, there is a strong possibility that some major banks will encounter liquidity problems or severe losses of income that could threaten their viability or credibility in the market place. This possibility becomes the stronger when one considers the magnitude of credit problems that will emerge as the world's economies struggle to reduce inflation. If a major bank should topple, or if several should appear wobbly, some domino or ripple effects are sure to ensue and have serious economic consequences.

This possibility raises a number of issues relating to what should or could be done in such an eventuality. Among these are so-called safety nets and lender-of-last resort facilities which I shall not examine. It also raises issues of what can be done by way of prudential prophylaxis.

The first issue under that agenda is an improved assessment of country risk. By that I refer to the measures that can or should be taken to encourage banks to recognize the risks in their international lending and the consequences of misjudgment or misadventures. The United States is, I believe, ahead of other nations in its supervisory policy on country risk exposures in banks. The essence of that policy is that diversification should be a key element in the banks' country lending just as it is with their credits to individual borrowers. No matter how healthy a country may be and no matter how glowing its prospects may appear, there is some point beyond which it becomes imprudent for a bank to concentrate more of its portfolio in credit in that country. The U.S. system asks, in effect, whether the bank knows what its exposure is in the countries in which it is lending, whether the bank has assessed the economic and political risks in lending in that country, and whether the bank is capable of withstanding problems caused by difficulties in that country. There are no regulatory limits set nor are countries graded by the supervisors. There are, of course, degrees of discomfort suffered by the supervisors when they encounter large exposures. In adopting this approach, the U.S. authorities sought to minimize interference with international credit flows and to retain the primacy of market decisions in the credit extending process.

There are a number of problems with the U.S. system, to be sure, and these will have to be resolved over time. Nevertheless, I believe that the system offers a reasonable approach to the problem. Moreover, it seems to me that a similar approach -- emphasizing portfolio diversification -- if it had been widely in place might have reduced the enthusiasm of many foreign banks in lending so heavily in a number of countries at such narrow spreads.

Supervisory efforts are under way in several countries to: (1) obtain more information about the country risk exposure of their banks; (2) determine the procedures used by their banks in assessing and monitoring country risk; and (3) develop a prudential policy on country risk exposure. The issue is how to develop and apply prudential standards without impeding necessary credit and capital flows.

The second major agenda item under the heading of prudential prophylaxis is the role of equity capital in the banking systems. Capital standards vary widely among countries and sometimes within countries. Those variations can and do affect the terms and conditions on which international lending take place.

Given all the uncertainties about international lending, if one is worried about the ability of the major banks to withstand the winds of adversity, the adequacy of their capital cushions needs to be examined. To the extent the banks believe those cushions will not be called upon -- that is, that governments will bail them out -- the market will not function efficiently in rationing credit among different risks. Similarly, to the extent capital costs and earnings are down played in the banking process, as many observers think they have been, the banks end up by not obtaining sufficient risk premia and again the allocative function is not adequately performed.

In the United States, capital standards are elusive and highly judgmental. The failure to establish clear standards reflects the existence of many different kinds of banks in a system that contains more than 14,000 banks and an unwillingness to discriminate among them. One result has been a more or less steady deterioration in the capital ratios of the major banks. In the United Kingdom, capital standards are also judgmental, though some of the considerations entering into the judgments have now been publicized. In continental Europe, complicated formulas remain the attraction, though until recently no capital requirements were applied to the operations of the banks outside the home country.

The objective of a multilateral examination would not be to seek uniform capital standards -- an unlikely possibility. Rather it would be to achieve a measure of agreement about the role of capital in the functioning of banks and about the kinds of risks for which capital is designed to provide the protection.

IV. THE SUPERVISION OF MULTINATIONAL BANKS

The status of the large banks as multinational firms has been widely recognized for some time. Their operations vary, of course, some operating large global networks, others being more selective. The essential fact, however, is that the major banks in each country conduct a significant part of their business across national frontiers. A continuing international regulatory issue is, as a consequence, the terms and conditions on which multinational banks operate in national markets. This issue involves such questions as: Who is allowed to enter a market? What standards are to be applied in determining entry? What sort of supervision should be given foreign institutions? What relative roles should home and host country supervisors play?

As many of you know, supervisors from a number of countries have been meeting regularly for several years under the sponsorship of the BIS to grapple with international regulatory issues. The first order of business of that group when it was formed was to try to thrash out the last two questions I just mentioned. The task was not an easy one. The result, which is now known as the Concordat, was a set of agreed general principles on the roles of the respective supervisors. The principal elements are: (1) all banks operating in international markets should be supervised institutions; (2) supervisory responsibilities are necessarily shared between host and home country supervisors, especially in such areas as liquidity; and (3) the home country supervisor has primary responsibilty for monitoring the health and solvency of the whole banking organization. A certain amount of imprecision attaches to these principles, and necessarily so, as the group discovered that supervisory responsibilities could not be neatly divided.

Since the Concordat was established, the International Banking Act of 1978 was passed. That Act gave the Federal Reserve a number of responsibilities over the operations of foreign banks in this country, including that of being a sort of residual supervisory authority over those operations. This immediately raised questions about the character of the foreign banks operating here as well as instituting a need for information about their operation in this country. To this end, the Federal Reserve proposed an annual reporting requirement for foreign banking organizations that would furnish, among other things, basic information about the financial condition of those organizations. This proposal was greeted by a number of European supervisors as a violation of the principles of the Concordat -- namely, that it suggested the Federal Reserve was invading their supervisory turf and was seeking to exercise supervision of the solvency of the foreign banks.

Putting aside some maladroitness of presentation and some unnecessary extensions of domestic reporting requirements in the Federal Reserve proposal, the European

258

criticism was, in my opinion, misplaced. A host authority has the responsibility of assuring itself that the foreign institutions operating in its market are sound and reputable institutions. To do so requires some continuing inquiry into the financial condition and activities of those institutions. The extent and quality of bank supervision varies widely around the world, and it is simply not acceptable to rely solely on the assurances of the home country supervisor. In addition, the European criticism ignored the aspects of the Concordat that emphasizes the sharing of responsibilities.

The reporting requirements were scaled back in the end and this blunted some of the criticism. I cite this incident as an illustration of one kind of problem we are going to be encountering as we go through the 1980s -- that of adjusting the relationships of the multinational banks to the various national authorities, especially as these banks become more deeply imbedded in national banking systems. The trick, of course, will be to assure that these banks are regulated to an extent that promotes a healthy banking system while avoiding over-regulation and conflicting regulations that interfere with their economic functioning. Part of the difficulty in this incident arose from requesting financial data that is regularly reported by banks in this country but which is often not made available by banks in foreign countries. This points up the disclosure issue. In recent years a lot of effort has gone into increasing the "transparency" of international lending. Very little has gone into increasing the "transparency" of the banks engaged in that lending.

V.   THE CHANGING INSTITUTIONAL SCENE

The issues I have identified so far arise in the context of commercial banks as the central international financing institutions. That viewpoint has been valid for the past 20 years and, in my judgment, commercial banks will continue to occupy a pivotal position in the 1980s. Nevertheless, we have to recognize that the institutional framework is changing. Certainly in this country the boundary lines between commercial banks and other financial institutions are becoming increasingly blurred. This development has started elsewhere as well and is sure to be copied even more widely.

As this development proceeds, regulatory attitudes and policies will have to be rethought, not only at the national levels but at the international level. Merrill Lynch is trying to develop a banking business overseas, in addition to their varied activities at home. Japanese securities houses are trying to get into banking outside Japan. What then becomes of the Concordat? How should these institutions be supervised as they assume the characteristics of banks? Knotty questions such as these are sure to be encountered with growing frequency.

VI. CONCLUSIONS

In these remarks, I have identified a few of the issues that I perceive on the international regulatory agenda in this decade. More could surely be listed: for example, I have not mentioned any of the problems that could be associated with the hoped-for winding down of inflation. Nor have I touched upon issues related to the changing technological aspects of international banking and finance. Those issues, too, will help crowd the agenda.

The sum of all this is to emphasize the need for cooperation in the international regulatory area. Cooperative efforts are not a sufficient condition for a healthy world banking and financing system, but they are certainly a necessary condition. Those cooperative efforts not only need to be deepened through existing consultative mechanisms, they also need to be extended to a wider group of countries. Progress in this direction, I am happy to report, is being achieved.

International cooperation is needed in order to address specific items such as I have identified on the international regulatory agenda. It is also needed in the broader sense of conscious recognition of the international implications of items on national regulatory agendas and a nonparochial attitude that will accommodate international interests when those issues are being resolved.

There will be quite enough to do and it will call for the thoughtful and imaginative resources of all those in the

private and public sector who are concerned about banking in
the broadest sense and its contribution to the world's work.

VI. NOTES

[1] The views expressed are those of the author and not necessarily those of the Federal Reserve System.

CHAPTER SIX

INTERNATIONAL TRADE IN BANKING SERVICES:

THE NEGOTIATING AGENDA

Geza Feketekuty

Assistant United States Trade Representative
for Policy Development

CONTENTS

I.   INTRODUCTION

Services are traded internationally much as goods. Much the same economic benefits are derived from services trade as from goods trade. Yet, as services trade becomes a more important adjunct to goods trade, restraints on services are becoming a new tool not only for protecting domestic service industries, but also for restricting imports of goods. These considerations lead to the question whether the standard tools of trade policy, designed to liberalize trade in goods, might not be applied to trade in services.

In the United States, the new interest in services trade found Congressional expression in the Trade Act of 1974.[1] A number of key provisions of the 1974 Trade Act were applied to trade in services.

Section 102 of the 1974 Trade Act authorizes the President to negotiate international agreements aimed at the reduction, elimination and harmonization of non-tariff barriers to international trade. Section 102(g)(3) defines the term "international trade" to include trade in both goods and services.[2] Services are also included under the other provisions of the 1974 Trade Act. Section 301 authorizes the President to retaliate against unjustifiable, unreasonable, or discriminatory actions by foreign governments which burden or restrict United States commerce.[3] Section 135 establishes private sector advisory committees to advise U.S. trade officials, and one of those committees is concerned with services.[4]

266

These provisions established an expectation on the part of Congress that U.S. trade officials would concern themselves with the trade problems of U.S. service industries, and would seek to negotiate international agreements limiting non-tariff barriers to trade in services. An effort was made in the recently concluded Tokyo Round of Multilateral Trade Negotiations to include services, but the concept proved too novel to achieve more than token results.[5] It became clear that a very considerable amount of analytical groundwork was needed before negotiations could succeed. The major industrial countries participating in the MTN accordingly agreed that they would undertake a serious study of the trade problems of service industries after the conclusion of the Tokyo Round. Such a study has been launched in the OECD.[6]

In a related vein, the U.S. Congress became concerned with the equality of competitive opportunities in international banking. The International Banking Act of 1978[7] established a comprehensive federal regulatory structure covering the operation of foreign banks in U.S. financial markets. The 1978 Act also directed the government to submit a report to Congress on "the extent to which [U.S. banks] are denied, whether by law or practice, national treatment in conducting banking operations in foreign countries, and the effect, if any, of such discrimination on United States exports to those countries."[8] It also asked the report to: "describe the efforts undertaken by the

United States to eliminate any foreign laws or practices that discriminate against [U.S.] banks...." The resulting Report to Congress on Foreign Government Treatment of U.S. Commercial Banking Organizations was submitted on September 17, 1979.[9]

This paper should be seen in the context of the current OECD effort to sort out the issues in services trade, and to establish a conceptual framework for future negotiations. To the extent that international discussions lead to broad principles, rules or procedures applicable to services in general, policy makers will need to ask whether those precepts apply to banking activities. To the extent the discussions lead to separate sectoral agreements for individual service industries, such as leasing or banking, the question for policy makers will be how those agreements can be integrated into a coherent whole.

The analysis of banking issues in the context of barriers to services trade is still at a rudimentary stage. The analysis in this paper, therefore, represents only a first attempt to frame the issues in banking.

Banking is probably the most difficult service activity to put into a trade framework for a number of reasons: (1) the regulation and control of banking activities is central to the management of the economy by national governments; (2) it is difficult to distinguish between trade in banking services and foreign investment in banking; (3) the dividing line between banking and other financial services varies from country to country; and, (4) the traditions surrounding international discussion of banking issues are very different from the approaches customarily used by trade negotiators.

An analysis of trade in banking services could begin by looking at theoretical issues. This is not the approach taken here, nor was it the approach taken in the OECD study. Services trade has become an issue because a number of U.S. service industries persuaded the Congress that their trade problems could be resolved through negotiations. For this reason, the United States urged that the OECD study begin with an analysis of the trade problems of service industries. For the same reason it is useful to begin this paper with a review of international trade problems in banking.

II. ISSUES RAISED BY U.S. BANKS.

The U.S. Government has compiled an inventory of foreign regulations that hamper the activities of American banks abroad. This inventory is based largely on information received from U.S. banks in response to surveys conducted by the Department of Commerce[10], by the Comptroller of the Currency[11] and by the USTR.[12]

Restrictions on American and other foreign banks fall into three major categories: (1) restrictions on entry; (2) discriminatory regulations that impose larger operating costs on foreign banks than on their local competitors, or that deny competitive opportunities to foreign banks; and,

(3) non-discriminatory government regulations aimed at non-banking objectives which hamper the operation of foreign banks.

Restrictions on entry include:

-- Complete prohibition on the establishment of any presence by a foreign bank;

-- Prohibitions on the establishment of any type of banking operation by a foreign bank other than a representative office or a correspondent relationship with a local bank;

-- Restrictions on the takeover of domestic banks by foreigners;

-- Limitations on the level of foreign equity participation in domestic banks or limits on the permissible degree of foreign control of domestic banks;

-- Prohibitions on the establishment of branches (but not subsidiaries) of foreign banks; and

-- Limitations on the type of domestic or international banking services that foreign owned banks are permitted to offer.

Discriminatory regulations that impose larger operating costs on foreign banks than on local banks include higher reserve requirements, higher capital-asset ratios, higher taxation, and more stringent or more restrictive enforcement of apparently nondiscriminatory regulations.

Discriminatory regulations that deny foreign banks competitive opportunities available to their local counterparts in foreign markets include:

-- Limits on government deposits;

-- Inability to participate in subsidized or guaranteed government export credit facilities;

-- Inability to use central bank rediscounting facilities;

-- Restrictions on the type of securities or other financial assets which can be acquired;

-- Restrictions on the ability of insurance companies to deposit funds in foreign banks;

-- Restrictions on local retail banking, including restrictions on the ability to accept local demand deposits as well as offer small business or consumer loans.

Nondiscriminatory government regulations aimed at non-banking objectives that hamper American and other third-country banks abroad include foreign exchange controls, immigration controls, and professional licensing requirements.

A preliminary inventory of these restrictions is included in Appendix A. This inventory is still tentative, and all details have not been verified. Nevertheless it provides a good basis for forming an overall impression of the types of restrictions faced by U.S. banks.

III. ISSUES RAISED BY FOREIGN BANKS

Concerns by foreign banks regarding their ability to do business in the United States arise primarily in two areas -- (1) limitations on interstate banking; and, (2) limitations placed on banks in the area of investment banking and securities brokerage services. Other concerns include deposit insurance requirements and burdensome reporting requirements on the activities of foreign banks both in the United States and abroad. For the most part, these restrictions apply to all banks operating in the United States.

271

Generally, the United States provides national treatment to foreign banks. Moreover, the United States is one of the very few countries that allows foreigners to acquire control of existing banks. The general complaint is not that the United States discriminates against foreign banks, but that the United States places more severe restrictions on all its banks than do other countries.

IV. REVIEW OF GOVERNMENT POLICY GOALS

In order to help determine the negotiability of foreign barriers identified by U.S. banks, it is first necessary to analyze the motives for imposing those measures. In many cases, measures identified as barriers are the result of legitimate government objectives. Each government needs to maintain control of banking functions both because of their impact on domestic economic activity and in order to protect depositors. In some cases, however, measures aimed at legitimate social objectives place a heavier burden on foreign banks. In still other cases, measures restricting the activities of foreign banks serve purely protectionist objectives.

Most governments maintain extensive regulations in the banking area in order to assure the sound financial condition of banks and to protect depositors. Most governments also seek to control the commercial lending activities of banks through a variety of regulations in order to manage the growth of overall money and credit. Some governments also use their control over banking to channel lending activity to certain sectors or regions of the economy. As a general matter, these fidiciary and credit regulations should apply equally to foreign and domestic banks. In some cases, however, regulations that in principle apply equally to both domestic and foreign banks could, in practice, prove discriminatory. For example, some governments limit the establishment of new banks, in order to preserve economies of scale and to prevent "over-banking" which could undermine the financial soundness of the banking system as a whole. Such controls on new entrants can be discriminatory in practice if foreign banks were prevented from establishing themselves in the past.

Some governments argue that certain discriminatory restraints on foreigners are necessary to assure effective regulatory control. For example, some governments require foreign banks to establish themselves through subsidiaries rather than through branches.

In other cases, government restrictions on foreign banks are motivated by a desire to prevent foreigners from exercising substantial control over domestic economic activity. This concern is particularly pronounced when the country in question is relatively small or less developed and the potential foreign banks seeking entry are quite large.

A closely related argument is the infant industry argument. It is said that domestic banks need protection

273

from foreign competitors for a transitional period so that they may grow and become more efficient. The infant industry argument, as applied to goods trade, has found some acceptance with respect to less developed economies, provided they make an accompanying commitment to trade liberalization as the local industry becomes more efficient. All too often, however, the lack of foreign competition eliminates any inducement for the local industry to improve its efficiency.

In still other cases, the protection of domestic banks is an explicit goal of the governments involved, and no effort is made to provide other justifications for such a policy.

Other policy measures viewed as restrictive by U.S. banks are aimed at policy objectives outside the banking areas. Foreign exchange control measures, for example, are usually aimed at balance of payments and exchange rate objectives. Immigration controls are aimed at various economic, social and cultural goals. Professional licensing regulations are aimed at assuring professional reliability and for protecting consumers. Such measures have traditionally been outside the scope of trade negotiations.

V.   EXISTING INTERNATIONAL ARRANGEMENTS IN BANKING

There are few international agreements in banking that could guide either private bankers or government officials seeking to reduce foreign barriers in banking. U.S.

274

bilateral treaties of Friendship, Commerce and Navigation (FCN), for example, have traditionally excluded commercial banking from commitments on national treatment, that is to say, commitments to treat foreign-owned firms on the same basis as domestic firms.

International banking issues are covered to some extent by the OECD Code on Liberalization of Capital Movements and Current Invisible Operations.[13] The liberalization obligations of the code, for example, apply to direct investment in banks, but not to administrative limitations placed on the right of establishment. The discipline of the code is weakened by a large number of national reservations, and by the absence of an effective mechanism for negotiating the elimination of such reservations. As is true of the OECD generally, implementation is based on moral suasion and peer group pressure, rather than a formalized process for enforcing code provisions.

Another OECD Agreement, the 1976 Declaration of International Investment and Multinational Enterprises, also covers banking. The Declaration provides for national treatment of foreign owned enterprises once they are established. This commitment is not binding, however, and as in all OECD instruments, there are no enforcement procedures. Implementation of the Declaration is discussed in the Committee on International Investment and Multilateral Enterprises (CIME). Individual issues regarding national treatment can be raised in the Committee, but this has not

275

proven to be an effective procedure for removing restrictions.

The OECD also has a Committee on Financial Markets (CFM), which from time to time discusses restrictions on the establishment and operation of foreign banks. Discussions in this Committee can lead to a better understanding of issues and can thereby facilitate unilateral steps by individual governments to adopt more liberal regulations. But it has not become a vehicle for negotiation of banking issues.

Foreign exchange restrictions are covered by the Articles of Agreement of the International Monetary Fund (IMF), and frequently become the subject of consultations between the IMF and member countries. While IMF rules permit the imposition of foreign exchange restrictions when warranted by balance of payments considerations, the rules can help to minimize abuse.

All in all, there are relatively few international agreements on banking that effectively cover establishment and operation of foreign banks. Most of the agreements have been negotiated within the OECD context and, as in all OECD instruments, have no effective enforcement provisions. Further, OECD arrangements are customarily limited to the developed countries.

VI. RELEVANT ARRANGEMENTS IN TRADE

Many U.S. service industries have pressed for negotiations in a trade context because "rules-of-the-road" already exist for trade. It is therefore useful to review the trade rules that are likely to be most relevant for banking.

The General Agreement on Tariffs and Trade (GATT), the basic "constitution" of the international trading system, contains a number of provisions that could prove relevant for banking. The central principle of the GATT is that barriers to trade must be at the border, must be applied on a non-discriminatory (most-favored-nation) basis to all countries, and must be subject to negotiated reductions. The national treatment concept of the GATT prohibits members from introducing domestic measures or financial charges that will discriminate against foreign products.

The GATT also provides a structured mechanism for dispute settlement. A country that questions whether the trade practices of another country are in conformity with GATT rules can initiate a dispute settlement procedure, and if such efforts fail, the offended party can obtain the right to retaliate by suspending concessions benefitting the offending party.

The recently concluded Tokyo Round of Multilateral Trade Negotiations resulted in the negotiation of a number of non-tariff codes. Perhaps the most relevant of these codes for banking is the Agreement on Technical Barriers to Trade (the Standards Code).

277

The Standards Code contains several provisions that may be relevant for a code of conduct for the banking sector. The relevance stems from the similarity between government-mandated standards for goods -- such as levels of quality, performance or safety -- and government regulations in the banking sector, which have the purpose of defining the quality, performance and safety of banking activities. The Standards Code has six key provisions:

1. A permanent committee which serves as a consulta-tive, information-sharing mechanism.

2. Agreement that signatories will not prepare, adopt or apply standards in a manner that would create obstacles to international trade.

3. The concept of national treatment.

4. Transparency of government policies and proce-dures.

5. Advance notification to other countries before new standards are adopted.

6. A dispute settlement procedure.

VII. CONCEPTUAL ISSUES

A number of conceptual issues need to be addressed before turning to possible negotiating objectives. Some of these issues have already been mentioned, but it is useful to address them explicitly before exploring solutions.

1. Does Trade Theory Apply to Banking?

A fundamental conceptual issue concerns the theoretical underpinning of any effort to liberalize international banking activity. Does the theory of comparative advantage, which has provided the theoretical foundation for all efforts to liberalize international trade, apply to trade in banking services? Are there economic gains from trade in banking services? This is a question that will have to be explored more deeply than is possible here. As a first approximation, however, it should be possible to view services provided by banks as the economic equivalent of traded commodities. To the extent some countries enjoy a comparative advantage in banking, the exports of banking services by such a country should lead to gains from trade as predicted by trade theory. There are any number of reasons why some countries could enjoy a comparative advantage in banking -- they may have had a long historical tradition in banking, they may have a legal and institutional environment conducive to banking, they may have built up a global banking network over the years, and so forth.

Arguments against free trade in banking services are based less on a rejection of the theory of comparative advantage, than on the contention that banking is so central to a nation's social, political and institutional fabric that it should not be viewed in strictly economic terms. Just as "national security" arguments are invoked to protect the shipbuilding industry, so "economic security" arguments are invoked to protect banking. Often lurking behind this contention is the view that the right to open a bank carries with it a guaranty of large profits -- and that such a valuable right ought to be reserved to established citizens.

2. Does Foreign Banking Benefit Trade in Goods?

A possible argument for the liberalization of foreign banking is that it could facilitate trade in goods, and conversely that restrictions on banking could have the effect of creating a trade barrier. This is a difficult argument to sustain without empirical research. One is struck, however, by the historical relationship between growth in international trade and growth in international banking. Common sense also suggests that a bank that has a presence in country X is in a better position to serve the needs of an exporter to country X than a bank that does not. While correspondent relationships can provide a substitute, such arrangements are not likely to provide the same quality of information about foreign markets and instill the same degree of confidence. On the other hand, a survey conducted by U.S. government agencies in connection with the Report to Congress on Foreign Government Treatment of U.S. Commercial Banking Organizations showed that few respondents felt that their export opportunities were limited by the absence of American banks in their export markets.[14] On balance, one suspects that the relationship between banking and trade is a positive one.

3. What is Trade in Banking Services?

If we want to pursue international banking problems in a trade context, we have to define trade in banking services. Banking services which are to be consumed in a foreign market have to be produced, at least in part, in that market. The local production of such services requires the presence of a locally established banking office; in other words, it requires investment in a banking entity. All issues regarding the operation of a foreign owned business enterprise have traditionally been viewed as investment issues, not as trade issues.[15] This is an important distinction. For while the GATT provides a systematic set of rules for the liberalization of trade, and procedures for enforcing the rules, the OECD Investment Code is based on other general principles, with no enforcement provisions.

One could take a narrow definition of trade in banking services. Under such a definition only services provided by the parent bank, or services provided by affiliated banks in third countries, would be considered in a trade context. Services falling within a narrow definition of trade would include services provided by outside banks to residents of the importing country, or services provided to banks estab-lished in the importing country. Services provided by the home office to a local branch or subsidiary bank would also fall within the trade category. But issues concerning services provided by locally established foreign banks would be considered investment issues.

Alternatively, one could adopt a broader definition of trade in banking services. One could consider all issues concerning the right to sell banking services as trade issues; only issues concerning the establishment of foreign-owned banking offices would be considered investment issues. Under this definition, trade rules would cover issues related to the right of a foreign financial institution to sell services under its name while investment rules would cover all issues related to ownership of a local banking enterprise. To the extent that a foreign financial institution used locally owned firms to sell services in its name, no investment issue would arise. For example, if an American financial institution arranged to have its travelers' checks or credit cards sold by local banks, its right to do so would be covered by trade rules and no investment issues would arise.

Perhaps distinctions between trade and investment will prove too artificial to provide a useful basis for formulating new international disciplines, and perhaps this will be true not only for banking but also for other service industries. If this conclusion were accepted at the outset, one could embark on an effort to construct a new type of discipline that made no distinction between trade and investment. Such a new discipline could build on the better features of existing international trade rules, including provisions for enforcement. Alternatively, one could build on the Invisibles Code in the OECD[16], which currently covers a broad range of service issues, although without the discipline and enforcement process of the GATT.

A decision to abandon all distinctions between trade

and investment would have important institutional implications. It would make it more difficult to use GATT as the
institutional base for negotiations: many countries are
reluctant to extend the GATT to cover investment issues,
even though the original charter for an International Trade
Organization (ITO) covered the whole range of trade and
investment issues.

4.   What Are Banking Services?

The definition of a bank varies from country to country. What are considered appropriate banking services in
one country are considered off limits in another. Stock
market brokerage services are a normal banking activity in
some countries, and a prohibited activity in other countries. A related definitional issue concerns services that
are frequently sold by banks, but do not fall within a
strict definition of commercial banking. Travelers check,
credit card, financial consulting and financial data services are examples in this area. The treatment of such
fee-based services sold by banks is becoming particularly
relevant, since American banks operating abroad are likely
to obtain an increasing proportion of their earnings from
the sale of fee-based services other than loans.[17]

5.   Reconciling Regulation and Liberalization of Banking

Most national governments consider the regulation of
banking a legitimate and essential function -- for the

achievement of fiduciary objectives (protection of depositors), for the achievement of monetary control objectives, and in some cases, for the allocation of credit.

The question is how such regulation can be reconciled with liberalization at the international level. In principle, if not in degree, this issue is no different from regulatory issues that arise with respect to trade in goods. Governments have established regulations concerning pesticides in fruit, emission of pollutants by autos, flammability of various materials. These regulations have been accommodated to the needs of international trade.

The Standards Code, concluded in the Tokyo Round of Multilateral Trade Negotiations, helps governments to reconcile their regulatory activities with their commitments to preserve open trade. The general approach in the Standards Code should prove helpful in devising an approach for reconciling the regulation and liberalization of banking. The Code accepts the legitimate right of every government to set its own social objectives and to develop a regulatory approach for achieving those objectives, but it commits governments to develop an approach that minimizes distortion of trade and avoids discrimination between foreign and domestic producers. In short, the Code asks governments to treat foreign producers on the same basis as domestic producers, a principle that is usually referred to as national treatment.

Two issues arise in connection with a national treatment approach in the Standards Code context. The first is that it could lead to very different opportunities for banking as between any two countries. If country A has a lenient approach to banking, while country B has a strict approach to banking, country B's banks will find better opportunities in country A than country A's banks will find in country B. This difference creates the appearance of an inequitable relationship; in response some would argue for equal treatment of foreign banks in both countries. An equal treatment approach at the international level, however, would lead to differences between the treatment of domestic and foreign banks within individual national markets. The only way to avoid the dilemma between equity within national markets and equity between national markets would be to negotiate a harmonization of national bank regulations, an overly ambitious objective.

The second issue raised by a national treatment approach is that basic differences in the position of domestic and foreign banks could mean that trade rules based on national treatment would lead to inequitable results. For example, restrictions on foreign exchange transactions could be particularly burdensome to foreign banks, since they engage in foreign exchange transactions whenever they have financial transactions with their parent bank. Further, foreign banks may be more specialized in international business that depends on foreign exchange transactions. One way out of this dilemma would be to cast the principle of non-discriminatory treatment in terms of equivalent treatment. National treatment would then be defined in terms of the achievement of "equivalent competitive opportunities" rather than identical treatment.

There is a subtle difference between the meaning of national treatment in a trade context and the meaning that the term has been given by some involved in the banking debate. National treatment in the GATT context applies to products that have been allowed to enter the country by virtue of earlier negotiations that led to the complete or partial elimination of trade barriers. National treatment as used by some in the banking community would require equivalent treatment not only of domestic and foreign banks that are already established within a country's borders, but also of foreign banks not presently in the country. In short, national treatment would cover free entry as well as equivalent treatment after entry.

6.   Reciprocity and National Treatment

One of the debates in the U.S. banking community concerns the merits of reciprocity as an international negotiating goal. More precisely, the debate has been over the relative virtues of reciprocity and national treatment as mutually exclusive goals. Since reciprocity has been a key building block of the international trading system, and since reciprocity has coexisted with the principle of national treatment in the GATT, this debate needs to be addressed.

Two observations are pertinent to banking issues. The first is that reciprocity has often been interpreted far more literally in the banking context than in the trade context. As used in banking, reciprocity has meant equal treatment at home and abroad. For example, if Germany permits American banks to establish branches throughout Germany, the banking definition of reciprocity would require the United States to allow German banks to establish branches throughout the United States, regardless of any restrictions placed on interstate banking by U.S. banks. Alternatively, it would give Germany the right to limit the geographic location of U.S. banks. Adoption of this concept would establish different rules for domestic and foreign banks and different rules for banks from different countries; it would also reduce the ability of individual countries to pursue their own regulatory goals. On the basis of this literal definition, it is not surprising that most observors have rejected reciprocity as an appropriate goal.

There is a broader definition of reciprocity, however, which has often prevailed in the trade context. The broader definition has meant the exchange of concessions perceived to be of equivalent value, the existence of equivalent competitive opportunities, or mutual adherence to a common set of "fair trade" rules. While these three variations of

287

the concept differ somewhat, they have generally meant that each country is giving and receiving commitments of equivalent value.

The national treatment principle says that governments should treat foreign firms on the same (or equivalent) basis as domestic firms. The national treatment principle is part of the GATT, and is fully compatible with the broad concept of reciprocity used in the GATT. Equal adherence to the national treatment principle by two countries constitutes an exchange of equivalent commitments between the two countries, and thereby meets the reciprocity test as used in the GATT. At the same time, it is also obvious that the literal definition of reciprocity, as used in the banking context, is at variance with national treatment.

Two policy issues arise from this discussion of terminology. The first is whether negotiators should seek the limited version of national treatment (providing nondiscriminatory treatment of goods or services that have been allowed into the country), or the broader version that has been assumed in some banking discussions (which includes the concept of free entry). If negotiators were to seek the limited version, they could then establish a second agenda for reducing barriers to entry. This second agenda would be comparable to the agenda on import barriers in the trade context. If negotiators were to seek a broader version of national treatment, no separate agenda on entry would be necessary. The advantage of the more inclusive

288

interpretation is that it would lead to the faster elimination of barriers to entry, should it prove negotiable. But the negotiation of entry conditions might well prove more difficult to achieve than the application of national treatment to established banks. In that event, separate negotiating tracks for the two issues might lead to more rapid liberalization.

The second issue which needs to be addressed is whether the broader (trade) definition of reciprocity should be adopted as an appropriate goal. It could be argued that a policy of admitting foreign banks into the United States is a desirable policy regardless of whether or not other countries are willing to admit U.S. banks. On the other hand, the United States is better off if its banks are allowed to operate overseas than if they are not, and reciprocity could be a useful concept for achieving this objective.

VIII. POSSIBLE ELEMENTS OF A NEGOTIATING AGENDA

Our analysis leads to an enumeration of some of the possible elements of a negotiating agenda for trade in banking services. Some of the possibilities are mutually exclusive, others are compatible and could be pursued simultaneously. No effort is made here to choose among them.

One obvious candidate for a negotiating agenda on

banking services is the national treatment concept. National treatment for established firms (including banks) is a principle that was included in the 1976 OECD Declaration on National Treatment. This principle is also embodied in the GATT. Perhaps adoption of this principle could be combined with the negotiation of a code along the lines of the MTN Standards Code. Such a code could be tailor-made for the banking sector, or could be cast more broadly to cover a broad range of service industries.

A negotiating agenda would also have to address restrictions on entry. Negotiations on such restrictions could be cast in terms of an effort to achieve a broad interpretation of national treatment, calling for unrestricted entry. Alternatively, entry could be negotiated on a bilateral basis, or on some multilateral basis. For example, countries might seek to negotiate the removal of reservations to the liberalization commitments in the OECD Code on Liberalization of Capital Movements and Current Invisible Operations.

A negotiating agenda could also address the liberalization of individual types of restrictions listed in the inventory of barriers in Appendix A. The agenda could include restrictions on government deposits, rediscounting, government subsidized or guaranteed export credits, deposits by insurance companies, and so forth. The agenda might also address issues concerning related fee-based services provided by banks, for example, travelers checks, credit cards, financial consulting services, financial data services, leasing, and portfolio management.

This enumeration should provide ample material for a lengthy, yet hopefully fruitful, negotiating agenda.

IX. NOTES

[1] Trade Act of 1974, P.L. 93-618, January 3, 1975.

[2] Ibid, p. 6.

[3] Ibid, p. 64.

[4] Ibid, p. 19.

[5] See Appendix A.

[6] The work in trade in services has been carried out by a number of committees and working groups in the OECD over the past two years, including the Trade Committee, the Invisibles Committee, the Insurance Committee, the Maritime Transport Committee and the Financial Markets Committee.

[7] International Banking Act of 1978, P.L. 95-369, September 17, 1978.

[8] Ibid, p. 17.

[9] Ibid, p. 18.

[10] Papers triggered by this study include, "Banking Regulation and Structure: An International Perspective," by Churck Heywood, and the following studies conducted by the American Bankers Association: "The Regulation of Capital Ratios in U.S. Banking"; "The Future Development of Foreign Banking Organizations in the U.S."; "The Future Development of U.S. Banking Organization Abroad"; and "The Environment of Non-Local Competition in U.S. Banking Markets". (all published January 1981).

[11] See, "U.S. Service Industries in World Markets," U.S. Department of Commerce, December 1976.

[12] See, "Report to Congress on Foreign Government Treatment of U.S. Commercial Banking Organizations," Department of the Treasury, September 1979.

[13] The survey material obtained by USTR was in response to a questionnaire prepared by USTR in conjunction with the U.S. Chamber of Commerce.

[14] Code of Liberalization of Current Invisible Operations, Organization for Economic Cooperation and Development, Paris, France, adopted 12 December 1961.

[15] "Report to Congress on Foreign Government Treatment of U.S. Commercial Banking Organizations," Department of the Treasury, September 1979, p. 394.

[16] See earlier discussion of OECD Invisible Code.

[17] *Ibid*.

APPENDIX A

A PRELIMINARY SURVEY OF
ENTRY RESTRICTIONS AND OPERATIONAL CONSTRAINTS IMPOSED ON FOREIGN BANKS
IN A PARTICULAR COUNTRY

TYPE OF RESTRICTION	PRACTICING COUNTRIES	COUNTRY SPECIFICS	IMPLICATIONS/COMMENTS
PROHIBITION BY LAW OF FOREIGN BANK PRESENCE IN ANY FORM	AFGHANISTAN BULGARIA CUBA CZECHOSLOVAKIA ETHIOPIA GUINEA IRAQ LAOS LIBYA MADAGASCAR SOMALIA NEPAL USSR	ALL OF THESE COUNTRIES HAVE WHOLLY NATIONALIZED BANKING SYSTEMS AND, THUS, PROHIBIT BOTH DOMESTIC AND FOREIGN PRIVATELY OWNED BANKING OPERATIONS	THE ABSENCE OF BANKING PRESENCE MAY INHIBIT THE DEVELOPMENT OF THE NORMAL CONTACTS THROUGH WHICH FOREIGN COUNTRIES BECOME FAMILIAR WITH ANOTHER COUNTRY'S MARKETS AND BUSINESS PROCEDURES AS A FIRST STEP IN ESTABLISHING AND ENHANCING TRADING RELATIONSHIPS
PROHIBITION BY CURRENT POLICIES OR LICENSING PRACTICES OF FOREIGN BANK ENTRY OF ANY FORM	BENIN KUWAIT NETHERLANDS ANTILLES SURINAM TANZANIA UNITED ARAB EMIRATES GUYANA	THE GOVERNMENTS OF U.A.E. AND GUYANA PREVIOUSLY PERMITTED FOREIGN BANKS. THEY HAVE DECIDED THAT THE NUMBER OF FOREIGN BANKS ALREADY PRESENT IS SUFFICIENT FOR THE SIZE OF THEIR RESPECTIVE BANKING MARKETS.	THE ABSENCE OF BANKING PRESENCE MAY INHIBIT THE DEVELOPMENT OF THE NORMAL CONTACTS THROUGH WHICH FOREIGN COUNTRIES BECOME FAMILIAR WITH ANOTHER COUNTRY'S MARKETS AND BUSINESS PROCEDURES AS A FIRST STEP IN ESTABLISHING AND ENHANCING TRADING RELATIONSHIPS.
PROHIBITION BY LAW OF ALL FORMS OF BANKING ENTRY EXCEPT REPRESENTATIVE OFFICES	ALGERIA BURMA COLOMBIA PORTUGAL SWEDEN SYRIA USSR YUGOSLAVIA VENEZUELA	SOME OF THESE COUNTRIES ALLOW PREVIOUSLY ADMITTED FOREIGN BANKS TO CONTINUE OPERATIONS (GRANDFATHER CLAUSE)	REPRESENTATIVE OFFICES CANNOT, BY DEFINITION, ENGAGE IN ANY TYPE OF BANKING BUSINESS AND ARE FREQUENTLY CONSTRAINED FROM ADVERTISING THE SERVICES OF THEIR PARENT BANK. ALTHOUGH THEY CANNOT TAKE DEPOSITS OR MAKE LOANS, THEY CAN SOMETIMES SOLICIT LOANS FOR THEIR PARENT AND ESTABLISH BANKING RELATIONSHIPS WITH LOCAL FIRMS.

USTR COMPUTER GROUP

294

A PRELIMINARY SURVEY OF
ENTRY RESTRICTIONS AND OPERATIONAL CONSTRAINTS IMPOSED ON FOREIGN BANKS
IN A PARTICULAR COUNTRY

TYPE OF RESTRICTION	PRACTICING COUNTRIES	COUNTRY SPECIFICS	IMPLICATIONS/COMMENTS
PROHIBITION BY CURRENT ADMINISTRATIVE PRACTICES OF ALL FORMS OF BANKING ENTRY EXCEPT REPRESENTATIVE OFFICES	PEOPLES REPUBLIC OF CHINA EL SALVADOR GERMAN DEMOCRATIC REPUBLIC GUATEMALA INDIA INDONESIA POLAND SAUDI ARABIA TRINIDAD & TOBAGO MEXICO NEW ZEALAND NORWAY	SOME OF THESE COUNTRIES ALLOW PREVIOUSLY ADMITTED FOREIGN BANKS TO CONTINUE OPERATIONS (GRANDFATHER CLAUSE)	REPRESENTATIVE OFFICES CANNOT, BY DEFINITION, ENGAGE IN ANY TYPE OF BANKING BUSINESS AND ARE FREQUENTLY CONSTRAINED FROM ADVERTISING THE SERVICES OF THEIR PARENT BANK. ALTHOUGH THEY CANNOT TAKE DEPOSITS OR MAKE LOANS, THEY CAN SOMETIMES SOLICIT LOANS FOR THEIR PARENT AND ESTABLISH BANKING RELATIONSHIPS WITH LOCAL FIRMS.

USTR COMPUTER GROUP

295

A PRELIMINARY SURVEY OF
ENTRY RESTRICTIONS AND OPERATIONAL CONSTRAINTS IMPOSED ON FOREIGN BANKS
IN A PARTICULAR COUNTRY

TYPE OF RESTRICTION	PRACTICING COUNTRIES	COUNTRY SPECIFICS	IMPLICATIONS/COMMENTS
PROHIBITION BY LAW OF FOREIGN BANKS ENTERING VIA BRANCHES	BERMUDA CAMEROON PEOPLE'S REPUBLIC OF THE CONGO COSTA RICA FINLAND GAMBIA GHANA HUNGARY ICELAND IRELAND NIGER PERU PHILIPPINES SOUTH AFRICA URUGUAY CANADA	SEVERAL OF THESE COUNTRIES PERMIT AFFILIATES. WITH THE EXCEPTION OF EC MEMBER COUNTRY BANKS PERMITS BANK SUBSIDIARIES PERMITS NEAR-BANK SUBSIDIARIES	MOST OF THE WORLDWIDE EXPANSION OF BANKING OVER THE PAST TWO DECADES HAS TAKEN PLACE THROUGH BRANCHES ELIMINATION OF THE BRANCH CHOICE MAY COMPLETELY DETER ANY ENTRY BY SOME BANKS WHICH FIND OTHER FORMS EITHER INADEQUATE, SUCH AS REPRESENTATIVE OFFICES, OR TOO EXPENSIVE OR UNWIELDLY, SUCH AS SUBSIDIARIES OR AFFILIATES.
PROHIBITION OF FOREIGN BANKS FROM PURCHASING ANY INTEREST IN INDIGENOUS BANKS	BANGLADESH COSTA RICA PAKISTAN PAPUA NEW GUINEA SURINAM		

USTR COMPUTER GROUP

A PRELIMINARY SURVEY OF
ENTRY RESTRICTIONS AND OPERATIONAL CONSTRAINTS IMPOSED ON FOREIGN BANKS
IN A PARTICULAR COUNTRY

TYPE OF RESTRICTION	PRACTICING COUNTRIES	COUNTRY SPECIFICS	IMPLICATIONS/COMMENTS
PROHIBITION OF FOREIGN BANKS FROM ACQUIRING CONTROLLING INTEREST IN INDIGENEOUS BANKS		MAXIMUM FOREIGN PARTICIPATION ALLOWED:	
	AUSTRALIA	10%	
	BERMUDA	40%	
	CANADA	10% CANADA PERMITS AN INDIVIDUAL FOREIGN PARTY TO OWN UP TO 10% OF A BANK, AND UP TO 25% OF ANY BANK MAY BE FOREIGN-OWNED	
	THE CONGO	49%	
	DENMARK	30% DENMARK REQUIRES A MERGER IF ANY PARTY, FOREIGN OR DOMESTIC, ACQUIRES 30% OR MORE OF A BANK	
	ECUADOR	20% FOR NON-ANDEAN PACT NATIONS	
	FINLAND	20%	
	GAMBIA	20%	
	JAPAN	5%	

USTR COMPUTER GROUP

297

A PRELIMINARY SURVEY OF
ENTRY RESTRICTIONS AND OPERATIONAL CONSTRAINTS IMPOSED ON FOREIGN BANKS
IN A PARTICULAR COUNTRY

TYPE OF RESTRICTION	PRACTICING COUNTRIES	COUNTRY SPECIFICS	IMPLICATIONS/COMMENTS
PROHIBITION OF FOREIGN BANKS FROM ACQUIRING CONTROLLING INTEREST IN INDIGENEOUS BANKS		MAXIMUM FOREIGN PARTICIPATION ALLOWED:	
	NIGERIA	40%	
	PHILIPPINES	30% 40% WITH PRESIDENTIAL APPROVAL	
	REPUBLIC OF KOREA	10%	
	UPPER VOLTA	49%	
	BAHRAIN	49%	
	DOMINICAN REPUBLIC	30%	
	GREECE	49%	
	ICELAND	49%	
	MOROCCO	50%	
	OMAN	49%	
	QATAR	49%	
	SINGAPORE	20%	
	SOUTH AFRICA	50% ONCE A FOREIGN-OWNED BANK REACHES U.S. $24 MILLION IN SHARE CAPITAL, IT MUST OPEN ITS SHAREHOLDINGS TO LOCAL PARTICIPATION, WITH THE GOAL OF EVENTUALLY REACHING 50% LOCAL OWNERSHIP	
	U.K.	15%	

USTR COMPUTER GROUP

298

A PRELIMINARY SURVEY OF
ENTRY RESTRICTIONS AND OPERATIONAL CONSTRAINTS IMPOSED ON FOREIGN BANKS
IN A PARTICULAR COUNTRY

TYPE OF RESTRICTION	PRACTICING COUNTRIES	COUNTRY SPECIFICS	IMPLICATIONS/COMMENTS
PROHIBITION OF FOREIGN BANKS FROM ACQUIRING CONTROLLING INTEREST IN INDIGENEOUS BANKS	CENTRAL AFRICAN REPUBLIC CYPRUS EGYPT ICELAND MALAYSIA MALAWI MALTA NETHERLANDS OMAN TRINIDAD & TOBAGO TUNISIA	NO MAJORITY CONTROL; NO SPECIFIC MAXIMUM:	

USTR COMPUTER GROUP

299

A PRELIMINARY SURVEY OF
ENTRY RESTRICTIONS AND OPERATIONAL CONSTRAINTS IMPOSED ON FOREIGN BANKS
IN A PARTICULAR COUNTRY

TYPE OF RESTRICTION	PRACTICING COUNTRIES	COUNTRY SPECIFICS	IMPLICATIONS/COMMENTS
PROHIBITION OR LIMITATION ON EXPANSION ON BRANCH NETWORKS	BRAZIL	SINCE 1964, BRAZIL HAS ALLOWED ONLY ONE NEW BRANCH FACILITY (1977).	BRANCH OPERATIONS ARE, HOWEVER, FREE TO RELOCATE
	GREECE	FOREIGN BANK BRANCHING IS BASICALLY LIMITED TO ATHENS. PIRAEUS AND THESSAL	WITHOUT FORMALLY DISALLOWING BRANCHING BEYOND THESE CITIES, THE CURRENCY COMITTEE HAS IN THE PAST DISCOURAGED FOREIGN BANKS FROM ESTABLISHING BRANCHES IN OTHER LOCATIONS
	INDONESIA	FOREIGN BANKS ESTABLISHED PRIOR TO THE EXCLUSIONARY POLICY ARE LIMITED TO ONE BRANCH AND ONE SUB-BRANCH OFFICE IN JAKARTA	
	IRELAND	FOREIGN BANKS MAY OPEN A SECOND OFFICE ONLY AFTER SEVEN YEARS OF OPERATION	
	KOREA	MORATORIUM ON FOREIGN BRANCH EXPANSION IN SEOUL	
	LEBANON	VERY LIMITED	
	MALAYSIA	EXISTING FOREIGN BANKS ARE NOT PERMITTED TO EXPAND THEIR BRANCH OPERATIONS	

USTR COMPUTER GROUP

300

A PRELIMINARY SURVEY OF
ENTRY RESTRICTIONS AND OPERATIONAL CONSTRAINTS IMPOSED ON FOREIGN BANKS
IN A PARTICULAR COUNTRY

TYPE OF RESTRICTION	PRACTICING COUNTRIES	COUNTRY SPECIFICS	IMPLICATIONS/COMMENTS
PROHIBITION OR LIMITATION ON EXPANSION ON BANK NETWORKS	MEXICO	SINCE 1930, MEXICO HAS LIMITED FOREIGN BANK ENTRY TO REPRESENTATIVE OFFICES. ONE FOREIGN BANK, ESTABLISHED IN MEXICO PRIOR TO 1930, CONTINUES TO BE ALLOWED TO OPERATE IN BRANCH FORM UNDER A GRANDFATHER CLAUSE. THIS BANK HAS FIVE BRANCHES IN MEXICO CITY AND HAS BEEN PROHIBITED FROM ESTABLISHING ADDITIONAL BRANCHES.	SOME COUNTRIES PROHIBIT ANY ADDITIONAL BRANCHING BY BOTH FOREIGN AND DOMESTIC BANKS. FOREIGN BANKS ARE USUALLY MORE ADVERSELY AFFECTED HOWEVER, SINCE THEY TYPICALLY HAVE FEWER ESTABLISHED BRANCHES THAN DOMESTIC BANKS.
	PAKISTAN	IT IS MORE DIFFICULT FOR FOREIGN BANKS TO OBTAIN APPROVAL TO EXPAND THEIR BRANCH NETWORKS THAN FOR DOMESTIC BANKS.	WHERE FOREIGN BRANCHES ARE SUBJECT TO CONSTRAINTS BOTH ON ACCEPTING CERTAIN TYPES OF DEPOSITS AND ON EXPANDING THEIR BRANCH NETWORKS, THE COMBINATION SEVERELY RESTRICTS THEIR ACCESS TO INEXPENSIVE LOCAL SOURCES OF FUNDS.
	PHILIPPINES	EXISTING FOREIGN BRANCH BANKS ARE NOT PERMITTED TO EXPAND THEIR NETWORKS	
	SINGAPORE	VERY LIMITED	
	THAILAND	LIMITS EXISTING FOREIGN BANK BRANCHING TO THE CAPITAL CITY.	
	TURKEY	APPROVAL TO EXPAND IS DIFFICULT TO OBTAIN	

USTR COMPUTER GROUP

A PRELIMINARY SURVEY OF
ENTRY RESTRICTIONS AND OPERATIONAL CONSTRAINTS IMPOSED ON FOREIGN BANKS
IN A PARTICULAR COUNTRY

TYPE OF RESTRICTION	PRACTICING COUNTRIES	COUNTRY SPECIFICS	IMPLICATIONS/COMMENTS
PROHIBITION OR LIMITATION ON FOREIGN BANKS' SOLICITATION OF CERTAIN KINDS OF DEPOSITS	COSTA RICA	ONLY STATE-OWNED COMMERCIAL BANKS ARE PERMITTED TO ACCEPT DEMAND AND TIME DEPOSITS	DEPOSITS ARE USUALLY ONE OF THE BANK'S LOWEST COST SOURCE OF FUNDS. TO THE EXTENT THAT DEPOSIT-TAKING LIMITATIONS FORCE FOREIGN BANKS TO USE MORE EXPENSIVE SOURCES OF FUNDS, THEY CONSTITUTE A SIGNIFICANT COMPETITIVE DISADVANTAGE TO FOREIGN BANKS.
	EGYPT	ONLY BANKS AT LEAST 52% OWNED BY EGYPTIANS ARE PERMITTED TO ACCEPT LOCAL CURRENCY DEPOSITS	
	EL SALVADOR	THE ONE FOREIGN BANK BRANCH OPERATING IN EL SALVADOR IS NOT PERMITTED TO ACCEPT SAVINGS DEPOSITS	
	FEDERAL REPUBLIC OF GERMANY	BRANCHES OF FOREIGN BANKS ARE NOT ALLOWED TO BECOME BANKS OF DEPOSIT FOR MUTUAL FUNDS.	
	INDONESIA	PROHIBITED FROM SOLICITING DEMAND DEPOSITS	

USTR COMPUTER GROUP

A PRELIMINARY SURVEY OF
ENTRY RESTRICTIONS AND OPERATIONAL CONSTRAINTS IMPOSED ON FOREIGN BANKS
IN A PARTICULAR COUNTRY

TYPE OF RESTRICTION	PRACTICING COUNTRIES	COUNTRY SPECIFICS	IMPLICATIONS/COMMENTS
PROHIBITION OR LIMITATION ON FOREIGN BANKS' SOLICITATION OF CERTAIN KINDS OF DEPOSITS	JAPAN	PROHIBITED FROM SOLICITING LOCAL DEPOSITS	DEPOSITS ARE USUALLY ONE OF THE BANK'S LOWEST COST SOURCE OF FUNDS. TO THE EXTENT THAT DEPOSIT-TAKING LIMITATIONS FORCE FOREIGN BANKS TO USE MORE EXPENSIVE SOURCES OF FUNDS, THEY CONSTITUTE A SIGNIFICANT COMPETITIVE DISADVANTAGE TO FOREIGN BANKS
	PHILIPPINES	FOREIGN BANKS ARE NOT PERMITTED TO SOLICIT RETAIL DEPOSITS	
	SPAIN	LIMITATION ON AMOUNT OF DEPOSITS A FOREIGN BANK MAY OBTAIN FROM SPANISH CUSTOMERS TO 40% OF ITS PORTFOLIO OF INVESTMENTS AND LOANS TO SPANISH ENTITIES, PUBLIC AND PRIVATE.	
	SUDAN	FOREIGN BANKS ARE EXCLUDED FROM TAKING INDIVIDUAL DEPOSITS FROM SUDANESE RESIDING IN SUDAN	
	TAIWAN	FOREIGN BANKS ARE NOT PERMITTED TO DEMAND AND TIME DEPOSITS.	

USTR COMPUTER GROUP

303

A PRELIMINARY SURVEY OF
ENTRY RESTRICTIONS AND OPERATIONAL CONSTRAINTS IMPOSED ON FOREIGN BANKS
IN A PARTICULAR COUNTRY

TYPE OF RESTRICTION	PRACTICING COUNTRIES	COUNTRY SPECIFICS	IMPLICATIONS/COMMENTS
RESTRICTION ON ACCESS TO GOVERNMENT DEPOSITS	BRAZIL	BANCO DE BRASIL IS THE SOLE BANKER FOR THE LARGE AND GROWING PUBLIC SECTOR	
	INDIA	ALMOST ALL GOVERNMENT AGENCIES AND PUBLICLY OWNED ENTERPRISES BANK WITH INDIAN BANKS	
	JAMAICA	NO ACCESS	
	LIBERIA	GOVERNMENT CORPORATIONS ARE OBLIGED TO KEEP THEIR FUNDS ON DEPOSIT WITH THE NATIONAL BANK OF LIBERIA	
	NIGERIA	NO ACCESS	
	PARAGUAY	NO ACCESS	
	PHILIPPINES	NO ACCESS	
	U.K.	FOREIGN BANKS DENIED ACCESS TO GOVERNMENT AND THRIFT INSTITUTION DEPOSITS.	

USTR COMPUTER GROUP

304

A PRELIMINARY SURVEY OF
ENTRY RESTRICTIONS AND OPERATIONAL CONSTRAINTS IMPOSED ON FOREIGN BANKS
IN A PARTICULAR COUNTRY

TYPE OF RESTRICTION	PRACTICING COUNTRIES	COUNTRY SPECIFICS	IMPLICATIONS/COMMENTS
NO ACCESS TO SUBSIDIZED FUNDS FOR EXPORT FINANCING	AUSTRIA	SUBSIDIZED EXPORT FINANCING PLACED ONLY WITH AUSTRIAN BANKS	
	JAPAN	THE JAPANESE EXPORT-IMPORT BANK AND THE BANK OF JAPAN HAVE PROGRAMS AND FACILITIES TO HELP FINANCE IMPORTS AND EXPORTS. FOREIGN BANKS ARE NOT ABLE TO PARTICIPATE	
	SOUTH KOREA		
	NIGERIA		
	PERU	FOREIGN BANKS IN PERU ARE REQUIRED TO CONTRIBUTE TO A FUND WHICH SUBSIDIZES FINANCING OF SOME EXPORTS, BUT ONLY DOMESTIC BANKS ARE ELIGIBLE TO WRITE THESE LOANS.	
	TAIWAN		
	U.K.	FOREIGN BANKS EXCLUDED FROM SOME PHASES OF THE EXPORT CREDIT GUARANTEE PROGRAMS.	

USTR COMPUTER GROUP

A PRELIMINARY SURVEY OF
ENTRY RESTRICTIONS AND OPERATIONAL CONSTRAINTS IMPOSED ON FOREIGN BANKS
IN A PARTICULAR COUNTRY

TYPE OF RESTRICTION	PRACTICING COUNTRIES	COUNTRY SPECIFICS	IMPLICATIONS/COMMENTS
LIMITATION OR DENIAL OF FOREIGN BANK ACCESS TO CENTRAL BANK DISCOUNT FACILITIES	DOMINICAN REPUBLIC	REDISCOUNT FACILITIES WITH THE CENTRAL BANK PERMIT THE REDISCOUNTING OF 100% OF LOCAL BANKS' CAPITAL AND RESERVES, BUT ONLY 90% OF FOREIGN BANKS.	PLACES FOREIGN BANKS AT A DISADVANTAGE IN MEETING LIQUIDITY NEEDS IN A TIMELY AND INEXPENSIVE MANNER. FORCING THEM TO HOLD A LARGER PORTION OF THEIR ASSETS IN LOWER YIELDING SECONDARY RESERVES.
	EGYPT	NO ACCESS	
	EL SALVADOR	THE ONE FOREIGN BRANCH OPERATING IN EL SALVADOR IS NOT PERMITTED TO REDISCOUNT MOST PAPER WITH THE CENTRAL BANK	
	GERMANY	REDISCOUNT QUOTAS LINKED TO BRANCH CAPITAL	
	INDONESIA	NO ACCESS	
	SOUTH KOREA	NO ACCESS	
	TAIWAN	NO ACCESS	
	U.K.	NO ACCESS - FOREIGN BANKS FORCED TO PAY A PREMIUM TO PLACE THEIR PAPER IN THE DISCOUNT MARKET.	

USTR COMPUTER GROUP

306

A PRELIMINARY SURVEY OF
ENTRY RESTRICTIONS AND OPERATIONAL CONSTRAINTS IMPOSED ON FOREIGN BANKS
IN A PARTICULAR COUNTRY

TYPE OF RESTRICTION	PRACTICING COUNTRIES	COUNTRY SPECIFICS	IMPLICATIONS/COMMENTS
POLICIES WHICH LIMIT THE SERVICES FOREIGN BANKS CAN OFFER	BANGLADESH	GOVERNMENT POLICY IS TO RESTRICT FOREIGN BANKING TO IMPORT/EXPORT FINANCING, FOREIGN EXCHANGE PROJECTS AND LOCAL CURRENCY LOANS FOR WHICH THE GOVERNMENT BANKS LACK SUFFICIENT LIQUIDITY	
	GUYANA	STATE CORPORATIONS AND GOVERNMENT EMPLOYEES ARE REQUIRED TO DO AS MUCH OF THEIR BANKING AS POSSIBLE WITH THE GOVERNMENT-OWNED BANKS.	
	INDONESIA		
	JAPAN	FOREIGN BANKS MAY NOT ENGAGE IN RETAIL BANKING	
		APPROVAL REQUIRED OF YEN LOANS TO NON JAPANESE BORROWERS.	
	SOUTH KOREA	PROHIBITS FOREIGN BANKS' ACCESS TO NEW CUSTOMERS.	
		KOREAN COMPANIES ARE REQUIRED TO DESIGNATE A "PRIME" BANK TO MANAGE CERTAIN ASPECTS OF THE COMPANIES FINANCING. THE USE OF FOREIGN BANKS FOR THIS PURPOSE IS DISCOURAGED.	

USTR COMPUTER GROUP

A PRELIMINARY SURVEY OF
ENTRY RESTRICTIONS AND OPERATIONAL CONSTRAINTS IMPOSED ON FOREIGN BANKS
IN A PARTICULAR COUNTRY

TYPE OF RESTRICTION	PRACTICING COUNTRIES	COUNTRY SPECIFICS	IMPLICATIONS/COMMENTS
POLICIES WHICH LIMIT THE SERVICES FOREIGN BANKS CAN OFFER	MALAYSIA	PROHIBITS FOREIGN BANKS' ACCESS TO NEW CUSTOMERS	
		LOCAL BORROWERS MUST DEAL WITH DOMESTIC BANKS	
		FOREIGN-CONTROLLED CORPORATIONS OPERATING IN MALAYSIA MUST GIVE AT LEAST HALF OF THEIR LOAN BUSINESS TO DOMESTIC BANKS	
	PHILIPPINES	PROHIBITS FOREIGN BANKS FROM PROVIDING TRUST SERVICES	
	SWITZERLAND	SWISS INSURANCE COMPANIES ARE (1) PROHIBITED BY LAW FROM DEPOSITING FUNDS IN OR INVESTING IN OBLIGATIONS OF FOREIGN BANKS; (2) EXCLUDED FROM THE SECURITY MANAGEMENT AND UNDERWRITING BUSINESS; (3) NOT PERMITTED TO MANAGE MUNICIPAL OR DOMESTIC BOND ISSUES.	
	TAIWAN	PROHIBITS FOREIGN BANKS FROM LENDING TO INDIVIDUALS	
	TRINIDAN & TOBAGO	GOVERNMENT CORPORATIONS ARE DISCOURAGED FROM DOING BUSINESS WITH FOREIGN BANKS	

USTR COMPUTER GROUP

308

TYPE OF RESTRICTION	PRACTICING COUNTRIES	COUNTRY SPECIFICS	IMPLICATIONS/COMMENTS
FOREIGN BANKS' LOAN CAPACITY LIMITED VIS A VIS DOMESTIC BANKS' AS A RESULT OF THE METHOD OF CALCULATING BANK ASSETS	DENMARK ITALY SOUTH KOREA SWITZERLAND	(1) (2) (1) (1) (1) (UNDER CERTAIN CONDITIONS THE BANK COMMISSION TOLERATES BRANCH LIABILITIES OF UP TO DOUBLE THE LIMITS)	BANKING REGULATIONS IN VIRTUALLY ALL COUNTRIES REQUIRE BANKS TO MAINTAIN A CERTAIN NET CAPITAL TO TOTAL LIABILITIES RATIO. THIS PERCENTAGE IS USUALLY THE SAME FOR BOTH DOMESTIC AND FOREIGN BANKS. YET THIS REGULATION DIFFERENTIALLY RESTRAINS FOREIGN BRANCH OPERATIONS IN THOSE COUNTRIES WHICH (1) BASE NET CAPITAL FOR DOMESTIC BANKS ON THE CAPITAL AND RESERVES OF THE WHOLE BANK, WHILE FOR BRANCHES OF FOREIGN BANKS IT IS BASED ON ONLY THE BANKS ASSETS WITHIN THE COUNTRY. SIMILIARLY, IN SOME COUNTRIES (2) BRANCHES OF FOREIGN-OWNED BANKS MUST REDUCE THEIR NET CAPITAL BY THE AMOUNT OF BRANCH CLAIMS ON THEIR HEAD OFFICE OR ANY OF THEIR SUBSIDIARIES OR BRANCHES OUTSIDE OF THE COUNTRY.

USTR COMPUTER GROUP

TYPE OF RESTRICTION	PRACTICING COUNTRIES	COUNTRY SPECIFICS	IMPLICATIONS/COMMENTS
SPECIFIED LOAN PORTFOLIO STRUCTURE	BOLIVIA	FOREIGN BANKS REQUIRED TO ALLOCATE 25 PERCENT OF TOTAL LOANS TO INDUSTRIAL AND MANUFACTURING TERM CREDIT. PERCENTAGE FOR DOMESTIC BANKS IS LESS.	
	ECUADOR	FOREIGN BRANCHES MUST INVEST 25 PERCENT OF THEIR PORTFOLIOS IN LOW YIELDING GOVERNMENT BONDS. THE REQUIREMENT FOR LOCAL BANKS IS ONLY 20 PERCENT.	
	PERU	FOREIGN BANKS ARE REQUIRED TO EXTEND TWO LINES OF CREDIT TO THE GOVERNMENT, ONE EQUAL TO TWICE THE FOREIGN BANKS LOCAL CAPITAL AND THE OTHER EQUAL TO THE AMOUNT OF DOMESTIC CURRENCY DEPOSITS HELD.	
POLICIES WHICH PLACE CONSTRAINTS ON FOREIGN BANKS' INVESTMENT PORTFOLIOS	BOLIVIA	REINVESTMENT OF EARNINGS MAY NOT EXCEED 5% OF CAPITAL ANNUALLY	
	BRAZIL	FOREIGN BANKS ARE PERMITTED TO HOLD ONLY UP TO 50 PERCENT OF CAPITAL STOCK AND UP TO 33 PERCENT OF VOTING SHARES IN BRAZILIAN FINANCIAL INSTITUTIONS	PRECLUDES FOREIGN BANKS FROM MATCHING THE MAJOR DOMESTIC BANKS DIVERSIFICATION INTO BANKING-RELATED ACTIVITIES.
	SPAIN	PROHIBITION OF FOREIGN BANK EQUITY PARTICIPATION IN SPANISH BUSINESS IN CONTRAST TO SPANISH BANKS, WHICH ALREADY CONTROL CLOSE TO 48 PERCENT OF PRIVATE INDUSTRY	LIMITS THE INVESTMENT PORTFOLIOS OF FOREIGN BANKS TO HOLDINIGS OF GOVERNMENT SECURITIES AND FIXED INTEREST OBLIGATIONS.

USTR COMPUTER GROUP

A PRELIMINARY SURVEY OF
ENTRY RESTRICTIONS AND OPERATIONAL CONSTRAINTS IMPOSED ON FOREIGN BANKS
IN A PARTICULAR COUNTRY

TYPE OF RESTRICTION	PRACTICING COUNTRIES	COUNTRY SPECIFICS	IMPLICATIONS/COMMENTS
DISCRIMINATORY OR EXCESSIVE CAPITAL REQUIREMENTS	BOLIVIA	INITIAL CAPITAL REQUIRED FOR FOREIGN BRANCHES IS TWICE THAT REQUIRED ON DOMESTIC BANKS	
	SOUTH KOREA	FOREIGN BANKS ARE REQUIRED TO CAPITALIZE EACH BRANCH SEPARATELY	
	SPAIN	BRANCHES OF FOREIGN BANKS MUST HAVE CAPITAL OF $10.7 MILLION, AND SUBSIDIARIES TWICE THAT AMOUNT (AS OF 1978).	THESE CAPITALIZATION REQUIREMENTS HAVE BEEN CRITICIZED BY FOREIGN BANKS AS TOO HIGH. IT SHOULD BE NOTED, HOWEVER, THAT THE CAPITAL REQUIREMENT FOR SPANISH BANKS IS EVEN HIGHER
DISCRIMINATORY OR EXCESSIVE RESERVE REQUIREMENTS	ECUADOR	FOREIGN BANKS MUST DEPOSIT A LARGER PROPORTION OF THEIR FOREIGN EXCHANGE WITH THE CENTRAL BANK	
	EGYPT	FOREIGN BANKS OPERATING IN EGYPT REQUIRED TO DEPOSIT 15 PERCENT OF THEIR CURRENCY WITH CENTRAL BANK	
	GREECE	FOREIGN BANKS MUST DEPOSIT U.S. $10 MILLION IN FOREIGN EXCHANGE WITH THE CENTRAL BANK FOR EACH BRANCH OFFICE ESTABLISHED	

USTR COMPUTER GROUP

311

A PRELIMINARY SURVEY OF
ENTRY RESTRICTIONS AND OPERATIONAL CONSTRAINTS IMPOSED ON FOREIGN BANKS
IN A PARTICULAR COUNTRY

TYPE OF RESTRICTION	PRACTICING COUNTRIES	COUNTRY SPECIFICS	IMPLICATIONS/COMMENTS
LIMITATIONS ON FOREIGN EXCHANGE TRANSACTIONS	AUSTRALIA	ALL FOREIGN EXCHANGE TRANSACTIONS MUST BE DONE THROUGH AUSTRALIAN BANKS AND AT RATES OF EXCHANGE FIXED OR AUTHORIZED BY THE CENTRAL BANK	THIS GIVES AUSTRALIAN BANKS A MONOPOLY ON FOREIGN EXCHANGE TRANSACTIONS TO THE COMPETITIVE DISADVANTAGE OF FOREIGN BANK SUBSIDIARY OPERATIONS LIMITATIONS ON FOREIGN EXCHANGE TRANSACTIONS ARE OFTEN THE PRODUCT OF GENERAL ECONOMIC AND BALANCE OF PAYMENTS POLICY MEASURES. IN SUCH INSTANCES, LIMITATIONS APPLY EVENLY TO ALL BANKS, FOREIGN AND DOMESTIC. YET THEY TEND TO HAVE A HARSHER IMPACT ON FOREIGN BANKS BECAUSE OF THE INTERNATIONAL ORIENTATION OF THEIR BUSINESS.

USTR COMPUTER GROUP

ENTRY RESTRICTIONS AND OPERATIONAL CONSTRAINTS IMPOSED ON FOREIGN BANKS
IN A PARTICULAR COUNTRY

TYPE OF RESTRICTION	PRACTICING COUNTRIES	COUNTRY SPECIFICS	IMPLICATIONS/COMMENTS
RESTRICTIONS ON REPATRIATION OF PROFITS OR FUNDS	BRAZIL	UP TO 12% OF EXISTING CAPITAL AND REINVESTMENT FUNDS MAY BE REMITTED EXCESSIVE AMOUNTS SUBJECT TO PROGRESSIVE TAX OF 65-85%.	
	BOLIVIA	PROFIT REPATRIATION MAY NOT EXCEED 20% OF CAPITAL ANNUALLY.	
	GHANA	DIFFICULT TO OBTAIN APPROVAL FOR REMITTANCE OF PROFITS	
	KENYA	DIFFICULT TO OBTAIN APPROVAL FOR REMITTANCE OF PROFITS	
	SOUTH KOREA	RETAINED EARNING REQUIREMENTS	
	LEBANON	RETAINED EARNING REQUIREMENTS	
	NETHERLANDS	RETAINED EARNING REQUIREMENTS	
	PAKISTAN	RETAINED EARNING REQUIREMENTS	
	PHILIPPINES	RETAINED EARNING REQUIREMENTS	
	SINGAPORE	RETAINED EARNING REQUIREMENTS	
	TANZANIA	RETAINED EARNING REQUIREMENTS	
	ZAMBIA	REPATRIATION OF PROFITS PROHIBITED	
		UP TO 30% OF EQUITY CAPITAL MAY BE TRANSFERRED ABROAD PROVIDED THAT THE AMOUNT IS LESS THAN 50% OF NET PROFITS	

USTR COMPUTER GROUP

A PRELIMINARY SURVEY OF
ENTRY RESTRICTIONS AND OPERATIONAL CONSTRAINTS IMPOSED ON FOREIGN BANKS
IN A PARTICULAR COUNTRY

TYPE OF RESTRICTION	PRACTICING COUNTRIES	COUNTRY SPECIFICS	IMPLICATIONS/COMMENTS
PERSONNEL RESTRICTIONS REGARDING FOREIGN PERSONNEL	AUSTRIA	WORK PERMITS OFTEN DIFFICULT TO OBTAIN	
	BRAZIL	BANK DIRECTORS MUST BE BRAZILIAN RESIDENTS. TWO-THIRDS OF A BANK PAYROLL MUST BE PAID TO BRAZILIANS OR TO "CERTAIN LEGAL EQUIVALENTS OF NATIONALS."	
	CAMEROON	MANAGERS OF FOREIGN BANKS MUST BE CAMEROONIAN	
	CHILE	IF A FOREIGN OPERATION EMPLOYS MORE THAN FIVE INDIVIDUALS, AT LEAST 85% OF THE STAFF MUST BE CHILEAN.	
	COLOMBIA	LAW 55 STATES THAT AFTER DECEMBER 1978 FOREIGN BANKS SHOULD NOT CONTINUE TO EXERCISE MANAGERIAL CONTROL OVER THEIR LOCAL AFFILIATES.	TO DATE, THE COLOMBIAN GOVERNMENT HAS NOT ENFORCED THIS POSITION
	FEDERAL REPUBLIC OF GERMANY	EACH BANKING OFFICE MUST BE RUN BY TWO FULL-TIME MANAGERS WITH KNOWLEDGE OF THE GERMAN LANGUAGE AND EXPERIENCE IN THE GERMAN BANKING SYSTEM	AS INTERPRETED BY THE GERMAN AUTHORITIES, THIS MEANS THAT MANAGERS MUST HAVE SPENT THREE YEARS IN A SENIOR POSITION WITH A GERMAN CREDIT INSTITUTION THIS OBLIGES THE HIRING OF SENIOR GERMAN BANKERS WHO ARE EXPENSIVE AND NOT ALWAYS EASY TO COME BY AND PREVENTS FOREIGN BANKS FROM SENDING THEIR OWN SENIOR STAFF INTO GERMANY AS IS CUSTOMARY IN OTHER COUNTRIES.
	IRELAND	A MAJORITY OF DIRECTORS OF NON-EC BANKS MUST BE IRISH OR NATIONALS OF OTHER EC COUNTRIES.	
	ITALY	WORK PERMITS FOR FOREIGNERS GRANTED ONLY WHEN AN ITALIAN CANNOT FILL THE POSITION.	EXCEPTIONS ARE USUALLY GRANTED IN THE CASE OF HIGH MANAGEMENT POSITIONS.

ENTRY RESTRICTIONS AND OPERATIONAL CONSTRAINTS IMPOSED ON FOREIGN BANKS
IN A PARTICULAR COUNTRY

TYPE OF RESTRICTION	PRACTICING COUNTRIES	COUNTRY SPECIFICS	IMPLICATIONS/COMMENTS
PERSONNEL RESTRICTIONS REGARDING FOREIGN PERSONNEL	NEW ZEALAND	WORK PERMITS SUBJECT TO A QUOTA IN SOME CASES	
	NIGERIA	EXPATRIATE QUOTAS EXIST TO LIMIT THE USE OF FOREIGN PERSONNEL	THIS STIPULATION HAS EFFECTIVELY DETERRED FOREIGN BRANCH ENTRY
	PAPUA NEW GUINEA	AT LEAST 70 PERCENT OF EMPLOYEES MUST BE LOCAL CITIZENS	
	SWEDEN	FOREIGNERS MAY NOT BE DIRECTORS OF SWEDISH BANKS	
	SWITZERLAND	WORK PERMITS ARE SOMETIMES DIFFICULT TO OBTAIN AND, CONSEQUENTLY, THE ABILITY OF A FOREIGN BANK TO DEVELOP STAFF AND MANAGEMENT MAY BE FRUSTRATED	THE WORK PERMIT RESTRICTION MAY HAVE DETERRED SOME FOREIGN BANKS THAT HAVE CONSIDERED DEVELOPING COMMERCIAL BANKING OR PORTFOLIO MANAGEMENT FACILITIES IN SWITZERLAND.
	TRINIDAD & TOBAGO	WOWRK PERMITS FOR FOREIGN NATIONALS ARE DIFFICULT TO OBTAIN	
	VENEZUELA	THE PRESIDENT AND THREE-FOURTHS OF THE EXECUTIVE OFFICIALS OF A BANK OPERATING IN VENEZUELA MUST BE VENEZUELANS RESIDING IN THE COUNTRY	
	ZAIRE	WORK PERMITS FOR FOREIGNERS, SUBJECT TO QUOTAS IN SOME CASES.	
DISCRIMINATORY TAXATION OF FOREIGN BANKS	INDIA	FOREIGN BANKS' PROFIT IS TAXED AT A HIGHER RATE THAN DOMESTIC BANKS (75% VS 60%)	
	SRI LANKA	FOREIGN BANKS REQUIRED TO PAY A SLIGHTLY HIGHER CORPORATE INCOME TAX THAN DOMESTIC BANKS.	

USTR COMPUTER GROUP

CHAPTER SEVEN

TAXATION OF INTERNATIONAL INCOME OF COMMERCIAL BANKS

A Comparison of Tax Systems in the
United States, the United Kingdom,
France, West Germany, and Japan

Thomas Horst

Taxecon Associates[1]

CONTENTS

TABLES

PART A

OVERVIEW

Judged by conventional standards, the rate of growth of international lending by U.S. commercial banks has been outstanding. Total assets of foreign branches of U.S. banks, the most common vehicle for international lending, grew from $8.5 billion in 1965 to $364 billion in 1979, an average compounded rate of growth of more than 30 percent per annum. In recent years, however, international lending by non-U.S. banks has been growing at an even more phenomenal rate, and the relative position of U.S. banks appears to be slipping. The Board of Governors of the Federal Reserve System recently began collecting data on international claims (e.g., a claim by a London branch against a French or a U.S. borrower) by the foreign and domestic branches of banks chartered in the United States. Between December 1977 and June 1979, such claims by U.S. banks relative to such claims by all banks reporting to the Bank for International Settlements slipped from 35 percent to 29 percent[2]--see Table 1. Even sharper was the decline over this 18-month interval in the U.S. banks' share of total claims against borrowers in OPEC countries, from 51 percent to 35 percent, and that against borrowers in non-OPEC LDC's from 48 percent to 38 percent.

The declining share of U.S. banks is all the more apparent in examining net new lending--gross new lending

319

TABLE 1: OUTSTANDING INTERNATIONAL CLAIMS OF BANKS REPORTING TO THE BANK FOR INTERNATIONAL SETTLEMENTS

Claims on:	Dec. 1975	Dec. 1977 Old Series	Dec. 1977 New Series[2] ($ billion)	Dec. 1978	June 1979
I. Group of Ten countries and Switzerland[3]	204	281	291	387	391
Non-US banks	150	207	217	302	310
US banks	55	73	73	84	81
(US share)	(27%)	(26%)	(25%)	(22%)	(21%)
II. Offshore banking centres	58	93	94	117	127
Non-US banks	24	34	35	51	62
US banks	34	59	59	66	64
(US share)	(59%)	(63%)	(63%)	(57%)	(51%)
III. Smaller developed countries[4]	38	66	71	84	87
Non-US banks	28	51	55	67	68
US banks	10	16	16	18	19
(US share)	(27%)	(24%)	(22%)	(21%)	(22%)
IV. Oil-exporting countries	14	35	39	56	58
Non-US banks	7	16	19	35	38
US banks	7	20	20	22	20
(US share)	(52%)	(56%)	(51%)	(39%)	(35%)
V. Non-oil LDCs	63	92	99	122	137
Non-US banks	29	45	52	72	84
US banks	34	47	47	50	52
(US share)	(54%)	(51%)	(48%)	(41%)	(38%)
VI. Eastern Europe[5]	23	36	42	53	56
Non-US banks	20	30	36	47	50
US banks	3	6	6	6	6
(US share)	(14%)	(16%)	(14%)	(11%)	(11%)
VII. Miscellaneous and unclassified	9	15	15	19	21
Non-US banks	4	9	10	11	12
US banks	5	5	5	8[6]	9
(US share)	(54%)	(36%)	(35%)	(43%)	(43%)
VIII. World total[3]	411	618	650	839	876
Non-US banks	263	392	424	584	624
US banks	148	226	226	255	252
(US share)	(36%)	(37%)	(35%)	(30%)	(29%)

Source: Rodney H. Mills, Jr., "U.S. banks are losing their share of the market," Euromoney, February 1980, Table 1.

Notes to Tables 1 and 2

[1] Banks in Belgium-Luxembourg, France, Germany, Italy, Netherlands, Sweden, Switzerland, United Kingdom, Canada, Japan, United States, and US bank branches in five offshore banking centres (Bahamas, Cayman Islands, Panama, Hong Kong, and Singapore); also banks in Austria, Denmark, and Ireland beginning December 1977, new series.
[2] Including banks in Austria, Denmark, and Ireland as reporters.
[3] Excluding claims on the United States.
[4] Western Europe other than Group of Ten countries and Switzerland, plus Turkey, South Africa and Australia.
[5] Including Yugoslavia.
[6] The increase over December 1977 largely reflects a change in reporting instructions for US bank foreign branches.
Figures may not add to totals because of rounding. Percentage shares were computed from unrounded numbers.

To allow full comparability with US data, the original BIS data have been adjusted to shift Yugoslavia from III to VI, New Zealand from III to VI, and Liberia from II to VII.
To allow full comparability with the BIS data, the US data as published by the Federal Reserve have been adjusted to (1) restore intrabank claims, which are netted out in the Federal Reserve series; (2) remove claims held by foreign branches of US banks on local customers, since these are not international claims from the BIS point of view; (3) remove claims held by US bank branches outside the BIS reporting area — i.e., outside the countries indicated in note 1.

Sources: Bank for International Settlements, quarterly reports on international banking developments; Board of Governors of the Federal Reserve System, Federal Reserve *Bulletin*, Table 3.20, issues beginning June 1979; author's adjustments to Federal Reserve data.

less repayments of outstanding loans--over the last few years. After undertaking almost 40 percent of net new lending in 1976 and 1977, the share of new lending by U.S. banks dropped to 20 percent in 1978 and turned negative in the first six months of 1979 as repayments exceeded gross new lending by $4 billion--see Table 2.

The last five years have hardly been periods of stagnant international loan demand. Indeed, OPEC oil price increases accelerated international lending, but unlike the mid-1970's, much of the recycling was undertaken by non-U.S. banks. Total cross-border claims of non-U.S. banks increased by 45 percent between June 1978 and June 1979--see Table 3. Note that the most rapid expansion in cross-border claims was by the U.S. branches of foreign banks, in obvious and sharp contrast with the decline in such claims by U.S. banks.

Increased competition from non-U.S. banks has squeezed lending margins in recent years. A Euromoney analysis of 769 syndicated loans made in 1979 found that such loans provided for an average margin of 0.8 percentage points over LIBOR and an average maturity of 8.1 years.[3] A similar survey for 1978 found that the average syndicated loan provided for a higher spread, 1.0 percentage points, and a shorter maturity, 7.0 years. Syndications led or co-led by U.S. banks generally provided for greater than average spreads, but for longer than average maturities.

The narrowing of lending margins and the stagnant

TABLE 2: NET INTERNATIONAL LENDING OF BANKS REPORTING TO THE BANK FOR INTERNATIONAL SETTLEMENTS

Lending to:	1976-77	1978	January 1978-June 1979[2] Jan-June 1979	Total
		($ billion)		
I. Group of Ten countries and Switzerland[3]	76	104	4	108
Non-US banks	57	85	8	93
US banks	19	26	−3	23
(US share)	(24%)	(25%)	negative	(21%)
II. Offshore banking centres	35	24	9	33
Non-US banks	10	16	11	27
US banks	25	8	−3	5
(US share)	(72%)	(32%)	negative	(16%)
III. Smaller developed countries[4]	28	15	−3	12
Non-US banks	23	12	−4	13
US banks	5	3	1	4
(US share)	(23%)	(17%)	—	(32%)
IV. Oil-exporting countries	21	18	1	19
Non-US banks	9	16	3	19
US banks	12	3	−2	1
(US share)	(58%)	(16%)	negative	(5%)
V. Non-oil LDCs	29	25	15	40
Non-US banks	16	20	12	32
US banks	13	4	2	6
(US share)	(46%)	(15%)	(15%)	(15%)
VI. Eastern Europe[5]	13	11	3	14
Non-US banks	10	11	3	14
US banks	2	2	−1	1
(US share)	(18%)	(18%)	negative	(9%)
VII. Miscellaneous and unallocated	5	4	2	8
Non-US banks	5	1	1	2
US banks	—	3[6]	1	4
(US share)	(4%)	(71%)	(50%)	(51%)
VIII. World total[3]	207	200	37	237
Non-US banks	129	160	40	200
US banks	78	39	−4	36
(US share)	(38%)	(20%)	negative	(15%)

Source: Rodney H. Mills, Jr., _Ibid_, Table 2.

TABLE 3: CROSS BORDER CLAIMS OF NON-U.S. BANKS

Location of banks	Annual average 1976-77	1978	Percentage increase — 12 months to June 1979	Outstanding in June 1979 ($ billions)
Belgium-Luxembourg	33	37	40	100.5
France	26	38	40	92.5
Germany	26	27	26	57.8
Italy	0	51	44	17.2
Netherlands	25	40	34	46.9
Sweden	14	3	24	5.1
Switzerland	22	37	26	53.2
United Kingdom:				
British banks[1]	18	33	30·	47
Other non-US banks[1]	27	26	35	110:7
Canada	14	23	22	23.9
Japan	3	54	43	35.9
United States: agencies and branches of non-US banks	17	105	58	51
Subtotal	22	38	45	641.7
Austria	n.a.	33	50	14.6
Denmark	n.a.	36	43	3.2
Ireland	n.a.	13	−52	.7
Total	n.a.	38	45	660.2[2]

[1] Based on data for mid-month report dates.
[2] This number exceeds the comparable figure of $624 billion in Table 1 because the claims in Table 4 include claims on the United States.

Sources: Bank for International Settlements; Federal Reserve System; Bank of England.

Source: Rodney H. Mills, Jr., Ibid., Table 4.

volume of international lending by U.S. banks had reduced the share of total earnings U.S. banks derive from their international operations. International earnings as a percentage of total earnings for the 10 largest U.S. banks have declined significantly in the last five years--see Table 4. Between 1977 and 1979, Citibank and Chase, the two U.S. banks traditionally deriving the largest share of total earnings from their international lending, both experienced a drop in their respective shares of nearly twenty percentage points.[4] The drop in those shares for the ten largest U.S. banks averaged almost 10 percentage points.

These recent changes in international banking represent a compounding of several economic factors. The foreign expansion of a country's banks often parallels the international trade and investment flows of manufacturing, resource extraction and other non-banking companies based in that same country. Banks follow their customers. During the 1970s, non-U.S.-based multinationals grew rapidly in all industries, not just in banking. The U.S. dollar depreciated against several foreign currencies, most notably the Swiss franc, the Deutchmark and the yen, which augments the apparent growth of international lending denominated in those currencies. Some U.S. banks may have reached their own lending limits with respect to specific foreign borrowers, thereby disqualifying themselves from competition for further lending.

A striking feature of published accounts of these

TABLE 4: INTERNATIONAL EARNINGS AS A PERCENT OF TOTAL
EARNINGS FOR THE TEN LARGEST U.S. BANKS, 1975-79

	1975	1976	1977	1978	1979
Citicorp	70.6	72.4	82.2	71.8	64.7
Chase Manhattan	64.5	78.0	64.9	53.2	46.9
Bank America Corp.	54.7	46.7	41.8	34.6	37.7
Manufacturers Hanover Corp.	49.1	59.3	60.2	51.2	48.8
J. P. Morgan & Co.	60.2	46.1	48.1	51.0	52.0
Chemical N.Y. Corp.	41.6	41.1	38.8	42.0	35.1
Bankers Trust N.Y.	58.6	60.4	82.8	67.9	51.5
First Chicago Corp.	34.0	17.0	21.0	16.0	3.5
Continental Ill. Corp.	13.4	23.0	16.6	17.8	18.5
Security Pacific Corp.	12.6	6.9	11.6	15.1	10.4
Composite	52.5	50.8	50.5	45.5	42.6

Source: Solomon Brothers, "Lending to LDCs: Mounting
Problems," April 2, 1980, Table 19, p. 24,
reprinted in C. Stewart Goddin and Steven J.
Weiss, "U.S. Banks' Loss of Global Standing,"
U.S. Comptroller of the Currency, Administrator
of National Banks, Staff Papers, 1980-3.

important changes in international banking is the virtually total disregard for income tax considerations. To be sure, the economic considerations aluded to above, together with the influence of national banking regulations, currency controls and other non-tax factors, carry far greater weight than income tax considerations. Moreover, until the mid-1970s, the banks themselves appear to have been relatively oblivious to the tax aspects of international lending. Critical decisions regarding the pricing and availability of credit and the funding of the loan portfolio were apparently made without explicit regard for the income tax consequences. The tax departments of most banks appear to have had the job of minimizing the tax cost of the decisions made by others. In recent years, however, as lending margins have narrowed, the larger U.S. and foreign banks have become increasingly aware of the ability of income taxes both to reduce the return on apparently profitable lending to an unacceptably low margin and to widen the effective margin on seemingly unprofitable lending to an acceptable level. The increasing awareness by the banks of the taxes they pay has not, by and large, been recognized by public commentators.

This study seeks to fill the gap by describing how the United States, the United Kingdom, France, Germany and Japan tax the income from international lending by commercial banks chartered under their respective laws. As of 1978, banks chartered in these five countries held 73 percent of the total deposits of the 100 largest banks in the free world.[5] The study covers not only lending by the head office (or a domestic branch) of a commercial bank, but also income derived by a foreign branch or subsidiary. Tax factors of particular significance to banks--e.g., the allocation of interest expense against foreign versus domestic income--are stressed, while those of less significance to them--e.g., depreciation allowances--are disregarded. Part B describes various countries' provisions and is necessarily tedious. Part C translates those tax rules into "minimum lending rates," a measure of the extent to which income taxes add to, or subtract from, the cost of lending for banks in various countries. Part D offers some criticisms of present practices and proposals for change.

INCOME TAX SYSTEMS

I. INTRODUCTION

Describing one country's income tax rules is difficult enough; comparing and contrasting five countries' systems is more difficult still. This survey begins with the way each country treats domestic income. The tax treatment of foreign income is often a straightforward extension of the treatment of domestic income. More importantly, the domestic tax consequences of earning additional foreign income and paying additional foreign taxes often hinges on the overall tax situation of a bank, and not just on the terms of its international loans.

The survey turns next to the tax treatment of foreign lending by the head office itself. In addition to describing each country's method for alleviating international double taxation, the survey describes how different countries' systems treat borrowing and lending denominated in a foreign currency. That discussion is followed by descriptions of each country's treatment of income derived by a foreign branch and a foreign subsidiary, respectively. Although non-tax factors may often dictate the form of a bank's international lending, the differential tax treatment may be paramount in other cases. The final part of this section describes countries' withholding taxes on interest paid to non-residents, a tax which regulates a bank's borrowing on international money and capital markets.

II. DOMESTIC INCOME OF A HEAD OFFICE

1. National Taxes

The United States taxes banks chartered under federal or state laws at progressive rate of up to 46 percent. Of particular significance to U.S. banks is the exemption from federal tax for interest received from a state or local government. U.S. banks (or domestic affiliates with which they file a consolidated tax return) also engage in substantial leasing which, because of accelerated depreciation allowances and the tax credit equal to 10 percent of qualifying investment, may shelter at least temporarily other income from U.S. taxation. Unlike the other four countries included in this survey, the United States does not attempt to eliminate the double taxation of earnings distributed by a bank or other corporation to individual shareholders.

The United Kingdom taxes the income of U.K. banks at progressive rates reaching a maximum of 52 percent. In addition, the United Kingdom imposes an Advanced Corporation Tax (ACT) currently equal to 30/70 of the cash dividend distributed to shareholders. The ACT serves as a withholding tax in the sense that a U.K. individual shareholder "grosses up" the cash dividend by, and claims a credit against his own tax liability of, the amount of the ACT.

The relief from double taxation arises because the U.K.

bank paying the dividend may also credit part or all of the ACT against its income tax liability. The maximum amount of ACT credit claimed in any year equals 30 percent of the income subject to corporate tax. ACT payments in excess of the current limitation may be carried back two years (i.e., applied against a similar tax liability which was not itself offset by the ACT), carried forward indefinitely, or "surrendered" to an affiliated company. The effect of this limitation is to leave a "mainstream" tax liability equal to 22 percent of corporate income which must either be paid or, as explained below, offset by a foreign tax credit.

To compare countries' tax systems accurately, taxation of shareholders, not just of corporations, ought to be described. Because that exercise is beyond te scope of this study, the next best procedure is to treat taxes, such as the ACT, which are legally imposed on corporations, but directly offset shareholders' tax liabilities, as shareholder level taxes. That is to say, the U.K. system can be considered the equivalent of a split-rate system which taxed a corporation's retained earnings at a rate of 52 percent and its distributed earnings at a rate of 31.4 percent, but allowed no imputation credit to shareholders.[6] The differential between the rate for retained earnings and that for distributed earnings equals the tax withheld at the corporate level and the tax creditable at the shareholder level.

France taxes the domestic income of the head office of a French bank at a flat rate of 60 percent. A French individual shareholder grosses the dividend income up by, and claims a tax credit of, 50 percent of the amount of the dividend, which also equals 50 percent of the underlying corporate tax on such income. Thus, the French system is, for present purposes, equivalent to a split-rate system which taxes retained earnings at a rate of 50 percent and distributed earnings at a rate of 25 percent. (International tax specialists are indebted to the French for their sense of symmetry and balance.)

West Germany relieves the double taxation of distributed earnings by a hybrid of a split-rate, shareholder-credit system. Domestic income is taxed at a rate of 56 percent, but 20 percentage points are refunded to the corporation upon a subsequent distribution of such income. That is to say, distributed earnings are taxed at a rate of 36 percent. A German shareholder grosses the dividend up by, and claims a tax credit of, the full 36 percentage points. Thus, the corporate level tax on distributed earnings are either refunded to the corporation or are creditable by the shareholder, so such earnings are, in effect, not taxed at the corporate level. That is to say, a split rate system which taxed retained earnings at a rate of 56 percent and levied no tax (and, correspondingly, allowed no shareholder credit) with respect to distributed earnings would impose the same economic burden as the German system

332

currently does. No other country has gone as far as Germany in this regard.

Japan also has a hybrid system, but the dichotomy in its treatment of retained versus distributed earnings is less pronounced than in West Germany. Retained earnings are taxed at a rate of 40 percent and distributed earnings at a rate of 30 percent. Japanese shareholders gross dividends up by, and claim a tax credit of, 10 percent of the net dividend, which effectively reduces the corporate-level burden to 23 percent of distributed earnings.

2. Subnational Taxes

Within the United States, states and certain local governments impose tax on income allocable to their respective jurisidctions. New York City taxes the allocable income of banks and other financial institutions at a rate of 13.82 percent, and New York State taxes at a rate of 12.0 percent. Neither jurisdiction exempts from taxation interest received from state and local governments (including their own). Because the New York City tax is deductible in computing income subject to New York State tax, the combined burden of the two taxes on income allocable to a head office in New York City is 24.2 percent (13.82 percent plus 12 percent of 86.2 percent).

The State of California taxes the business income of banks and other financial institutions attributable to California at a rate which varies from year to year, but is set in such a way as to equalize the overall tax burden of financial corporations vis-à-vis that of non-financial corporations. For fiscal years ending in 1980, the rate was 11.6 percent. Because state and local taxes are deductible in computing federal taxable income, the combined (local, state and federal) tax on income allocable to a head office in New York City is 59.1 percent, and the combined tax on a head office in California is 52.3 percent.

As has been widely noted, state and local governments within the United States are not bound by uniform rules in determining the amount of income allocable to their respective jurisdictions. New York City and New York State allow corporations to allocate income and deductions to their jurisdictions on the basis of separate accounting for each branch or office. California, by contrast, allocates a portion of the consolidated worldwide income of a "unitary business" to California. The consolidated activities of a U.S. bank or a bank holding company, including domestic and foreign subsidiaries, would generally be considered a "unitary business" by the California Franchise Tax Board and would therefore be subject to apportionment. The California portion of total income is based on the average of three ratios: the value of property (e.g., the principal amount of a loan) attributable to California relative to the value of total property; employee compensation in California relative to total employee compensation; and sales (e.g., gross interest on a loan) attributable to California relative to total sales.

Many states in addition to California compute income for state tax purposes by using a formula to apportion the income of a "unitary business". However, the methods of defining a unitary business, computing total income subject to apportionment, and calculating the apportionment factors vary substantially from state to state. Corporations with multistate or multinational operations have protested the states' failure to follow internationally accepted norms. The U.S. Supreme Court has, however, recently upheld the states' rights to apply formula apportionment in cases involving Mobil and Exxon. The states succeeded in convincing the Senate not to ratify a proposed U.S.-U.K. tax treaty which contained an article precluding formula apportionment of the non-U.S. income of a U.K. corporation. Likewise, legislative proposals to restrict the application of formula apportionment have so far had no success in the Congress.

Subnational taxes have not created similar problems outside the United States. There are no subnational taxes in the United Kingdom or France. Municipalities in West Germany impose a Trade Tax on income at rates varying from 12 to 21 percent. If a German bank has branches or other places of business in more than one municipality, a common tax base is apportioned among the municipalities based on the payroll of employees in each municipality. Because Municipal Trade Taxes are deductible from income subject to that same tax, a nominal rate of 15 percent (which is often

335

taken as a typical rate) is equivalent to an effective rate of 13.0 percent (15 percent divided by 115 percent). Because the Municipal Trade Tax is also deductible from income subject to Federal tax, but is not rebated upon a distribution to a German shareholder, the combined municipal-federal tax burden on retained earnings is 61.7 percent, and on distributed earnings it is 13.0 percent.

In _Japan_, prefectures impose two separate taxes on income. An Enterprise Tax is imposed at a nominal rate of 12 percent and, because it is deductible from its own base, an effective rate of 10.7 percent (12 percent divided by 112 percent). If a Japanese bank has offices in more than one prefecture, its income is apportioned among the prefectures based on the number of employees in each. The Enterprise Tax is deductible from income subject to national tax and is unaffected by the retention or distribution of earnings. In addition, an Inhabitants Tax equal to 17.3 percent of the national income _tax_ is imposed and, if necessary, apportioned among prefectures based on the number of employes in each. The combined burden of the Enterprise, national, and Inhabitants taxes is 52.6 percent with respect to retained earnings and 36.3 percent (net of the shareholder credit) with respect to distributed earnings.

III. FOREIGN INCOME OF A HEAD OFFICE

Unless prevented by banking or foreign-exchange controls, a head office may lend directly to a foreign borrower. Interest received with respect to such a loan is typically subject by the country where the borrower is resident to a withholding tax equal to a fixed percentage of the gross interest income (i.e., no deductions are allowed). The rates of taxation under most statutory laws are typically 20-30 percent, but these rates are often reduced and in some instances eliminated entirely under bilateral tax treaties.

All five countries included in this survey subject such income received by a head office to domestic tax, but, with certain restrictions noted below, allow the foreign withholding tax to offset the tax with respect to that income. Countries differ, however, in their criteria for determining what foreign taxes are creditable, the amount of foreign tax available for credit, and, most importantly, the method by which the foreign tax credit limitation--the amount of national tax imposed on foreign income--is calculated. Also described below are special tax preferences or incentives countries provide with respect to such lending, the treatment of gains and losses which may arise if borrowing or lending are denominated in a foreign currency, and the application of subnational taxes to such income.

1. Foreign Tax Available for Credit

The criteria for determining what foreign taxes are

337

creditable, rather than merely deductible in computing taxable income, has been particularly controversial in the United States. The U.S. Internal Revenue Service allows a credit for foreign withholding taxes provided the scope of such a tax is limited to interest not attributable to a local branch or other "permanent establishment" within the country imposing the tax. A tax imposed on all gross interest, regardless of the residence of the recipient, such as that imposed by subnational governments in Mexico, is not creditable under I.R.S. rules because no deduction is allowed for the interest and other expenses of earning such income. After some hestitation, the I.R.S. ruled that the withholding tax imposed by the national government of Mexico on interest paid by Mexican residents to foreign banks was a creditable tax. Under Mexican banking law, foreign banks may have representational offices, but not branches, in Mexico (the Citibank branch, which was established prior to the Mexican ban, was "grandfathered"). The issue which caused the I.R.S. to hesitate was whether the activities conducted by the Mexican representational offices of U.S. and other banks were, in fact, substantial enough that under international standards for taxing foreign banks the interest income of U.S. banks "should have been" taxed on a net, rather than a gross, basis.

In 1978, the Internal Revenue Service ruled that U.S. banks could claim a foreign tax credit for only a portion of the 25 percent withholding tax imposed by Brazil. To bring

338

down the high cost to Brazilian borrowers, including itself, the Brazilian government began in 1975 rebating to the Brazilian borrower 85 percent of the withholding tax on a foreign lender. After ruling in 1976 that U.S. banks could credit the full 25 percent, the I.R.S. reversed its position in 1978 and ruled that credit could be claimed only with respect to the portion of tax which was not rebated (i.e., 15 percent of the 25 percent tax applied to the nominal interest payment). Because of its prior favorable ruling, the I.R.S. "grandfathered" through 1979 the treatment of outstanding loans. In 1980, the Brazilian government temporarily increased the rebated portion of the withholding tax to 95 percent, and then cut it back to 40 percent.

The U.S. position with respect to the Brazilian withholding tax contrasts with that in the other four countries. Unlike the United States, each of those countries has entered into bilateral tax treaties with developing countries, including Brazil, which provide for "tax sparing" -- see Table 5. Under a standard tax sparing formula, the developing country (e.g., Brazil) reduces its actual withholding tax rate (e.g., from 25 percent to 15 percent), but the developing country (e.g., West Germany) will allow a credit for not only the tax imposed (15 percent), but also the tax spared (10 percent in this example). Unwilling to spare taxes under a bilateral treaty, the United States was, in essence, also unwilling to allow Brazil (or any other country) to impose unilaterally a tax-sparing scheme.

339

TABLE 5. BILATERAL TAX TREATIES OF THE UNITED KINGDOM, FRANCE, WEST GERMANY AND JAPAN SPARING WITHHOLDING TAX ON INTEREST.

Treaty Partner	United Kingdom	France	West Germany	Japan
Algeria		X		
Barbados	X			
Belize	X			
Botswana	X			
Brazil		X	X	X
Cyprus	X		X	
Fiji	X			
Ghana	X			
Gilbert I.	X			
Greece		X	X	
India		X	X	X
Indonesia	X			
Israel	X	X	X	
Jamaica	X		X	
Kenya	X			
Korea	X			X
Liberia			X	
Malaysia	X			X
Malta	X		X	
Morocco			X	
Pakistan	X	X	X	X
Philippines		X		
Portugal	X	X		
Singapore	X	X	X	X
Spain	X		X	
Sri Lanka				X
Sudan	X			
Thailand				X
Trinidad & Tobago	X		X	
Zambia				X
Fr. West African Countries		X		

SOURCE: International Bureau of Fiscal Documentation, _The Taxation of Companies in Europe_, and Price Waterhouse & Co., _Doing Business in Japan_, October 1975.

The United Kingdom, France, West Germany and Japan all
allow a credit for the full 25 percent withheld by Brazil
from the gross interest payment. The latter three countries
all have treaties with Brazil which provide for tax sparing
and, thereby, reduce the tax actually paid even further.
The United Kingdom, which has no treaty with Brazil, but has
tax sparing rovisions in numerous other treaties, has
expressed concern about the Brazilian scheme, but has agreed
to allow a credit for the full 25 percent.

Finally, it should be noted that France provides no
foreign tax credit under its statutory law. Although a tax
credit would be available under French treaties with more
than 50 countries, taxes withheld by a non-treaty country
(e.g., Mexico, Argentina, Korea, Indonesia) could be deducted from the taxable income of a head office of a French
bank, but could not be credited against the French tax
liability.

2. Limitation on the Amount of Foreign Tax Credit

All five countries seek to prevent foreign taxes from
offsetting that portion of their own tax attributable to
domestic income. The foreign tax credit limitation is
generally computed according to the following formula:

$$\frac{\text{Foreign-source taxable income}}{\text{Worldwide taxable income}} \times \text{Total tax before credit}$$

The key difference among countries' foreign tax credit
limitations are: (1) the extent to which separate items of
foreign-source income and the related foreign tax are

341

combined or segregated in applying the limitation formula; (2) the amount of interest, head-office and other expense which must be allocated against foreign-source interest income in computing the numerator of the above formula; and (3) the treatment of foreign taxes in excess of the limitation.

The United States imposes the limitation separately with respect to several special categories of foreign income, but U.S. banks are subject for all intents and purposes to a single, overall limitation. That is to say, all foreign income taxes are combined and allowed to offset the U.S. tax on all foreign source income. The overall limitation is advantageous in that high taxes on one source of income may be offset against the U.S. liability on other foreign income subject to low foreign tax or exempt from such tax altogether.

The United States does require, however, that interest, head-office and other expenses and certain losses be allocated against foreign source income. In early 1977, the United States issued detailed regulations for making such allocations. Although the 1977 regulations appeared to require more research and development and certain other expense to be allocated to foreign source income than before and, thus, to reduce the foreign tax credit limitation, the regulations apparently allowed U.S. banks to allocate less interest expense than before. Prior to 1977, the common practice apparently was to allocate the interest expense on specific liabilities against the interest income from the foreign loans such liabilities had funded. The 1977 regulations, however, took the view that because "money is fungible," "tracing" specific liabilities to specific assets produced an artificial result, and that total interest expense should simply be apportioned to foreign versus domestic income based on the total value of assets or total gross income. Because U.S. banks, like other banks, are funded in part by shareholders' equity and by demand and other deposits bearing little or no interest, both of which were typically traced to domestic assets prior to 1977, apportionment under the 1977 rules resulted in less interest expense being allocated against foreign source income and, thus, a larger foreign tax credit limitation.

Finally, it should be noted that the foreign tax credit cannot exceed the total U.S. tax liability. Because the rate of interest received on tax-exempt bonds is typically a few percentage points less than the cost of funds to a U.S. bank, a U.S. bank with substantial holdings of such bonds or with a domestic leasing affiliate generating tax losses would report an overall, domestic-source loss. If this loss were a substantial fraction of its foreign source income, the amount of foreign taxes which are actually creditable may be substantially less than 46 percent of foreign-source taxable income.

Whether the limitation is set by the U.S. tax attributable to foreign source income or by the total U.S. tax liability, foreign income taxes in excess of the limitation may be carried back two years or forward five years. The option to deduct all foreign income taxes from taxable income, rather than crediting them against the tax liability, is rarely advantageous.

The United Kingdom applies the foreign tax credit limitation separately with respect to each "source" of foreign income, a particular loan constituting a single source. Thus, foreign tax in excess of the limitation with respect to interest on one foreign loan cannot offset the U.K. tax with respect to interest on a second loan. However, the U.K. does not require any interest, head-office or other expense or loss to be allocated against foreign interest income, and few, if any, countries levy withholding tax at rates in excess of 52 percent. Thus, the limitation would rarely be binding.

The U.K. Board of Inland Revenue's concern about the method of calculating the limitation was manifest in a paper circulated in 1979 to U.K. banks. The Inland Revenue paper, which was widely discussed in various financial journals,[7] noted that U.K. banks had recently made loans with negative margins--i.e., the interest received net of foreign withholding tax was less than the cost of funding the loan. As explained more fully in Part C below, such lending may be profitable from a U.K. bank's standpoint because the withholding tax, which is often inflated by the tax-sparing provisions of a U.K. tax treaty, can be offset against the

U.K. "mainstream" tax. The Inland Revenue paper also noted that some U.S. banks shifted their Brazilian loans to London branches or subsidiaries after the 1978 I.R.S. ruling disallowing a U.S. credit for the rebated portion of the Brazilian tax. The Inland Revenue paper did not propose any remedy for the alleged abuse, but suggested that Inland Revenue's concerns would be allayed if U.K. banks stopped lending at negative margins.

In essence, the U.K. corporate income tax is divided into two distinct parts: that portion (30 percent of taxable income) which may be offset by the ACT, but not the foreign tax credit; and the residual portion which may be offset by the foreign tax credit, but not the ACT. This overall limitation, which is computed by reference to the "mainstream" tax on all income, and not by reference to income derived from foreign sources, appears to provide for all practical purposes the real limitation on the foreign tax credit.

France, which allows a foreign tax credit only by treaty, generally requires that the credit for a particular tax be applied only against French tax on income from the same treaty country. That is to say, a "per-country" limitation applies. French banks and other financial institutions are permitted, however, to calculate a single, overall limitation with respect to foreign withholding taxes imposed on interest income. A primary effect of this exception is to allow withholding taxes imposed by countries

345

with which France has a tax treaty (e.g., West Germany) to be offset against the French tax on interest derived from a country with which France does not have a tax treaty (e.g., Mexico).

In computing the foreign tax credit limitation, French banks are required to allocate interest expense to foreign source income, but not head-office or other expenses unless they bear a specific relationship to foreign source income. However, withholding taxes which are either not creditable because France has no treaty with the country imposing the tax, or creditable under a treaty, but in excess of the foreign tax credit limitation, may be deducted. The implicit effect of this rule is to allocate such expenses against French source income. As shown in Part C, the tax benefit of deducting foreign taxes in excess of the limitation is hardly trivial.

In addition to its regular corporate income tax, France applies a levy, the precompte mobilier, on dividends which are considered to be paid out of income which has not borne French corporate tax at a rate of at least 25 percent. The precompte is similar in its effect to the U.K. ACT, and like the ACT, its impact is mitigated by deeming dividends to be paid first out of income which has borne corporate tax. However, unlike the U.K., France under its tax treaties allows foreign taxes to offset the precompte and, thus, to reduce the individual shareholder's, and not just the parent corporation's, income tax liability.

West Germany appears to impose the most stringent foreign tax credit limitation of any country included in this survey. The German limitation applies to each foreign country separately, so a high rate of taxation in one country cannot offset German tax on income subject to a low rate of taxation in a second country. Germany also requires funding costs and, in some instances, administrative costs to be allocated against such income. Whether a German bank would have to allocate more or less expense against foreign income than a comparable U.S. bank is uncertain.

Germany, like France, imposes additional tax on a corporation paying a dividend out of income which has been subject to German corporate income tax at a rate of less than 36 percent (the rate of gross-up and credit for a German shareholder). As in other countries, the impact of this rule is mitigated by an ordering rule under which earnings that have been subject to domestic tax are deemed to be distributed first. Under its statutory law, Germany does not allow the foreign tax credit to be applied against the additional tax on a distribution of income not taxed in Germany.

Like the United States, Japan allows its banks to aggregate foreign taxes paid to all countries and compute a single, overall limitation. Foreign taxes may be deducted, rather than credited, but if the deduction approach is selected all foreign income taxes must be deducted. In principle, interest and head office expenses must be allocated against foreign source income. Because precise regulations have not been formulated, how liberal or stringent the allocation requirement will prove in actual practice cannot be determined.

3. Tax Incentives for Foreign Lending

As noted above, the United Kingdom, France, West Germany and Japan have agreed to tax-sparing provisions in bilateral tax treaties with developing countries. In addition, under its statutory law, Japan allows its banks to take a deduction and establish a reserve with respect to certain foreign loans. The reserve is maintained for five years and then included ratably in taxable income from the sixth to the tenth year. The amount of the reserve equals 15 percent of loans extended to companies with their head offices in a developing country (or, in certain instances, a Japanese company established for the purpose of investing in such a company), 40 percent of loans extended to a "natural resources development company," and 100 percent of loans extended to a "natural resources prospecting company."

4. Foreign Currency Gains and Losses

Most borrowing or lending denominated in a foreign currency would be undertaken by a foreign branch or subsidiary of a domestic bank, and the tax treatment of those entities' gains and losses is described below. A head office is, however, typically a foreign currency dealer and may have other reasons for borrowing or lending foreign currency on its own account. Under U.S. tax accounting rules, gains and losses are generally recognized only when realized (i.e., an asset is sold, a liability discharged, etc.). Dealers, including U.S. banks dealing in foreign exchange, may, however, value their dealer inventories at current market value, rather than historical cost. Because of the way in which the deduction for cost of goods sold is computed, this inventory valuation rule allows dealers to recognize unrealized gains and losses with respect to such inventory. These rules may not be applied, however, to other (non-dealer) foreign-currency-denominated items.

Although realization ordinarily triggers recognition, a U.S. court has found that a gain arising on discharge of a foreign-currency-denominated liability with depreciated currency was "gain on the discharge of indebtedness," which a U.S. taxpayer may elect not to recognize, providing reduces its basis in assets by a corresponding amount. Until recently, U.S. corporations would reduce the basis of their stock in foreign subsidiaries or other nondepreciable assets and thereby obtain an indefinite deferral of the U.S. tax liability on such gains. Under legislation enacted in 1980 and pertaining primarily to tax consequences of bankruptcy, U.S. corporations were obligated to reduce their basis in depreciable assets, which effectively shortened but did not eliminate the deferral of U.S. tax on such gains.

A key issue on which U.S. law is unsettled is the

349

impact of a foreign exchange gain or loss on a U.S. bank or other taxpayer's overall foreign tax credit limitation. In December 1980, the Treasury Department issued a "discussion draft" which proposed that a foreign exchange gain or loss on a foreign-currency-denominated asset be treated like an adjustment in interest income received with respect to that asset, that a comparable gain or loss on a foreign-currency-denominated liability be treated like an adjustment in interest expense with respect to that liability, and that a gain or loss on a forward exchange contract be treated by reference to the treatment of the gain or loss on the item the contract was hedging. The Treasury proposal did not address the treatment of gains and losses from dealing in foreign currency, but instead reserved that subject for further consideration. Thus, the Treasury proposal would, if adopted, apply to the ordinary borrowing and lending of U.S. banks, but not to their activities as foreign exchange dealers.

The United Kingdom, like the United States, generally recognizes gains and losses only upon their realization. Gains and losses on trading assets and liabilities (e.g., deposits) are combined with similar gains or losses in computing trading income. Gain or loss in the sale of capital assets receives special treatment: a portion of a net capital gain (regardless of the holding period) is exempted from tax, which reduces the effective tax rate on the total gain to a maximum of 30 percent; a capital loss

350

can be offset against a current capital gain or carried forward to offset capital gains in future years, but cannot be offset against ordinary income. Gains or losses on non-trading liabilities, such as a subordinated debenture that a U.K. bank might issue to improve its overall capital position, are, in Inland Revenue's view, excluded in computing either trading income or capital gain. Because the pound sterling was until recently depreciating against the dollar, the Deutchmark, the Swiss franc and most other currencies available on international capital markets, U.K. banks and other taxpayers were deprived of tax relief for the substantial losses often incurred with respect to such liabilities. U.K. taxpayers are litigating Inland Revenue's position, but the issue has yet to be resolved by the courts.

In France, gains and losses on outstanding foreign-currency-denominated payables and receivables are accrued at the official exchange rate at the end of the bank's taxable year. That is to say, foreign exchange gains and losses are recognized regardless of whether or not they are realized. Although similar treatment is generally accorded to long-term financial assets and liabilities, the Consul d'Etat has ruled that losses incurred with respect to long-term liabilities used to finance fixed assets (e.g., a real property mortgage) should be reflected in the basis of that asset and not recognized currently. Whether similar treatment also applies to gains on the discharge of such liabilities is uncertain.

In _German_ tax accounting, net income is computed from the increase in net worth shown on the balance sheet which in turn is calculated using assymetrical valuation rules for assets and liabilities. The rules are designed to accelerate losses and defer gains. Debt claims and portfolio securities, like certain other assets, are valued at the lower of cost or "going concern" value (which generally equals market value). Conversely, accounts payable are valued at the _higher_ of cost or going-concern value. The effect of these rules is to accrue currently unrealized foreign exchange losses, but to defer recognition of foreign exchange gains until their realization. Thus, even if the head office of a German bank matched every foreign currency asset with a liability denominated in the same currency, any change in the value of that currency would result in the accrual of a foreign exchange loss. (If the foreign currency depreciated against the Deutsche mark, a loss would be accrued on account of the asset, and the gain on the liability would be deferred; if the foreign currency appreciated, the loss would be accrued on account of the liability, and the gain with respect to the asset deferred.) The losses recorded on account of this assymetrical valuation rule allow a temporary deferral, but not a permanent exemption, from German tax. However, in periods where exchange rates are highly volatile, even a temporary deferral of tax on a substantial gain may yield significant tax savings.

A head office of a *Japanese* bank with short-term receivables or payables denominated in a foreign currency may choose either to accrue the foreign exchange gains and losses currently or to let recognition await realization. The choice between the two must be applied consistently to items denominated in the same currency, but items denominated in one currency may be accrued while those in a second currency may be recognized only upon realization. The foreign exchange gain or loss with respect to long-term receivables and payables is accrued currently only if the change is "remarkable" or if the Japanese bank has obtained special permission to do so. The criteria for identifying "remarkable" changes or obtaining permission to accrue other gains and losses are uncertain.

5. Subnational Taxes

Within the United States, New York City and New York State apply their income tax to the interest earned by a foreign loan made by a head office located within their taxing jurisdiction, and no credit or deduction is allowed with respect to foreign withholding tax. That such taxes represent a substantial barrier to foreign lending by New York banking entities is manifest in the willingness of both taxing jursidictions to exempt the proposed International Banking Facilities (IBFs) from such taxes.

If the head office of a bank located in California makes a foreign loan, the net income from that loan would be included in the total income subject to apportionment. In apportioning that income, the principal amount of the loan would be considered California property, and the interest would be California "sales." As explained more fully in Part C, if the loan terms yield the bank just an average return, relative to property, payroll and sales, the entire net income from the loan is effectively allocated to California. But if the loan terms result in a higher-than-average return, as it might happen because apportionable income is gross of foreign withholding tax, a portion--but not the entirety--of the "excess" net income will be allocated to California.

As noted earlier, neither the United Kingdom nor France have subnational income taxes. In West Germany, the Municipal Trade Tax would apply to interest received from a foreign borrower by the head office of a German bank, and no credit or deduction would be allowed for foreign withholding taxes. Comparable interest received by the head office of a Japanese bank would be similarly subject to the 12 percent Enterprise Tax, and neither a deduction nor a credit would be allowed for the foreign withholding tax. However, a foreign withholding tax may be credited not only against the national income tax, but also against the Inhabitants Tax, which is computed as a portion (17.3 percent) of the national tax. The Japanese Inhabitants Tax is the only subnational tax encountered in this survey which alleviates double taxation of foreign income received by a head office.

IV. INCOME OF A FOREIGN BRANCH

1. Basic Approach

Income derived by a foreign branch of a bank chartered in the United States is taxed by the federal government under the same rules as are applied to income derived by a head office. That is to say, the amount of foreign tax available for credit, the application of the overall foreign tax credit limitation, and the allocation of interest and other expense against foreign-source income, do not depend on whether the income is derived by a domestic versus a foreign entity. The special accounting rules applied when a foreign branch keeps its books in a foreign currency are described below.

The United Kingdom also taxes income attributable to foreign branches as it is earned and allows a foreign tax credit for income taxes paid by the branch (including those withheld on gross interest by a third country). However, the foreign tax credit limitation would be applied to the branch's income net of interest and other deductions, rather than to each source of gross income. Consequently, U.K. banks would appear to have a significant tax incentive to undertake foreign lending subject to high foreign withholding taxes through a head office in London rather than an overseas branch.

Under its statutory law, France exempts from corporate taxation the income attributable to a foreign branch. Because of that exemption, however, dividends paid by a

French bank out of those earnings are subject to the precompte, which cannot be offset by foreign taxes imposed on that income. That is to say, the precompte can be offset by foreign withholding tax of a treaty country on interest paid to the French head office, but not by similar taxes imposed on interest paid to a foreign branch.

A French bank may, however, apply to be taxed in France on its worldwide income, including that attributable to its foreign branches. Because foreign taxes paid by the branches could then be credited against the precompte, this option could be attractive even though some additional French tax might be imposed on branch income. Reportedly, the few French corporations which are taxed in this way are concentrated in the natural resources sectors and not in banking. Whether the absence of French banks is attributable to tax costs in excess of benefits, the reluctance of the French tax authorities to approve applications from French banks, or some other factor is uncertain.

Under its statutory law, West Germany taxes income attributable to a foreign branch, and allows a credit for foreign taxes paid by that branch. Such taxes would be combined with withholding taxes on interest paid to the head-office and any other taxes paid to that country in applying the per-country limitation.

The application of German tax to the income of a foreign branch of a German bank is, however, limited. Under its many bilateral tax treaties, Germany exempts income

356

attributable to a permanent establishment in the treaty country from German tax. When a German bank pays a dividend out of such income (income taxed in Germany is deemed to be distributed first), Germany imposes a tax of 36 percent. German corporations have reportedly brought suit claiming that their exemption from German tax under bilateral tax treaties applies not only to the regular, 56-percent tax, but also from the 36-percent tax subsequently imposed on distributions out of exempt income.

Income attributable to a foreign branch of a Japanese bank is subject to Japanese tax, and a foreign tax credit is allowed for interest withholding taxes and income taxes paid by the branch. No exemption is available by statute or by treaty. Japan allows its corporations to disregard a loss attributable to a foreign branch in computing its foreign-source taxable income and, thus, its overall foreign tax credit limitation. In that sense, Japanese corporations benefit from the combined advantages of an overall and a per country limitation. This treatment is particularly advantageous to Japanese petroleum and other natural-resource-extraction companies, but also may benefit a Japanese bank incurring significant start-up costs in establishing a new branch or encountering unforeseen losses in its established foreign branches.

357

2. Translation of Foreign Currency Accounts of a Foreign Branch

A foreign branch often keeps its books in its local currency, and rarely is it practicable to compute its income in the domestic currency of the head office by translating each transaction of the branch at the exchange rate on the date the transaction is recorded. Instead, financial statements for the branch are prepared in the local currency of the branch, and the cumulative end-of-the-period results, rather than the separate transactions, are translated into the currency of the head office.

The profit or loss of the branch stated in the currency of the head office is usually computed in one of two ways. Under a profit-and-loss method, the profit or loss as stated in the local currency of the branch is translated at an average or year-end exchange rate into the currency of the head office. Under a net-worth (or balance sheet) method, profit or loss equals the increase in net worth, which, in turn, is computed by translating the various assets and liabilities of the branch at an appropriate exchange rate.

The critical difference between these two methods was vividly illustrated by rules for financial accounting promulgated by the U.S. Financial Accounting Standards Board (FASB) in 1975. The 1975 FASB rules mandated a net-worth method under which the financial assets and liabilities of a foreign branch or subsidiary of a U.S. corporation were translated at exchange rates for the date of the balance sheet. If a foreign branch's financial assets denominated

358

in the foreign currency exceeded its liabilities so denominated, and the local currency had appreciated against the dollar, the branch's income would include a foreign exchange gain; if the local currency had depreciated in value, the branch's income would reflect a foreign exchange loss.

The 1975 FASB rules were heavily criticized on two counts. The practice of translating financial assets and liabilities at current rates and other items (inventory, plant and equipment, stock in a subsidiary) at "historical" exchange rates (i.e., the exchange rate for the date on which they were acquired), it was argued, distorted financial reports and encouraged hedging of reportable, but unreal, foreign exchange exposures. U.S. banks were particularly concerned that the sharp fluctuations in quarterly earnings reports due to foreign exchange rate changes would confuse their depositors and creditors and impugn their own credit-worthiness.

U.S. banks strongly supported an August 1980 FASB proposal which would replace the net-worth method with a profit-and-loss method based on the "functional currency" of a branch or subsidiary. The "functional currency" would ordinarily be the currency in which books of record were kept, but another currency (e.g., the U.S. dollar) could be designated if that other currency were more representative of the economic environment in which the entity operates. The 1980 FASB proposal would also require that foreign exchange gain or loss measured by translating all assets and liabilities (not just the financial items) at current exchange rates be shown on the balance sheet as an adjustment ot shareholders' equity, but not in the more conspicuous profit-and-loss statement. Public hearings on the FASB proposal were held in December 1980, but final rules have not yet been published.

Tax accounting rules do not adhere as closely to financial accounting rules (or vice versa) in the United States as they do in other countries. The Internal Revenue Service published two Revenue Rulings in 1975 setting forth a net-worth method and a profit-and-loss method, either one of which could be used in computing the income attributable to a foreign branch. In its December 1980 "discussion draft," the Treasury Department proposed to adopt the notion of a "functional currency," which would preclude the use of a net-worth method except in those cases where the branch's books were kept in a local currency, but the U.S. dollar was the branch's functional currency. It is too soon to say whether U.S. banks and other taxpayers will endorse this approach, or whether the Treasury Department will continue to support it.

In the United Kingdom, tax accounting rules generally conform to financial accounting rules, and the net profit or loss of a foreign branch of a U.K. bank may be computed using either a profit-and-loss or a net-worth method. As noted above, France exempts income attributable to the

360

foreign branch of a French bank and, thus, has not developed rules for translating the branch's profit or loss into French francs.

Because the domestic income of a <u>German</u> corporation is measured by the increase in its net worth, it is hardly surprising that income attributable to a foreign branch would be computed under a net-worth method, rather than a profit-and-loss method. The German rules are similar to the 1975 FASB rules in translating fixed assets and inventories at historical, rather than current, exchange rates. Like-wise, the income attributable to a foreign branch of a <u>Japanese</u> bank is also computed under a net-worth method. Because the Deutchmark and the yen have tended to appreciate against most other currencies, the net-worth method would ordinarily result in less taxable income attributable to foreign branches of German and Japanese banks than would a profit-and-loss method.

3.   <u>Subnational Taxes</u>

In the <u>United States</u>, New York City and New York State allow banks and other corporations to use separate entity accounting in computing income subject to their respective taxes. Thus, income and deductions allocable to a foreign branch would have no effect on the New York City or State tax of a U.S. bank.

The result under California's unitary apportionment approach is less certain. The property (loan principal), payroll and sales (interest income) of a foreign branch would not be attributed to California, but its income gross of withholding or other income taxes would be included in total income subject to apportionment. As a consequence, if the foreign branch's pre-tax income were higher relative to property, payroll and sales than average for the unitary business, its income would attract additional California tax. Conversely, if its pre-tax income were lower than average, California tax would be reduced.

Interest attributable to a foreign branch of a German bank is exempt from the Municipal Trade Tax, and that attributable to a foreign branch of a Japanese bank would be exempt from the Enterprise Tax. The Japanese Inhabitants Tax would, however, apply to the income of a foreign branch, but may be offset by a foreign tax credit.

V.   INCOME OF A FOREIGN SUBSIDIARY

1.   Actual Dividends

The United States taxes foreign corporations, including foreign subsidiaries of U.S. corporations, only with respect to income "effectively connected" with a trade or business within the United States and U.S.-source dividends, interest, rents, royalties and certain other types of income. U.S. shareholders are, however, subject to U.S. tax with respect to dividends, interest or other income received from a foreign corporation. In addition to the credit for foreign taxes withheld from such dividends, etc., a U.S.

parent corporation may claim a "deemed paid" foreign tax credit for taxes paid by a foreign subsidiary with respect to earnings subsequently distributed to the U.S. parent. The deemed-paid credit is available for taxes paid by a first-, second- or third-tier foreign subsidiary, providing the U.S. parent corporation holds directly or indirectly at least 10 percent of the voting shares of the subsidiary. The amount of the credit is calculated according to the following formula:

$$\frac{\text{Dividend received}}{\substack{\text{Accumulated profits in excess} \\ \text{of foreign income tax}}} \quad X \quad \text{Foreign income tax paid}$$

Because the dividend must be grossed up by the amount of the deemed-paid credit, the deemed-paid credit as a percentage of the grossed-up dividend income equals the foreign income tax as a percentage of pre-tax earnings. That is to say, if the rate of taxation of the foreign subsidiary equals or exceeds that of its U.S. parent, no additional U.S. tax will be imposed on the distribution of earnings. Deemed-paid taxes are combined with other foreign income in computing the overall limitation on the foreign tax credit.

Dividends received from a foreign subsidiary by a U.K. parent corporation are taxed in the United Kingdom in much the same way as they would be in the United States. The U.K. parent must have a 10 percent interest in the foreign subsidiary, but the credit extends to taxes paid by a subsidiary in any tier, providing the 10-percent test is met. Each subsidiary of a U.K. parent corporation is

363

considered a separate source of income, so taxes paid or deemed paid with respect to a dividend from one subsidiary are subject to a separate foreign tax credit limitation. A U.K. parent corporation can, however, "average" foreign taxes paid by different subsidiaries by interposing a foreign holding company between the U.K. parent and its foreign subsidiaries. Dividends and the associated "deemed paid" taxes are combined when paid to the holding company and constitute a single source upon redistribution to the U.K. parent. As with other foreign income taxes, "deemed paid" taxes can be credited against the "mainstream" corporate tax, but not the portion of that tax which can be offset only by the ACT.

Dividends received from a foreign subsidiary by a French parent cororation are exempt from the regular corporate income tax in France, provided the French parent holds at least a 10 percent interest in the subsidiary. Expenses of the parent corporation equal to 5 percent are allocated against such dividend income, which has the effect of increasing French tax by 2.5 percent of a dividend from a treaty country. Withholding taxes imposed by a treaty country cannot be credited against that additional tax, but may be credited against the precompte on the redistribution of those dividends to the shareholders of the French parent.

West Germany's treatment of dividends received from a foreign subsidiary of a German bank is analogous to its treatment of income derived by a foreign branch. Under its

364

statutory law, dividends are subject to German tax, but a "deemed paid" credit is allowed for income taxes paid by a first- or second-tier subsidiary, provided the German parent owns directly or indirectly at least 25 percent of the shares, that the subsidiary is engaged in a banking, insurance or other business, and provided that certain other conditions are met. In applying its per-country limitation, West Germany "looks through" a foreign holding company to determine the country to which foreign taxes were actually paid. Unlike a U.K. parent corporation, a German parent cannot "average" foreign taxes paid by subsidiaries in different countries by interposing a holding company between itself and its subsidiaries.

The German foreign tax credit with respect to a dividend received from a subsidiary in a developing country is, however, equal to the German tax on such income, even if the taxes actually paid are less. That is to say, such dividends are effectively exempt from German tax. Under its tax treaties, Germany exempts dividends received from subsidiaries resident in the treaty country. Thus, German tax applies to dividends received only from developed countries with which Germany has no treaty.

Japan also taxes dividends received by a Japaneses bank from its overseas subsidiaries. Japan allows its corporations to claim a deemed-paid credit, but only with respect to taxes paid by first-tier subsidiaries in which the

Japanese parent holds at least a 25 percent interest. Unlike many other aspects of its international tax system, Japan's "deemed paid" credit appears more restrictive than comparable provisions in other countries.

2. Deemed Dividends

To limit the avoidance of taxes through tax-haven subsidiaries, the countries covered by this survey have enacted or are presently contemplating provisions under which earnings may be deemed to have been distributed to domestic shareholders and may thereby be subject to domestic tax. The United States considers a foreign corporation to be controlled by U.S. shareholders when those U.S. shareholders who separately (directly or indirectly), own 10 percent or more of the voting shares, collectively own 50 percent or more of such shares. If such a "controlled foreign corporation" derives more than 10 percent of its gross income from "tainted" sources, or makes certain tainted investments in the United States (e.g., a loan to an affiliated U.S. corporation), it is deemed under Subpart F of the Internal Revenue Code to have paid a dividend equal to its tainted income or investment. A deemed-paid credit may be claimed for taxes paid on such income. Although tainted income generally includes dividends, interest and certain other types of passive income, such income is not tainted (and, thus, not deemed distributed) when derived in the conduct of banking, financing, or similar business.

366

The United Kingdom is the only country in this survey which has not yet enacted legislation similar to the U.S. Subpart F provisions. In January 1981, the U.K Board of Inland Revenue released a "consultative document" indicating that it was actively contemplating such legislation. Under the Inland Revenue proposal, U.K. shareholders with a 10 percent or greater interest in a controlled corporation could be deemed to receive their pro rata share of tainted income. Income would be tainted if (1) the subsidiary was resident in a country which exempted income from tax or taxed it at a rate significantly lower than the rate in the U.K., and (2) arrangements were made or transactions were entered into with the object of avoiding tax. As in other countries, however, income attributable to genuine trading activities, including banking, would not be subject to the deemed dividend treatment. A novel feature of the U.K. proposal is that income would be deemed distributed only at the discretion of the Board of Inland Revenue.

In January 1980, France enacted deemed-dividend provisions. French parent corporations holding a 25 percent interest in a company domiciled in a tax haven and whose principal activity is rendering services are deemed to receive their pro rata share of the subsidiary's income. "Rendering services" would not, however, include a bona fide banking business, so the income derived from such would not be deemed distributed. A deemed-paid credit, the only such credit in the French system, is allowed for income taxes paid by the subsidiary.

West Germany deems a dividend to be paid if a subsidiary is located in a country taxing income at a rate of less than 30 percent, the income is not derived from a business, and a German shareholder or affiliated group of shareholders owns at least 50 percent of the shares in the subsidiary. Because banking and other financial services would be considered a business, income derived from such activities would not be deemed distributed.

Japan deems Japanese shareholders to receive their pro rata share of the undistributed income of certain foreign subsidiaries. In order for a deemed distribution to occur, Japanese shareholders who separately own 10 percent or more of the total shares must collectively own 50 percent or more of the total shares of such a subsidiary, and the foreign country must tax the income of the subsidiary at a rate of less than 25 percent or, while taxing domestic income at a higher rate, must exempt income derived outside its territory. Moreover, the provisions do not apply if the subsidiary has an office of fixed place of business in the foreign country, manages and controls its business from within that country, and, in the case of a bank and certain other types of business, conducts its business mainly with unrelated persons (i.e., with persons other than its parent corporation, sister subsidiaries, etc.).

3. Foreign Currency Issues

The computation of a deemed-paid foreign tax credit gives rise to two foreign-currency issues: (1) should taxes paid by a subsidiary be translated at the exchange rate for the date the taxes were paid or the date the dividend is subsequently paid to the parent; and (2) should the profits or earnings out of which a dividend is paid (the denominator of the deemed paid credit formula) be calculated under a net-worth or a profit-and-loss method? These questions are significant because dividends are considered to be paid out of undistributed earnings from the most recent year and therefore a large distribution (e.g., upon the liquidation of a subsidiary) may be considered to include earnings from several years or even decades ago when exchange rates were very different from their current value.

In the United States, the practice with respect to actual dividends has been to translate the taxes paid by the subsidiary and the profits out of which the dividend is paid at the exchange rate at the time of the distribution. However, the deemed-paid credit arising on a deemed dividend is calculated under different rules: the foreign tax is translated at an average exchange rate for the year, and earnings are calculated under a net-worth method. The difference between the two sets of rules gives rise to opportunities for manipulation by sophisticated taxpayers and, more often, to confusion and inconsistency when an actual distribution is made out of previously taxed

369

earnings. In its December 1980 "discussion draft" the U.S. Treasury proposed to change the rules with respect to deemed dividends to conform to those presently applied to actual dividends.

The author has not been able to determine how these issues are treated under other countries' tax systems.

4. Subnational Taxes

In the United States, New York City and State both exempt from tax the dividends a parent receives from its subsidiaries providing the parent corporation owns at least 50 percent of the subsidiary's shares. California would generally consider the activities of a foreign subsidiary to be part of a bank's unitary business, and thus its income would be subject to apportionment. As with a foreign branch, the income of a foreign subsidiary would attract California tax only if its taxable income relative to its property, payroll and sales were higher than average for the unitary business.

The application of subnational taxes in foreign countries to dividends received from foreign subsidiaries is similar to their application to earnings derived by a foreign branch. Neither the Municipal Trade Tax in Germany, nor the Enterprise Tax in Japan, applies to a dividend received from a foreign subsidiary by a German or a Japanese bank, respectively. The Japanese Inhabitants Tax would be applied, but may be offset by the Japanese bank's foreign

370

tax credit.

VI. WITHHOLDING TAX ON INTEREST PAID BY A BANK

Under their statutory law, all five countries covered by this survey impose withholding taxes on interest derived from a domestic source and paid to nonresident corporations, individuals or other entities. Because banks often fund international lending by borrowing in Eurocurrency and Eurocapital markets, the application of withholding taxes has particular significance for internationally oriented banks.

The United States withholding tax rate on U.S.-source interest paid to an individual, corporation or other entity not resident in a country with which it has a tax treaty is 30 percent. Unless a U.S. corporation derives 80 percent or more of its income from outside the United States, interest paid by its head office or a foreign branch is considered U.S.-source and, therefore, is subject to U.S. tax. However, interest paid by a U.S. bank on the deposit of a non-resident, whether the deposit is with a domestic or foreign branch, is considered foreign source and, thus, exempted from the tax. In addition, the United States seeks to eliminate its withholding tax on interest in its bilateral tax treaties in exchange for a reciprocal exemption from foreign tax for U.S. recipients. Many U.S. corporations, including U.S. banks, have established finance subsidiaries in the Netherlands Antilles or other tax-haven

371

jursidictions which have a tax treaty with the United States in order to avoid the U.S. withholding tax.

Like the United States, the United Kingdom imposes a withholding tax on interest at a rate of 30 percent, but eliminates such taxes reciprocally under many of its bilateral tax treaties. All interest, not just that on deposits, paid by a corporation carrying on a bona fide banking business within the United Kingdom is exempt from withholding tax. In addition, interest paid by a foreign branch of a U.K. bank is not considered U.K.-source and is therefore exempt from the U.K. withholding tax.

By statute, France imposes withholding tax at a rate of 25 percent. Although the withholding tax has been eliminated in a limited number of tax treaties, in most treaties it remains at 10 percent. A 1978 protocol to the French treaty with the United States eliminated both the French and U.S. withholding taxes on interest paid by banks. And under its territorial tax system, no withholding tax applies to interest paid by a foreign branch of a French bank.

German statutory law imposes withholding tax on certain interest at a rate of 25 percent, but the scope of that tax is limited. Interest paid on debt secured by real property, convertible bonds, and bonds evidenced by individual certificates (as opposed to a single universal certificate) are taxed. Interest paid on bank deposits or on loans is exempt. Moreoever, like the United States and the United Kingdom, Germany prefers to eliminate reciprocally withholding taxes on interest in its bilateral tax treaties.

Japan imposes by statute a withholding tax on interest at a rate of 20 percent, which is usually reduced to 10 percent, but never eliminated entirely, under its tax treatites. Although no special exemption is provided for bank deposits or bank interest generally, interest paid to finance trade under a letter of credit is considered foreign source and is therefore exempt from withholding. Moreover, following the practice of countries other than the United States, interest paid by a foreign branch of a Japanese bank is considered foreign source and exempt from withholding.

PART C

ECONOMIC ANALYSIS

Rather than simply summarizing the many complex rules described above, this section shows how those rules combine to determine a "minimum lending rate" for a head office or a foreign branch of a bank chartered by, and with its head office located in the United States, the United Kingdom, France, West Germany or Japan. The minimum lending rate is the rate of interest gross of all costs and taxes which a bank would have to charge in order to obtain a specified profit margin net of taxes. The calculations below assume that the only variable non-tax cost of lending is interest on borrowed funds at a rate of 15 percent per annum. The foreign country in which the hypothetical borrower resides is assumed to withhold tax equal to 20 percent of gross interest, and the bank is assumed to require a net margin of 1 percent of the loan principal. Thus, if the interest income were exempt from all tax except the withholding tax, the minimum lending rate would be 20 percent per annum.

The minimum lending rate does not indicate how banks domiciled in various countries actually price loans. That decision reflects a variety of factors other than interest and tax expenses -- factors such as the maturity of the loan, the reputation of the borrower, any special relationship between the bank and the borrower, and so forth. Rather, the minimum lending rates are intended only

374

to indicate how income taxes affect the cost of lending for various banks.

The minimum lending rates for a bank domiciled in New York City, California,[8] the United Kingdom, France, West Germany and Japan are shown in Table 6. (See the Technical Appendix for a more detailed explanation of how the minimum lending rates are calculated.) Table 6 shows the minimum lending rates for a loan originating from the head office or from a foreign branch of the bank (the foreign branch is assumed to pay no local taxes either because it is located in a tax haven or because the country where it is located allows a foreign tax credit for the withholding tax). In addition, Table 6 shows how the minimum lending rates vary according to whether the bank has a deficit of tax credits or a surplus of tax credits. If a bank has a deficit of credits, it can offset the full amount of the foreign withholding tax against its domestic tax liability, so that the net tax cost of making the loan equals the tax liability (before credit) in its home country. If a bank has an excess of credits, that excess is assumed to be sufficient to offset the additional domestic tax liability arising from the new loan, so the net tax cost of making the loan equals the withholding tax imposed by the borrower's country. Whether a bank domiciled in various countries will have a deficit rather than an excess of credits depends partly on the rules described in Part B above and partly on a bank's own individual circumstances.

375

TABLE 6: MINIMUM LENDING RATES FOR A LOAN SUBJECT TO
FOREIGN WITHHOLDING TAX EQUAL TO 20 PERCENT
OF GROSS INTEREST MADE BY A BANK DOMICILED IN
NEW YORK CITY, CALIFORNIA, THE UNITED KINGDOM,
FRANCE, WEST GERMANY OR JAPAN

Domicile of Bank	Head Office	Foreign Branch
	(percent per anum)	
New York City		
Deficit of Credits	17.4	16.9
Excess of Credits	22.1	20.0
California		
Deficit of Credits	17.0	16.9
Excess of Credits	20.5	20.3
United Kingdom		
Deficit of Credits	16.7	16.7
Excess of Credits	20.0	20.0
France		
Deficit of Credits		
Treaty	16.6	20.0
No Treaty	20.8	20.0
Excess of Credits	18.3	20.0
West Germany		
Deficit of Credits	16.6	16.4*
Excess of Credits	21.0	20.0
Japan		
Deficit of Credits	16.8	16.6
Excess of Credits	20.8	20.0

The computation of minimum lending rates is explained in
the Technical Appendix.

* Minimum lending rate for branch located in non-treaty
country. A branch located in a treaty country is exempt
from German tax and, thus, has the same minimum lending
rate as that when the German bank has an excess of credits.

A New York City bank with a deficit of credits could absorb the foreign withholding tax (i.e., credit the withholding tax against its federal tax liability) and have a minimum lending rate of 17.4 percent per annum. The 1.4 percent differential between the cost of funds, 15 percent, plus the required margin, 1 percent, goes to pay New York City, New York State and federal income taxes (as noted above, the combined rate of tax is 59.1 percent). Because the foreign withholding tax can be fully offset against the bank's U.S. tax liability, the minimum lending rate is the same as it would be for a loan to a domestic customer whose interest payments are subject to no withholding.

If a New York City bank has an excess of foreign tax credits, it is effectively exempt from the U.S. federal income tax on foreign income, but must reflect the foreign withholding tax, the New York City and the New York State income taxes in its minimum lending rate. Because the New York City and State taxes allow neither a deduction nor a credit for the foreign withholding tax, those taxes are imposed on the additional gross interest necessary to cover the cost of the withholding tax, and the withholding tax is imposed on the additional gross interest necessary to cover the cost of the City and State taxes. This double taxation pushes the minimum lending rate to 22.1 percent, almost 5 percentage points higher than the rate for a New York City bank with a deficit of credits and the highest rate shown in Table 6.

377

The second column of Table 6 shows the minimum lending rates if the same loan originates from a foreign branch in a third country (e.g., the London branch of the New York bank), rather than from the head office. Interest received by the branch is assumed to be subject to the same withholding tax as that on interest received by the head office, but to no additional taxes in the country in which the branch is located. If the New York City bank has a deficit of foreign tax credits, its foreign branch's minimum lending rate of 16.9 percent is 0.5 percentage points lower than its head office's rate. If the New York City bank has an excess of credits, the foreign branch's 20.0 percent minimum lending rate is 2.1 percentage points lower than its head office's rate. In both instances, the foreign branch's advantage is its exemption from New York City and State income taxes, an exemption which is particularly valuable when the minimum lending rate reflects a foreign withholding tax for which the City and State income taxes allow no deduction.

Table 6 also shows the minimum lending rates for a California bank. Under California's unitary apportionment system, the income from a new loan will increase the total income subject to apportionment. If the loan is made by the California head office, the portions of the bank's total property, sales, and perhaps payroll (if additional employee compensation results from making or servicing the loan) attributed to California will increase; if the loan is made by a foreign branch, those portions attributable to

378

California will decrease. The net effect on income apportioned to California depends on how the income from the loan
relative to the additional property, payroll and sales
created by the loan compares to the bank's total income
relative to its total property, payroll and sales. If the
loan generates an average amount of taxable income relative
to these three factors, the unitary apportionment approach
has the same result as separate entity accounting would--the
entire income from the loan is attributed to the entity
making the loan. If the loan carries a higher than average
return, a fixed portion of the excess return is attributed
to California irrespective of whether the loan originated
from the head office or a foreign branch.

The amount of income subject to tax in California
cannot, thus, be determined without reference to specific
information about a bank's own situation. For the sake of
the analysis here, it is simply assumed that a loan which
generated taxable income equal to 1 percent of loan principal would be average, and that 50 percent of any taxable
income over and above that 1 percent would be apportioned to
California regardless of which entity originates the loan.
The relatively low margin of 1 percent reflects the fact
that banks have substantial overhead costs which do not vary
with the volume or location of its lending, and consequently
that the average margin on all outstanding loans would be
less than the margin expected on an additional loan.

As shown on Table 6, a California bank has a lower

minimum lending rate than a New York City bank with respect to a loan made by its head office, but a slightly higher rate with respect to a loan by a foreign branch. The advantage with respect to a head-office loan derives from the lower rate of local income tax (11.6 percent in California versus 24.2 percent for the combined New York City-State tax) and from the apportionment to California of only 50 percent of the "excess" profit on a loan. That apportionment of "excess" profit also applies, however, to a loan by a foreign branch of a California bank, whereas a branch of a New York City bank would be exempt from City and State tax.

Because of its imputation system, the tax on a United Kingdom bank depends on the portion of its income paid out as dividends and, thus, the portion of the regular corporate income tax offset by the ACT. The assumption in calculating minimum lending rates in Table 6 is that half of pre-tax income is retained and half distributed, so the corporate level tax is 41.7 percent (a simple average of the 52 percent rate of tax on retained income and the 31.4 percent rate on distributed income). If a U.K. bank has a deficit of foreign tax credits, its minimum lending rate is 16.7 percent; if it has an excess of such credits, its minimum lending rate would be 20.0 percent.

Because there are no subnational income taxes, the minimum lending rates are the same for a foreign branch as for the head office of the U.K. bank. It should be recalled, however, that the expenses of a foreign branch of

380

a U.K bank are allocated against its gross income in computing the per-source limitation on the U.K. foreign tax
credit, whereas the expenses of a head office are not.
Thus, the same loan could result in excess credits if made
by the foreign branch, but not if made by the head office.

If a French bank has a deficit of tax credits with
respect to its combined interest income, and if the 20
percent withholding tax is imposed by a country with which
France has a tax treaty, the minimum lending rate for a head
office loan would be 16.6 percent. (As above, it has been
assumed that half of pre-tax income is distributed, so the
overall rate of tax is a simple average of the rates with
respect to retained and distributed income.) If the foreign
tax was paid to a non-treaty country and could not be
credited, the minimum lending rate would be 20.8 percent.
If the French bank had an overall excess of foreign tax
credits with respect to its foreign interest income, the
minimum lending rate would be 18.3 percent, regardless of
whether or not the tax was creditable under a treaty.
Because the head office of a French bank with excess credits
can deduct the excess against its French-source income, it
can partially absorb the foreign withholding tax, a benefit
banks outside of France do not enjoy.

Under its territorial tax system, France unilaterally
exempts a foreign branch of a French bank from French
taxation, so the minimum lending rate for the branch is 20.0
percent regardless of whether the head office has a deficit

or excess of credits or whether the tax is paid to a treaty or non-treaty country. Because excess credits can be deducted against French source income if the loan originates from a head office in France, but not from a foreign branch, a French bank has an incentive to originate loans generating excess credits from the head office.

The German foreign tax credit limitation is applied country by country, so the possibility is remote that a German bank would have a deficit of foreign tax credits with respect to a country imposing a 20 percent withholding tax on interest. Should it somehow have such a deficit, its minimum lending rate would be 16.6 percent on a loan originating from its head office. Although the interest would be subject to the Municipal Trade Tax, the national tax on distributed corporate earnings is either rebated to the corporation or creditable by German shareholders, so the corporate burden is relatively low. If, as is more likely, the German bank has excess credits with respect to the country in which the hypothetical borrower is resident, the minimum lending rate would be 21.0 percent to cover the cost of the foreign withholding tax and the German Municipal Trade Tax. This minimum lending rate reflects the same type of international double taxation as the analogous rates for New York City and California banks do.

If the German bank undertook the loan through a branch (or a subsidiary) in a country with which Germany had a tax treaty, the income would be exempt from German tax, and the minimum lending rate would be 20 percent. The same minimum lending rate would also apply to a branch in a non-treaty country if the German bank had an excess of foreign tax credits with respect to the country imposing the tax. Only if there were no treaty exemption and the bank had a deficit of credits would the minimum lending rate for the branch be reduced to 16.4 percent.

The pattern and absolute levels of minimum lending rates for a bank domiciled in Japan are similar to those for a German bank. The key difference between the two is that Japanese banks (like U.S. banks) are subject to an overall limitation, rather than a per country limitation, so they are more likely to have a deficit of foreign tax credits than German banks are. Although the Japanese prefectural Inhabitants Tax may be offset by a credit for foreign withholding taxes, the Enterprise Tax cannot be offset, and thus gives rise to double taxation.

The above calculations assume that the foreign with-holding tax is imposed at a rate of 20 percent of gross interest. As noted in the previous section, the United Kingdom, France, West Germany and Japan (but not the United States) have agreed under various bilateral tax treaties to allow a credit not only for withholding taxes paid to developing countries, but also for taxes "spared." Often a developing country will refuse to lower its withholding tax unless a developed country agrees to a tax-sparing provision.

In order to see the potential impact of tax sparing, suppose a developing country reduced its withholding tax on interest paid to a United Kingdom bank from 20 percent to 10 percent, but the United Kingdom agreed to allow a foreign tax credit equal to 20 percent of gross interest. Under the same assumptions as above, a U.K. bank with a deficit of foreign tax credits would have a minimum lending rate of 14.3 percent compared to 16.7 percent absent the tax-sparing provision. That is to say, if the United Kingdom bank were content with a 1 percentage point margin net of taxes, it could afford to set its lending rate gross of the foreign withholding tax at 0.7 percent less than its cost of funds (and its lending rate net of the foreign withholding tax at 2.1 percentage points below the cost of funds). If the U.K. bank had an excess of foreign tax credits, the tax-sparing provision per se would not affect its minimum lending rate, but the reduction in the tax actually paid from 20 percent to 10 percent of gross interest would allow the minimum lending rate to be reduced from 20 percent to 17.8 percent.

Tax sparing has a comparable impact on the minimum lending rates of banks domiciled in France, West German and Japan.

Japan is the only country included in this survey offering tax incentives other than tax-sparing to foreign lending. As noted above, a Japanese bank may establish a reserve equal to a 15 percent of loans extended to a company with its head office in a developing country, 40

384

percent of loans extended to a "natural resources development company," and 100 percent of loans extended to a "natural resources prospecting company." The amount of the reserve may be deducted from taxable income in the year the loan is extended, maintained for five years, and then included in taxable income ratably from the sixth to the tenth year.

A reserve such as this is tantamount to an interest-free loan by the Japanese treasury to the Japanese bank in the amount of the deferred tax. For example, a reserve equal to 40 percent of the loan principal for a head office whose income was subject to prefectural and national tax at the combined rate of 43.7 percent would result in an interest-free loan to the Japanese bank equal to 17.5 percent of the amount the bank loaned to a natural resources development company. Thus, its cost of funding that loan would be reduced by 17.5 percent, or from 15 percent per annum to 12.4 percent per annum. Under the same assumptions which underlie the computations in Table 6, the minimum lending rate for the head office of a Japanese bank with a deficiit of credits would be reduced from 16.8 percent to 14.2 percent per annum, and that for a bank with excess credits would be reduced from 20.8 percent to 17.4 percent. Thus, this "temporary deferral" of income tax has a substantial impact on the Japanese bank's cost of making a loan that qualifies for a special reserve.

385

PART D

CONCLUSIONS

Several conclusions can be drawn from this analysis. The many differences in countries' systems for taxing the income of commercial banks from foreign lending translate into substantial differences in banks' minimum lending rates, a measure of the cost of making various loans. Banks appear to be increasingly aware of the income tax consequences of their lending -- a long overdue development.

The reason why income taxes have assumed greater importance derives from the changing economics of international lending. As gross interest rates have risen and net margins have narrowed, the amount of withholding tax imposed by the country where a borrower is resident has grown to be several times larger than the tax on net income by the country in which the bank is domiciled. This, in turn, has strained banks' ability to absorb foreign withholding taxes and, by implication, has strained the rules for computing the foreign tax credit limitation in different countries.

The capacity of banks chartered in one country to absorb high foreign withholding taxes relative to the capacity of banks chartered in other countries cannot be assessed with any precision. U.K. banks are singularly advantaged by not having to allocate any interest or other expense against foreign interest income in calculating their per-source limitation. However, the aggregate foreign tax

386

credit of a U.K. bank cannot exceed its mainstream tax, which, in turn, is a fraction of its total tax. Head offices of French banks are allowed a credit only for taxes paid to countries with which France has a tax treaty, but may deduct from French-source income both creditable taxes in excess of the limitation and all non-creditable taxes. Both Japan and the United States impose an overall limitation on the foreign tax credit claimed by their banks, and this allows excess credits with respect to one source of income to be applied against a deficit with respect to another. The United States requires its banks to apportion total interest expense between foreign and domestic income based on its total assets or gross income, a procedure which results in a smaller allocation of such expense (and, thus, a larger foreign tax credit limitation) than that under the traditional "tracing" method. Whether U.S. banks must allocate more or less total expense against foreign interest income than comparable French, German or Japanese banks cannot be determined, however, without more precise information on those countries' requirements. The most stringent foreign tax credit limitation apparently applies to German banks: they must calculate their limitation country by country and, unlike U.K. banks, allocate interest and other expenses against foreign income.

The extent to which limitations on the foreign tax credit have actually affected patterns of international lending is difficult to say. The combination of high current interest rates, high withholding taxes unreduced by an extensive treaty network with developing countries, and narrowing lending margins, may well have produced significant excess credits for the larger U.S. banks with substantial international loan portfolios. If so, they would be hard pressed to match the lending terms of those foreign banks and smaller U.S. banks still able to absorb high foreign withholding taxes against their domestic tax liabilities. The ability of the international banking system as a whole to absorb high withholding taxes imposed is, however, limited. Tax considerations may, therefore, lead to more widespread resistance to narrow loan margins in the next few years than they have in the recent past.

The imbalance between foreign withholding taxes and domestic taxes based on net income has been a tax policy concern in some countries, but apparently not in others. The United States is the only country which has developed stringent criteria for the creditability of foreign taxes and has disallowed credit for significant foreign taxes in the process. In addition, the United States has continually refused to accept tax-sparing provisions and thereby limited its treaty network with developing countries. The U.S. opposition to tax sparing reflects both a more general objection to tax incentives for foreign investment not enjoyed by domestic investment, and a concern over the possible revenue cost to the U.S. Treasury. The United Kingdom has expressed concern over U.K. banks lending at negative margins to countries covered by tax-sparing treaty provisions. The United Kingdom's concern appeared to focus, however, more on the adverse impact of such loans on the balance of payments than on the loss of tax revenues.

However desirable it may be, it seems unlikely that many countries will unilaterally reduce or eliminate high withholding taxes on interest. For many developing countries, withholding taxes are a significant source of tax revenue and entail little collection cost. If the U.S. tax policy concern is a loss of U.S. tax revenues, a better solution might be to allow a credit for foreign taxes spared, but to limit the credit to the U.S. tax attributable to net income from that country. This approach, which Germany takes, reduces the need to differentiate between creditable and non-creditable foreign taxes, avoids unnecessary conflicts with developing countries, and secures a reduction in excessive withholding taxes at little or no real cost to the domestic treasury.

Subnational taxes are also particularly deserving of comment. State and local income taxes within the United States, the Municipal Trade Tax in West Germany, and the Enterprise Tax in Japan are all imposed on the foreign income of a head office or domestic branch, and none allows a deduction, much less a credit, for foreign withholding taxes. A California bank may be subject to California tax not only with respect to the foreign income of a head office or branch in California, but also with respect to income

389

attributable to a foreign branch or subsidiary which the state deems to be part of the same unitary business. This often results in double taxation. The combined burden of the New York City and New York State income tax is almost 25 percent; together they result in an increase in the minimum lending rate (as computed above) for the head office of a New York City bank from 20.0 percent to 22.1 percent. The practical effect of these taxes is to shift banks' international lending to offshore branches, obviously not the objective of the tax. A better solution may be modeled on the Japanese Inhabitants Tax, a prefectural tax which is imposed on foreign income, but which can be offset by foreign income taxes in excess of those creditable against national income tax.

PART E

ADDENDA

I. TECHNICAL APPENDIX

This Appendix explains how the minimum lending rates shown in Table 6 and in Part C of the text are derived. The general formula for the minimum lending rate is:

$$g = c + n + wg + s(g-c) + t(g-c)(1-s) - f$$

The symbols are defined as follows:

g = minimum lending rate

c = cost of borrowed money to the bank

n = income net of all taxes and costs

w = rate of foreign withholding tax on gross income

s = rate of subnational tax on gross income less cost of borrowing

t = rate of national tax on gross income less cost of borrowing and subnational taxes

f = foreign tax credit

If the bank has a deficit of foreign tax credits, $f = wg$; if the banks has a excess of credits, $f = t(g-c)(1-s)$. Unless otherwise indicated, it is assumed that $c = .15$, $n = .01$ and $w = .2$. The values of s and t, which determine the minimum lending rate, g, vary from country to country.

For a New York City bank, $t = .46$. For a loan originating from a head office, $s = .242$; for a loan originating from a foreign branch, s = 0.

For a California bank, the basic formula had to be modified to accomodate California's unitary apportionment system. For a loan made by the California head office, the additional California tax arising from the loan would equal:

$$s(a + p(g-(c+a)))$$

where a is the amount of income, assumed to be .01, which is attributed to California on account of the increase in California property, payroll and sales attributable to the loan, and p is the average ratio of California property, payroll and sales to worldwide property, payroll and sales, respectively. The value of s = .116 and of t = .46. For a loan by a foreign branch, the value of g would be computed by setting a = 0.

For a United Kingdom bank, s = 0 and t = .417, the latter rate being a simple average of the rate on retained income, .52, and that on distributed income, .314.

For a French bank, s = 0 and t = .375, the latter rate being a simple average of the rate on retained income, .5, and that on distributed income, .25. If the French bank has a deficit of foreign tax credits and the withholding tax is paid to a country with which France does not have a tax treaty, then the basic formula must be modified to:

$$g = c + n + wg + t(g-c-wg)$$

392

For a foreign branch of a French bank, which is exempt from French tax, the basic formula is:

$$g = c + n + wg$$

For a West German bank, $t = .28$, half the rate on retained income, .56 (distributed income is effectively exempt from tax). For a loan from a head office, $s = .13$; for a loan from a foreign branch, $s = 0$.

For a Japanese bank, the prefectural Inhabitants Tax, which is computed as a surtax of 17.3 percent of the national tax, was included in the national tax. Thus, $t = .369$, a simple average of the rate with respect to retained income, .469, and that for distributed income, .270. For a loan from the head office, $s = .107$; for a loan from a foreign branch, $s = 0$.

If a U.K. bank made a tax-spared loan, $w = .1$, but if the bank has a deficit of credits, $f = .2g$. Otherwise, the parameters are as stated above.

If a Japanese bank could establish a tax-deferred reserve equal to 40 percent of principal, the value of c would be reduced by 17.5 percent from 15 to 12.4 percent per annum for the reasons indicated in the text. Other parameters used in computing the minimum lending rate, g, would be as indicated above.

II. <u>NOTES</u>

[1] The author was Director of the International Tax Staff in the U.S. Treasury Department's Office of Tax Analysis from 1977 to 1980 and is now a partner in Taxecon Associates. This survey of foreign countries' tax laws is based on English-language secondary sources listed under the References. Although considerable effort was made to check sources against one another and with individuals having particular expertise on various points, misrepresentations doubtless remain.

The author has received many thoughtful comments and criticisms and is particularly grateful for the technical corrections made by Hugh Ault, John Chown and Marcia Field. Unfortunately, the author alone bears responsibility for any remaining errors.

[2] These statistics are drawn from Rodney H. Mills, Jr., "U.S. banks are losing their share of the market," <u>Euromoney</u>, February 1980, pp. 50-62.

[3] "The year of the gunslinger," <u>Euromoney</u>, May 1980, pp. 64-73.

[4] Solomon Brothers, "Lending to LDC's: Mounting Problems," April 2, 1980, Table 19, p. 24, reproduced in C. Stewart Goodin and Steven J. Weiss, "U.S. Banks' Loss of Global Standing," Comptroller of the Currency, Administrator of National Banks, Staff Papers, 1980-3, note 10.

[5] "500 Largest Banks in the Free World," <u>American Banker</u>, annual listing.

[6] The equivalent rate of tax on distributed earnings equals the tax imposed on the corporation if all earnings are distributed, 52.0 percent in this instance, less the portion of that tax which is available as a credit to the shareholders, 30/70 of 48 percent, or 20.6 percent, in this instance. The equivalent rate of tax on distributed earnings in other countries is computed in a similar fashion.

[7] See, e.g., Pamela Clarke, "How the British taxpayer gives London banks a handout," <u>Euromoney</u>, August 1979, pp. 121-22.

[8] A bank domiciled in New York City or California in-
     cludes a bank chartered under either federal or state
     law with its head office located within those jurisdic-
     tions.

III.   REFERENCES

Anonymous, "The year of the gunslinger," Euromoney, May 1980, pp. 64-73.

Bryan, Greyson, "The Tax Implications of Japanese Multinational Corporations," Journal of International Law and Politics, Spring 1976, pp. 152-209

California Franchise Tax Board, Guideline for Apportionment of Income of Banks and Financial Corporations, FTB 1036, April 1976.

Commerce Clearing House, Inc., Guidebook to California Taxes, 1980.

Commerce Clearing House, Inc., Guidebook to New York Taxes, 1980.

Goodin, C. Stewart and Weiss, Steven J., "U.S. Banks Loss of Global Standing," U.S. Comptroller of the Currency, Administrator of National Banks, Staff Papers, 1980-3.

Horst, Thomas, Income Taxation and Competitiveness, National Planning Association Committee on Changing International Realities, 1977.

International Bureau of Fiscal Documentation, The Taxation of Companies in Europe, Looseleaf series updated continuously.

Mills, Rodney H., Jr., "U.S. banks are losing their share of the market," Euromoney, February 1980, pp. 50-62.

Peat, Marwick, Mitchell & Co., Bank Taxation in Europe, Second Edition, Frankfurt/Main, 1979.

Peat, Marwick, Mitchell & Co., Foreign Tax Credits Available to Banks in Europe, London, 1979.

Peat, Marwick, Mitchell & Co., Tax Treatment of Exchange Gains and Losses in Selected Countries, Paris, 1979.

Price Waterhouse, Doing Busines in ....., Country series updated periodically.

Tax Bureau, Ministry of Finance, An Outline of Japanese Taxes, 1979.

TAXATION OF INTERNATIONAL INCOME OF COMMERCIAL BANKS

Thomas Horst, Taxecon

COMMENT

John Chown

J. F. Chown and Company, Ltd.

CONTENTS

Tom Horst's paper is an excellent and detailed account of comparative banking taxation. Relatively small taxes such as withholding taxes can be of strategic importance to banks which make their living by borrowing and relending 20 times their capital base: a fractional change in margin can make all the difference between profit and loss.[1]

For years I had to apologize for being a tax economist: if I was neither a lawyer nor an accountant, I must be a quack! Today, happily, a panel of two lawyers and two economists (Tom and myself) is considered a normal balance. Our training and approach produces insights different from, and complementary to, those of the lawyers. And there are certain subjects where we have a "comparative advantage." It is a commonplace amongst economists that the dollar, the pound, and the mark are not stable measuring rods but change in value from day to day, and we have less difficulty than the lawyers and the accountants (particularly those who caused so much trouble with the nonsense of FASB 8!) in understanding the interactions between taxes, inflation and currency risk.

I.   THE ROLE OF THE TAX ADVISOR

Like Tom, I have found the combination of tax and currency risk fascinating. Unlike him, I cut my teeth by advising not banks but corporate borrowers. Corporations that have separate departments and advisors for tax problems on the one hand and currency problems on the other have unnecessarily lost billions of dollars in the last decade, while those (mainly in my experience the oil and resources companies) that have a "systems" approach, have saved themselves similar sums.

Some of you are concerned with the public policy aspects of bank regulation and international aspects of bank regulation and international money. Tax factors cannot be ignored. The British Revenue attitude to the Marine Midland case, and the U.S. Treasury stand on "fungibility" (a term they misused) both seemed to be mere technical tax issues, but have far-reaching implications for the subject we are discussing here.

How should banks use tax advisors? In my work, and on the conference circuit, I meet many of the in-house international tax advisors to major corporations and banks. There is an important difference between the typical American and the typical European in-house international tax man.[2] The typical European regards his job as knowing about foreign taxes in the various countries in which his corporation does business, but gives too little attention to the effect of foreign operations on the domestic tax position, leaving that to his humbler colleague who looks after home taxes. The typical American who considers himself an international tax specialist, is usually a specialist in the United States tax treatment of international income rather than an expert on foreign taxes. His characteristic fault is to concentrate on the centre and ignore the periphery.

400

The ideal tax advisor then, must be a cross of an American with a Dutchman, with some economist's blood in his veins. He will have to advise you not only on how best to conduct your tax planning in a particular country, but also whether it is advisable that you take advantage of all the opportunities apparently open to you, having regard to the requirements of good corporate citizenship and of good political and public relations at the local level.

How should you use this paragon of an advisor? Tom has shown that the after-tax margin available on loans to certain foreign countries can vary dramatically according to whether the loan is booked in New York, the Bahamas, London, Paris or elsewhere -- and that the best answer contrary to popular superstition is <u>not</u> always Nassau! He has also shown that banks based in other countries may be at a competitive advantage or disadvantage compared with an American bank with the same funding costs making the same loan.

The obvious lesson (which most banks have learned) is that you should look at tax factors when deciding where to <u>book</u> the loan. Many have not mastered the second lesson namely, that tax factors should also influence <u>whether</u> to make the loan at all. Instead most banks only consult the tax department <u>after</u> they have decided to make a loan, leaving the tax people just to decide where to book it. The better approach is to treat tax as a strategic factor in making the loan decision itself. It is, as we have shown, an important factor although less important than other factors, country risk for example. The tax department should work together with the rest of management in setting guidelines. If you need 15 percent on a domestic one-year loan, you may need 18.5 percent for a loan to Brazil booked through head office to give the same after-tax return and before adding on any risk premiums. If the best place to book the loan is London where the break even yield figure is 17.5 percent, you should know that even before you start the negotiations. These yardstick figures can vary quite sharply with changes in tax rules or the worldwide tax mix of the bank. There is, as Tom has shown, an optimum tax mix that gives the best profits but you are only likely to achieve this if you regard tax as a central and strategic managment factor rather than a fringe activity.

The tax team should also monitor the tax treatment of banks in other countries. If you have established that 17.5 percent is the break-even point for a loan into Brazil and your tax people tell you that because of a tax break, British banks can lend at 17, you might as well save yourself the cost of a flight to Rio. And when the British change the rules, a previously closed market would be opened up: it could be worth something to have that information a few days ahead of the competition!

A speaker yesterday suggested that "recycling" would be easier if we could get regional banks in on the act. This could be helpful if the smaller banks could acquire the tax skills already deployed by the larger ones.

II. RESERVE REQUIREMENTS

Another factor affecting the booking decision is not
tax but reserve requirements. Indeed, from an operational
point of view, reserve requirements are a tax in disguise,
just as your old interest equilization tax was an exchange
control in disguise. Exchange controls are themselves
another factor to be built into any international tax
planning model. From a public policy point of view, reserve
requirements, rather than tax laws, have to be watched if we
are to bring the "offshore" bank back onshore -- to New York
or wherever. And, as John Forsyth pointed out yesterday,
the UK "windfall tax" on bank profits is a retrospective
reserve requirement.

III. EXCHANGE RISK

So far we have concentrated on where to book loans. In
the case of my corporate borrowers, I have found one of the
more important decisions to take is where, and in what form,
to bear (or to cover) exchange risks.[3] Exchange risks are
not always treated symmetrically. UK Revenue law does not
recognize capital gains and losses on long-term liabilities
-- Marine Midland fell badly into this particular (and well
documented) tax trap, but British companies, too, lost the
odd billion between them in a non-tax deductible form. In
other countries, the rules may be symmetrical in the long

run but there are timing differences so that, for instance, unrealized losses may be recognized while unrealized profits are carried forward. At today's rates of interest, tax postponed is tax saved and there are very useful economies to be achieved by attention to this particular detail.

I am well aware of an investigation into the foreign exchange practices of one of your banks a couple of years back. I have my own views on what is and what is not ethical and/or expedient. However, good tax planning does not mean being a bad corporate citizen. If your competitors are taking tax advice and you are not, you risk either being shut out of potentially profitable markets or, still worse, being tempted into markets only to find that you lost money even in after-tax terms.

IV. LEASING

We have discussed leasing. In your country and mine, fixed asset leasing is allegedly a powerful tax planning tool. It certainly saves a lot of tax -- more strictly it postpones tax but at the present interest rates this often comes to much the same as saving tax. The "cost" is that it involves making finance available more cheaply. Tom points out that the name of the game is not to reduce taxes but to maximize after-tax profits. By this criterion and by my calculations, leasing is far less effective as a shelter than is commonly supposed. A rational and comprehensive analysis of all the alternatives available internationally

404

would in my experience often cause a bank to reduce its commitment to leasing and increase its use of international tax efficient lending procedures.

This can have adverse political consequences. The new UK Budget imposed a "windfall tax" on banks at 2.5 percent (non-deductible so therefore approximately equal to a 5 percent tax-deductible levy) on an average of non-interest bearing domestic sterling deposits. Yet (by my calculations) the big banks had only just preserved their real capital base (after tax and inflation) before the tax and would fail to do so afterwards. In this case, the conventional bank practice of having a "provision for future tax" that was calculated on "conventional" (but inaccurate) accounting principles may have impressed the stockholders but politically it cost them money!

V. <u>NOTES</u>

[1] My technical comments have been incorporated into the published version of the main paper.

[2] I am indebted to my friend Professor Sven Olof Lodin of Uppsala for drawing my attention to this insight.

[3] See John Chown, "The Treasurer", May 1981.

TAXATION OF INTERNATIONAL INCOME OF COMMERCIAL BANKS

Thomas Horst

COMMENT

Henry S. Conston

Walter, Conston, Schurtman & Gumpel, P.C., New York

In the conduct of their daily business, banking executives frequently do not ascribe to taxes the importance that should be attributed to them. Thus, it is often left to the lawyers and tax advisers to cope with, and minimize the impact of, taxation after transactions have beem completed.

Nevertheless, the influence of taxation has played an ever-increasing role in the way banks engage in business. Dividends from foreign subsidiaries are timed and coordinated for maximum foreign tax credit utilization. Complex new financing structures, such as lease financings, are developed in order to enable banks to benefit from advantageous tax attributes. Advantages that may arise as a result of differences in characterization of legal entities in different countries are taken advantage of to minimize the overall impact of taxation on major transactions.

During the past four years, regulations issued by the Internal Revenue Service (Section 1.861.8(e) and Section 1.882-5) threatened to have such a devastating effect on the U.S. branch operations of foreign banks that several of the banks seriously considered shutting down their branches if the regulations were allowed to remain in effect and were upheld by the courts.

The regulations which became effective in 1977 would have required foreign banks to calculate the interest cost deductible against income of their U.S. branches at the banks' world-wide average interest cost rate. The rule was based on the theory that all money is fungible. It

408

disregarded the effect of differences in interest rates for different currencies, and it failed to acknowledge the fact that a bank branch must operate as a separate profit center and must independently cover its loan funding requirements.

After a major effort by the affected banks, the regulations were amended early this year to substitute a complex formula for the determination of deductible interest expense. While the new formula does not present an ideal solution, it does avoid the absurd results of the prior method.

These comments address just a few of the areas of interest in international tax planning. Banks engaging in international business should make full use of creative tax planning opportunities available to them.

CHAPTER EIGHT

THE OUTLOOK FOR OFFICIAL EXPORT CREDITS

Axel Wallen

Director-General, The Swedish Export Credits
Guarantee Board[1]

and

John M. Duff, Jr.

Senior Vice President, Direct Credits and
Financial Guarantees, Export-Import Bank
of the United States[1]

CONTENTS

411

I.   HISTORICAL BACKGROUND (Wallen)

1.   Developments Before the Consensus

As early as the 1920s, some major exporting countries became aware of the necessity to provide official support to exports when credit was a dimension of the transaction. This was the genesis for the creation of official export credit guarantee institutions like EGCD in the U.K., OND in Belgium, and others. This development continued in the 1930s and 1940s, but was limited to covering political risk, sometimes combined with commercial risk. The credits that were guaranteed usually had short maturity terms.

As exports of capital goods to developing countries grew in the 1950s, the demand for longer term credits on large transactions correspondingly increased. Official support began to take the form of guarantees to banks on loans provided to foreign buyers. Well into the 1960s, one could find that many major exporting countries offered financing or refinancing of medium term and long term export credits at fixed interest rates, independent of market rate fluctuations. Thus the financial package came to be an element of competition and soon a real "under-bidding" in officially supported export interest rates took place.

This development was first seen as an important problem within the shipbuilding field. Intense competition between European and Japanese shipyards caused a situation where low fixed rates (5.5%) were matched by, and later combined with, long credits -- up to eight years. As early as 1963 a

412

special working group (Working Party 6 also known as WP6) of the OECD was entrusted with the task of finding ways to limit subsidization within the shipbuilding sector. From 1967 to 1969 negotiations within the group were directed at reaching an agreement on common credit terms for the export of ships. In 1969 WP6 finally succeeded in creating the OECD Understanding on credit for ships. The United States did not adhere to the Understanding. The understanding has remained in effect since 1969, but with some interesting changes over the years.

The Understanding spells out in eight short paragraphs all the necessary elements in an agreement on export credit terms: interest minima, minimum downpayment, credit length maxima, permitted matching, relation to aid, etc. It is quite natural that European and Japanese views on a broader consensus on export credits were greatly influenced by these first steps taken on the path to harmonization of export credit terms in the shipbuilding sector.

While this development took place at the end of the 1960s within WP6, more general discussions in the export credit field were being held in another expert group in the OECD, the group on export credit and guarantees (Export Credit Group). This group had been established in 1963 with the aim of limiting official subsidization in export promotion. Up to the beginning of the 1970s, the group's main goal seems to have been to discuss an information and consultation procedure for transactions where the credit period was to be longer than the normal maximum, at that time a term of five years. Some efforts were also made to create reliable and moderate terms for credits less than five years. In this second area the main work has, however, devolved on the international Union of Credit and Investment Insurers (Berne Union).

The Berne Union has devoted much effort since the Second World War to the design of common international norms so as to avoid official support for transactions on abnormal terms. Since 1959, the reporting of export credit guarantees for transactions with more than a five-year repayment term has had a certain restraining effect on the credit race and has provided an essential factual basis for reviewing the development of export credits.

In 1972 the Export Credit Group (ECG) in the OECD agreed on a system for information and consultation, which increased the possibilities for member countries to obtain information on terms provided by other countries and thereby to adapt their own terms to international trends or to match each other's terms. Signs were evident in the beginning of the 1970s of increasing competition between rival financial packages, with subsidized interest rates playing a growing role. In 1972, therefore, it was suggested within the ECG that the group should take a closer look at the problems of this kind of subsidization. In 1973, a first review was made of official export credit facilities, and a conclusion was dared that some kind of agreement on

414

minimum interest rates would be useful if not necessary.

The thinking and aims within the ECG were suddenly pushed forward by external events. The oil crisis in the autumn of 1973 drastically exposed the vulnerability of the western exporting countries and propelled them to even fiercer credit competition in the markets of Eastern Europe and developing nations. At the same time, the necessity to provide long-term credits as one means of accomodating the oil shock became greater. Fearing an immediate credit war, ministers from Germany, France, Italy, Japan, the United Kingdom and the United States initiated talks and discussions at an IMF meeting in Nairobi in September 1973 on a so-called gentlemen's agreement that would aim at limiting the credit race. Export credit issues were stressed in the trade declaration issued by the OECD Ministerial Council in May 1974. In the autumn of 1974 a very simple agreement was signed in Washington, implying a minimum interest rate of 7.5%. The agreement was, however, a very rough one and it was immediately realized that much more thorough work had to be done to create an effective bulwark against increased subsidization.

The ensuing work was mainly done under the guidance of Dr. Geberth from the German Ministry of Economics who at that time was also Chairman of the ECG. It was extremely difficult work to find solutions on all elements in a package which could be acceptable to every member. The work was done at several general meetings in the period 1974 to

415

1976 and led to the unilateral declarations in the spring and summer of 1976 which constituted the "Gentlemen's Agreement".

The agreement of 1976 (which had been awaited so long that the London Financial Times had said in 1975: "Gentlemen prefer subsidies") was a series of seven unilateral declarations of the same concept and about the same wordings, made by the six countries which had met in Nairobi in 1973 plus Canada.

2. The Consensus (1976)

The Gentlemen's Agreement of 1976, often called the "Consensus" as it was not a formal agreement, set forth the following guidelines:

(a)   At least 15% of the contract price of the export should be paid before the starting point (as defined by the Berne Union) of the credit period.

(b)   The credit length should not be extended over 5 years for exports to countries in Category I ("relatively rich" countries), 8.5 years for exports to countries in Category II ("intermediate" countries) and 10 years for exports to countries in Category III ("relatively poor" countries).

(c)   The officially supported interest rate (namely the refinancing rate in a supplier credit transaction or the financing rate in a buyer credit transaction) should not be lower than the relevant rate set forth in a matrix that ranged from 7.25% to 8.00%. The rates in the matrix depended on the length of the credit and the country categorization: the shorter the credit and the poorer the importing country the lower rate.

(d)   If any member wished to derogate from these guidelines, it had to give prior notification to other members. Further, if any member wished to provide a tied aid credit with a grant element of less than 15% it had to give prior notification.

The classification of countries was one of the more difficult tasks the negotiators faced when creating the Consensus.   In the end they agreed on a list in which groupings were made based on World Bank 1973 gross national product per capita figures.   Countries with GNP per capita of more than $3,000 were in Category I, countries with per capital figures of $1,000 to $3,000 were in Category II, and countries below the $1,000 level were in Category III.   Even though current GNP per capita figures at the end of the 1970s would place countries in different categories than they were in 1973, the political difficulties of revising the categories has proved too arduous, and countries remain in their original categories.

The relationship between the credit length and the interest rate minima created an especially difficult problem for the countries involved in the Consensus discussions. This resulted mainly from the fact that some European countries with relatively small capital markets had introduced interest rate subsidization but wished to keep credit periods relatively short, while the North American countries which provided relatively little interest rate subsidization but had deep capital markets wished to allow longer credit periods to reflect the cash-flow of the project, irrespective of the country of destination. Therefore, the European demand for a maximum of five years credit to countries in Category I was long rejected by the United States and Canada. These different approaches are reconciled in the present Arrangement through the compromise that a decision on a longer credit in such a case does not constitute a full derogation but does call for advance notification.

Another difficult task was the use by some European countries (mainly France) of official cost escalation guarantees. The United States wished to have rules against this practice inserted in the Consensus but eventually had to abandon its efforts in the end in order to reach agreement. The question of restricting the use of tied aid credits (mixed credits) with a grant element below 25% underwent the same fate, as it was not possible to force

418

France to accept a prior notification procedure for transactions with a grant element above 15%.

3. The Arrangement (1978)

During 1977, the Consensus guidelines were adopted by most OECD countries. At the end of the year, however, it was evident that there were rather large differences of view on the Consensus as between the European Community and the United States. The United States wished to see the Consensus as a first step towards the reduction of export subsidization, while the Community hesitated to accept major changes in the existing guidelines, such as a matrix requiring higher interest rates or stricter rules for the use of mixed credits. At three meetings in rather quick succession, from December 1977 to February 1978, the present Arrangement was elaborated with much more detailed guidelines than the earlier Consensus. Throughout these meetings, the United States reserved on its participation in the still-being negotiated Arrangement, in hopes of reaching substantive change in the guidelines. In the end, the United States accepted that no changes in the matrix were able to be made, nor could any improvements on mixed credits or cost escalation be achieved, but found relief in the fact that a greater discipline was introduced by the detailed derogation and matching procedures in the Arrangement. In addition, rules were clarified on local cost financing, mainly in accordance with an old OECD agreement. Like the

Consensus, the Arrangement excluded certain categories of exports: military equipment, agricultural commodities, aircraft, nuclear power plants, and ships covered by the WP6 Understanding on export credit for ships. Special rules were stipulated on the treatment of prior commitments. On the whole, the Arrangement was regarded as a step forward as it was more comprehensive and more precise than the Consensus had been and constituted for the first time a uniform document to which all members of the ECG subscribed.

4. Post-Arrangement Efforts

The Arrangement has probably stabilized competition in official export credits, but unfortunately at a high level of official subsidization. It probably has also made competition more equal in some respects. In addition, there have been rather few outright derogations. Continuous efforts have been made during the three years of the Arrangement to make it a more effective instrument. This has mainly been done in the course of the annual reviews.

The efforts have been aimed specifically in four directions; namely, to change the interest rate matrix, to change the rules on mixed credits, to change the rules for special excluded sectors (which will be discussed in another section), and to find some acceptable rules for "side financing", i.e. commercial financing used in combination with official export credits in such a way that the total financial package exceeds one of the Arrangement guidelines.

420

(a) <u>The Interest Rate Matrix</u>. The United States has been especially interested in the first two points, and brought the Arrangement to a crisis at the end of 1978 when it asked for, among other things, an increase of the matrix minima of 0.50% to 0.75%. This request was resisted by the European Community, although average market interest rates had increased considerably since 1976 when the matrix was initially adopted. In the discussion on the matter, Austria strongly argued that the whole matrix concept with the same interest rates for all currencies without relation to the varying market rates of the different currencies involved was intellectually unsatisfactory and could not in the long run be made to work. At the same time, the inadequate definitions in the Arrangement of "interest rate" and "official support" were felt increasingly unsatisfactory.

At a moment when a total deadlock threatened, the Swedish delegation proposed that the group should try to study the problems of the present matrix, taking into account the Austrian views and the definitional problems. Another reason for such a study was the need to have more factual preparation undertaken by the OECD Secretariat between meetings. The Participants had great difficulty in making decisions at the meetings without adequate prior preparation and such preparation could be done only through Secretariat reports. After some hesitation, the proposal on an interest rate study was accepted and a mandate worked out, basically aimed at evaluating the matrix system, taking into account market rates, inflation, exchange risks, etc. The head of the Swedish delegation, Axel Wallen, one of the authors of this paper, was put in charge of the study.

The work on the report was done during 1979. A preliminary report on the outlines was discussed at a meeting of the group in May 1979. The report was completed in the second half of 1979 and discussed at a meeting in February 1980. The main conclusions of the report were not surprising. They indicated a relationship between exchange risk, inflation and market rates in such a way that high inflation currencies tended to have relatively high market interest rates and relatively low risk of appreciation against other currencies (low exchange risk), while the converse was true of low inflation currencies. According to the Arrangement matrix system then, countries with high inflation currencies and low exchange risk were allowed to subsidize more than others. A system with subsidization in relation to each market rate would obviously be more equal and would substantially reduce the amount of subsidization.

At the meeting in February 1980, the authors of the study were asked to expand some of the basic ideas. They did so in a short report which was discussed at the meeting in May 1980. Two basic ideas were presented: one more far reaching, providing for different minimum interest rates for each currency, based on market rates (the differentiated rate system or DRS), the other less radical, providing a single minimum interest rate for all currencies but one which would move automatically according to changes in average market rates (the uniform moving matrix or UMM).

At the meeting in May 1980, some participants gave their support to a DRS system, others to a UMM. The participants with low market rates -- below the matrix -- found advantages in the DRS. The European Community, however, did not want to indicate a clear preference. For the moment, a way out of the deadlock was found through the revision of the matrix by an increase effective from 1 July 1980 of 0.75% for rich and intermediate countries and 0.25% for poor countries, bringing the range of rates to 7.50% - 8.75%. This caused the matrix to look then (and still today) as follows:

	2-5 years	5-8.5 years	8.5-10 years
Relatively Rich	8.50%	8.75%	N/A
Intermediate	8.00%	8.50%	N/A
Relatively Poor	7.50%	7.75%	7.75%

It was also decided in May 1980 to continue the efforts to reach a mutually acceptable solution for adjusting the interest rates, with a deadline of 1 December 1980. Many participants, eager to find a definite solution based on the alternatives set forth in the interest rate study, attached great importance to this decision. This decision was later confirmed both at a meeting at the Ministerial level in the OECD in June 1980 and in the communique issued after the summit meeting in Venice at the end of June, which referred to a "solution covering all aspects of the Arrangement" including bringing the interest rates closer to market conditions.

After a meeting in early October, which was mainly devoted to technical discussions of the two alternatives, it was quite obvious that the only solution which then had a possibility of acquiring total support was a UMM solution. In the course of the autumn, however, it became more evident that the European Community would have great difficulties in reaching a common mandate. At the last moment before the deadline of 1 December, the Community gave the European Commission, its negotiating arm, a mandate based on an increase of the matrix of 1.0% for relatively rich and intermmediate countries and of 0.6% for relatively poor countries. At a meeting in the last days of November no agreement could be made, as the majority of Participants wanted a decision at least along the lines of a UMM, which the Community resisted. Participants agreed to "stop the clock" and meet a fortnight later to continue the discussions.

At the meeting in December a problem that had become more and more visible during the preceding half year became quite clear to every Participant. The problem related to currencies with market rates below the matrix. This problem surfaced dramatically when the Japanese found that an increase of the matrix along the lines proposed by the European Community would leave the Yen at market rates below the matrix or at least somewhere within the range. This would consequently mean that the Japanese interest rate subsidization scheme had to be abandoned. The Japanese delegation therefore proposed that Participants with market rates below the matrix should be entitled to provide subsidization of the same relative proportion that the high interest rate countries could provide. This is a variant of the DRS system suggested in the interest rate study, but the proposal was strongly rejected by all other Participants at the December meeting. After consultation with Tokyo, the Japanese delegation withdrew its request to be allowed to subsidize below Japanese market rates but insisted on being able to at least lend at Japanese market rates. It was evident that the Japanese and other Participants with below-matrix currencies wanted a clear statement in the Arrangement that their exports could be financed at market rates. This would be in addition to the practice -- never formally approved by the Participants but accepted in practice by all -- of permitting low-interest rate countries to offer insurance or guarantees only ("pure cover") at interest rates which could be below the matrix.

When the Participants were presented a draft pointing in this direction of permitting low interest rate countries to lend at their market rates, the United States, Canada and some smaller countries did not object, but the Community asserted that this would open the back door for a DRS and rejected the proposal. This meant a total failure to reach an agreement on any increase of the matrix minimum. This was unfortunate, as most market rates had risen tremendously during 1980 and thus the amount of subsidization had increased accordingly. Participants, however, agreed on a number of subjects to be further investigated and explored in the 1981 review session, scheduled for May 1981. Special attention was to be devoted to the submatrix problems, taking into account the structure and accessibility of the markets of the low interest rate countries.

(b) Mixed Credits. Another of the subjects on which the OECD Secretariat was asked in December 1980 to concentrate more preparatory work was the field of tied aid credits or mixed credits. As already mentioned, this subject has long been an intricate one, dating back to the negotiations on the "Gentlemen's Agreement."

According to established practice built on decisions within the OECD, "genuine aid" or official development assistance has been defined as a transaction in which the grant element, calculated in a prescribed way using a discount rate of 10%, amounts to at least 25% of the total value of the transaction. This grant element can be achieved, for example, by a suitable combination of low interest rate (say 3%), a long credit period (for example 15 years), and a "grace period" before amortization starts (for example 4 years). No objection has been raised to the fact that special rules should apply to genuine aid transactions and that such transactions should not in any way be regarded as commercial sales. It has therefore been accepted in the Arrangement that no prior notification need be given if a country intends to accept the heavy burden of providing credit which has a grant element of at least 25%. When discussing this matter in the early 1970s, it was obvious, however, that France had an aid scheme whereby it "mixed" official export credits and official aid on transactions to old French colonies and to some other developing areas, with a resulting grant element as low as 15%. France refused to accept a proposal from other countries who desired to be able to match the French mixed credits that all transactions with a grant element below the genuine aid level of 25% should be looked upon as commerical transactions and therefore notified in advance as a deviation from normal terms. The wish to make this change is shared by all participants outside the European Community, but to date it has not proved possible to negotiate this change.

In the last five years, many countries have started their own mixed credit schemes in order to offer the same possibility of winning attractive transactions with a relatively small amount of aid and thus circumvent the basic idea of the Arrangement. In light of this competitive deterioration, it will be interesting to see whether conditions for discipline might be better now than earlier.

(c) Side Financing. Side financing is private financing provided outside and above the official export credit and originates from the same country as the export.

In principle, there are no objections to private financing, but when it is provided over and above a heavily subsidized credit, the question has been raised whether international rules aimed at the equalization of subsidies should not be established for the use of side financing. Not all kinds of side financing have caused concern. Financing through banks without recourse to the exporter has generally been regarded as acceptable (e.g., a credit covering the down payment). On the other hand, there have been many negative comments regarding the use of double credits, whereby only the publicly supported credit is adapted to the Arrangement rules, and a second credit is privately financed or guaranteed by the exporter on terms that would violate the Arrangement if it were publicly supported. The problems of side financing are for the moment being analyzed within the Export Credit Group in a subgroup of experts under the leadership of Mr. Gilbert Morleghem of Belgium, a former chairman of the Export Credit Group.

II. TYPES OF EXPORT CREDIT PROGRAMS (Duff)

Export credit agencies come in many different shapes and sizes. One of the difficulties in reaching some form of harmonization of the different systems has been the tremendous degree of institutional difference among the various export credit agencies, as well as the resulting lack of knowledge of another country's system. Despite almost continuous meetings of the major export credit agencies, it

428

remains true that enormous gaps of information and knowledge separate one country from another.

1.   United Kingdom

The Export Credit and Guarantee Department (ECGD) of the Secretary of State for Trade of the U.K. Government is the grandfather of the export credit agencies and has in fact served as the model for other agencies. Formed in the 1920s, its purpose was to provide political and commercial risk insurance ("cover" as it is known in the trade) to exporters selling overseas. As an insurer, its approach tended towards spreading the risks assumed over many countries. The premium for the insurance was borne by the insured which normally passed it on to the buyer by increasing the price of the goods being sold by a like amount. Since ECGD was a risk-taker, its instincts were to keep exposure limited by insisting on short repayment terms, generally not exceeding five years.

This insurance business at ECGD has generally thrived over the years. The attempt at running it at no significant cost to the public "fisc" seems generally to have worked, although underwriting losses in recent years ($60.7 million in 1979, $265.4 million in 1980) have strained that goal somewhat. ECGD recently increased its premium rates in order to raise premium income about 15% in 1981.

Providing "cover" alone, however, has not proved sufficient from the point of view of export-dependent countries.

429

Foreign buyers want and generally need financing for their imports and they prefer, not surprisingly, financing bearing low interest rates fixed for the life of the loan. This preference for fixed-rate financing is particularly sharp today when most commercial lenders have adapted to the hardships of inflation by offering interest rates that vary or "float" with an agreed index. Borrowers have observed the difficulties of paying a spread over the U.S. prime rate or the London inter-bank offering rate when those indices have been as high as 20%. It may become one of the minor anomalies of our time that the only fixed-rate lending available will be from export credit agencies.

In any event, beginning in the 1960s, ECGD offered buyers subsidized fixed-interest rate loans. An option available to ECGD at that time was to extend the loans itself, acting like a bank such as the U.S. Eximbank. Given the background of ECGD as an insurer, it is perhaps not surprising that ECGD chose to remain a third-party to the transaction. Commercial banks would finance the transaction and the British Government (initially the Bank of England and later ECGD itself) would refinance it at subsidized rates.

This approach worked fairly well as long as commercial interest rates were not significantly higher than the refinancing rate ECGD felt necessary to maintain for competitive reasons. As rates rose in the late 1970s, the budgetary cost of the refinancing operation became quite high.

Understandably, the demand for 7.5% to 8.5% money at a time of 15% to 20% private rates was enormous.

Desiring to reduce the budgetary impact of ECGD, and also to reduce the growth of sterling-denominated claims against foreigners, in 1978 the U.K. Government offered a lower interest rate for foreign currency transactions (principally those denominated in U.S. dollars) than for sterling and, at the same time, abandoned the refinancing scheme for U.S. dollar deals. Instead, ECGD offered the commercial banks an "interest make-up" in dollars sufficient to enable the banks to charge interest rates of 7.5% to 8.5%. In 1980 the make-up scheme was extended to sterling. Today, therefore, the budget impact of export credit subsidization has been reduced in the sense that budgeted funds are not necessary to refinance a loan but only to subsidize its rate. That is not to imply a budget saving: the cost of the subsidy has risen from £220 million ($418.0 million) in 1978 to £357 million ($749.7 million) in 1979 to an expected £500 million ($1,150.0 million) in 1980. As interest rates have declined recently, the British appear to feel that they have weathered the worst and that the cost of the subsidization will be less over the next few years. Nonetheless they would appear to want to move the Arrangement minimum rates up somewhat.

2.   _France_

If cost were the criterion, the French system would win
all prizes. The interesting point, though, is that no one,
probably even including the French, really knows the cost of
the French system. The French seem to have concluded some
time after the first oil price rise in 1973-1974 that the
subsidization of exports through credits was a beneficial
government investment. They perhaps felt that it was
cheaper -- and more beneficial for the value of the franc --
to subsidize jobs through export credits than to subsidize
the absence of jobs through unemployment compensation. This
approach is consistent with the strong mercantilistic
tradition which France has followed at least since the days
of Colbert. Although the cost of this investment seems to
have more than doubled from something in the neighborhood of
$400 million in 1974 to approximately $1 billion in 1978
(and presumably even more in 1979 and 1980), the French
continue to view the investment as desirable.

COFACE provides political and commercial risk protection much the same way ECGD does. Funding comes either from
the commercial banks when the maturity is seven years or
less or from the Banque Francaise du Commerce Exterieur
(BFCE) when the maturity exceeds seven years. Both BFCE and
the commercial banks discount their loans with the French
central bank, Banque de France, at a discount rate, presently 3.5%. The amount of the loan eligible for discount
is set to arrive at an interest rate to the borrower equal

432

to the applicable minimum interest rate of the Arrangement. In addition to their strong philosophical aversion to raising the Arrangement minimum by more than a minor amount, the French, being conservative by nature, are always wary of international agreements that might change their administrative system or arguably reduce their exports.

The French system of subsidization is thus in some ways similar to the British, but the difference is that the subsidy does not appear as an expense in the French government budget. Rather, it appears in the first instance as money creation by the central bank, and, in the second instance, as lower central bank earnings for a given amount of money creation. The Banque de France has argued unsuccessfully for many years that it is difficult to control the money supply when there is an unknown but ever-increasing demand for export credit funds at 3.5%. Clearly the system entails an enormous real cost, even if the cost does not show up on the government budget. Some recent rumblings suggest that the refinancing mechanism might be modified and replaced by an interest make-up system similar to ECGD's. If this occurs, the amount of the subsidy may become more visible.

3.   United States, Canada and Japan

Other export credit agencies have structured themselves quite differently from the insurers and refinancers of Europe. The U.S. Export-Import Bank may have little to do with imports, but it is in fact a bank. Although it started offering insurance programs similar to those of Europe in 1961, in the main it still operates as a bank, lending money directly to the borrower. As a bank it looks at the viability of the project, employing a staff of loan officers, engineers and economists to assist in analyzing the technical aspects of a project and the ability of the borrower to repay the loan. Further, its bankish nature makes it inclined to operate at a "profit". In almost each of the last 20 years the Bank has had annual operating income in excess of $100 million. Since 1945 it has remitted dividends to its sole shareholder, the U.S. Treasury, slightly in excess of the $1 billion investment made by the Treasury in 1945. All these characteristics make Eximbank's approach to the business of export credits quite different from that of the Europeans.

The Canadian export credit agency, Export Development Corporation is, if anything, even more commercial than Eximbank. Its emphasis on attempting to lend at rates higher than its borrowing costs has, in recent years, forced EDC to offer longer repayment terms than permitted by the Arrangement in order to compensate for higher Canadian interest rates. Of course, when the competition learns of the longer terms offered by EDC, the competition offers to increase its repayment term to match, but regretably does not raise its interest rate to the higher Canadian rate.

The Japanese Export-Import Bank is modelled after the

434

U.S. version but is bigger and more active. Its assets of approximately $20 billion are funded by its revenues, by capital subscribed by the Japanese Government, and by borrowings from the Government's postal savings trust fund. These borrowings seem to be made at below government market rates so that the Japanese Eximbank can show an operating profit more easily than the U.S. Eximbank or EDC of Canada, which both borrow at government rates.

As bankers, the export credit agencies of the United States, Canada and Japan approach lending from similar vantage points. They are keen on project analysis and -- at least in the case of the United States and Canada -- offer repayment terms consistent with the economics of the project. As lending institutions, they are probably more sensitive than the insurers of Europe to the need to lend at rates higher than borrowing costs. Further, as lenders they are much more subject to budgetary constraints than the insurers of Europe. While this has not proved a serious constraint for an export-minded nation like Japan, it has severely limited the United States and Canadian export credit agencies.

4. Mixing of Export Credits with Development Aid

Many exporters in the United States and other countries have blasted the French for violating the terms of the Arrangement. Although there is undoubtedly some cheating around the edges of the Arrangement by a number of countries, many practices that are thought of as cheating are in fact sanctioned by the Arrangement. The principle example is the "mixed credit", a blending of a smaller part of development aid on highly concessionary terms (e.g., 3.5% per year interest rate, 20 year repayment term) with a larger part of export credit.

One can well ask why -- at a time when export credit rates are below those of the World Bank -- a device offering even more concessionary financing is required. The French argue that the amount of money they use each year on mixed credits is small (approximately $500 million for the aid portion) and that this small amount provides them dispropor- tionately large benefits. When former President Giscard went to Mexico or Brazil, he could lay on the table this form of concessionary financing amidst much fanfare. When another country subsequently tries to compete in Mexico or Brazil, it is confronted with the French mixed credit. A better price and product are rarely enough to counteract 3.5% money. The effectiveness of this device can be seen from the gradual adoption of such programs by other countries. In 1975, there were approximately five mixed credit pro- grams, including the French; today there are at least ten.

The United States has from time to time matched the French terms. In Cyprus, matching by the Eximbank enabled the U.S. exporter to win a contract which otherwise would have been out of reach. In Tunisia, the United States offered a line of credit to match the concessionary French terms. In Mexico, Eximbank retained its normal interest rate but extended its repayment term to 22 years to win a large railroad project that otherwise could well have gone to the French exporter who had the advantage of a mixed credit line.

The Canadians have recently announced a $750 million, three-year scheme of mixed credits to be used defensively against others. The United Kingdom has also come up with a small defensive war chest. Japan -- to the great consternation of all concerned -- has announced a new program of unspecified amount to match other countries' programs. Sweden, Norway, Spain and Holland all offer mixed credits of one form or another.

It seems clear that if the French agreed not to use mixed credits the practice would disappear, as every other country has adopted the practice for defensive reasons. The United States and most other countries have pressed hard for many years to eliminate or reduce mixed credits. But the only progress has been the step achieved in 1976 when mixed credits with a "grant element" (a measure of concessionality based upon a 10% discount rate) of less than 15% were required to be notified in advance of use. This prior notification enables other countries to match and seems to have had the effect of drying up mixed credits with a grant element of less than 15%. Since most export credits already retain a grant element of 7% to 8%, in one sense the more concessional a mixed credit the better: it costs the donor

437

more and is less likely to be confused with normal export credit.

The failure to achieve restraint through negotiations suggests that the mixed credit vehicle may be here to stay. Pressures in the U.S. Congress to devise some sort of fund for Eximbank to match mixed credits will undoubtedly abate during the present period of budget cutting, but will resurface as other countries are perceived to be stealing the business. The mixed credit is clearly a bad idea and it is regretable that such a bad idea survives and flourishes simply because one country thinks it is a good idea.

5.   Other Types of Export Credit Programs

In addition to insurance coverage, subsidized financing and mixed credits, many export credit agencies offer additional programs. The most popular is insurance protection against exchange risk. Almost every major agency other than the U.S. Eximbank offers some variation of exchange rate insurance. However, in recent years, notwithstanding the wide fluctuations among currencies, the usage of these prorams has been limited, suggesting that export credit agencies have priced these programs at high rates. For example, almost all such programs require the insured to bear the exchange risk for the first two years and to share in the risk if the fluctuation exceeds a defined band.

The other program offered which has attained some notoriety is the inflation insurance coverage offered by the

438

French and British. The idea is to protect the exporter against cost increases during production in excess of a certain percentage each year (6.5% in the case of the French, 7% for the British). Although the French program was quite attractive when established, restrictions adopted in 1977 have reduced demand somewhat. Whether this type of proram constitutes an unfair export subsidy is under review in the General Agreement on Trade and Tariffs (GATT).

The last two or three years have not seen a proliferation of new programs, but rather an increasing use of existing one. The recent high cost of operating the interest rate subsidies probably has forced agencies not to stretch their resources any further with new programs.

III. CURRENT PRESSURES RESTRAINING EXPORT CREDITS (Duff)

It appears that official export credits will be the last segment of the economic world to adjust to an inflationary world. While traditional long-term fixed rate lenders are shortening their maturities because of the risks of inflation, and while commercial banks have conditioned their borrowers worldwide to accept floating interest rates, official export credit agencies have ignored the world around them and instead have responded to "competitive" pressures by adhering to fixed interest rates well below current and anticipated market rates. Indeed, the minimum Arrangment rates are all now well below the standard World Bank rate. Australia and the United States, two rich

439

countries that are ineligible for World Bank assistance, can receive export credits at 8.75%, compared with the World Bank rate of 10.60%. A poorer country that is eligible to receive World Bank credits at 10.60% can obtain export credits at 7.75%.

In this topsy-turvy world, it is not surprising that some countries might experience budgetary and cost restraints. Perhaps none experiences these restraints more dramatically than the U.S. Eximbank. Eximbank has borrowed funds from the public (via the U.S. Treasury) and has endeavored to lend at rates slightly in excess of its borrowing costs. This worked well as long as the borrowing costs to the Bank were not significantly higher than the rates offered by other official export credit agencies. For many years the Bank was able to borrow at 5% or 6% and lend at 6% or 7%. So successful was the Bank that it earned $3 billion on the Treasury Department's original investment of $1 billion. In addition, it was able to structure its financing offers so that generally half the financing was provided by commercial banks at floating interest rates and the other half was provided by Eximbank at fixed rates. The resulting blended rate to the borrower was substantially equivalent to the all fixed-rate loans then being made by foreign official export credit agencies.

High inflation in the United States and concurrent high interest rates have made a shambles of the Eximbank's desire to operate in a commercial way and at the same time provide competitive offers.

On the one hand, Eximbank's borrowing costs have skyrocketed to 15% and the Bank has felt, with considerable evidence to support the view, that loans extended at rates of 15% or 16% would simply be non-competitive and would rarely if ever be accepted by a borrower. As a result, the Bank has felt constrained by competitive pressures to keep its lending rate much lower than its borrowing costs. Until July 1981 its lending rates had been 8.75% for non-aircraft transactions and 9.25% for aircraft transactions; in July 1981 those rates were raised to 10.75% and 12%, respectively.

One the other hand, the traditional sharing of the financing with the commercial banks does not provide a competitive package when commercial rates exceed 15%. The Bank has felt constrained to respond to this by increasing the amount of its participation from one-half up to all of the financing (after payment of the required 15% "cash payment" by the borrower).

This increased participation has resulted in tremendous strains upon the Bank's budget. Each year an annual limitation is adopted on the amount of loans that the Bank can authorize in that fiscal year. Since the Bank is included in the unified federal budget, disbursements under authorized loans result in budgetary outlays. Although disbursements do not generally occur in the same year as the loans are authorized, but rather occur in the three or four

441

succeeding years, the control of authorizations results in the control of disbursements in subsequent years. Thus a $1 billion cut in the authorization level for fiscal year 1981 would result in a reduction of the deficit of only approximately $80 million in fiscal 1981 and of $300 million in fiscal 1982.

Efforts to reduce federal expenditures are probably not a temporary phenomenon and therefore Eximbank will continue to face limitations created by budget presssures. Many argue that a different budget treatment of the Bank would result in greater resources. This appears to be a red herring. The Bank's budget properly should be controlled in some fashion and whatever the form of control the result will be some sort of rein on the Bank's lending authority.

The income constraints on the Bank are as severe as the budget pressures. As mentioned earlier, the Bank has enjoyed operating income of at least $100 million in almost every one of the last 20 years, but the Bank has announced its expectation that fiscal year 1982 will produce the first operating loss in the Bank's history. The Bank has capital and surplus of slightly more than $3 billion and it would take many years of losses before that reserve was depleted. Even after depletion the Bank could continue to operate by borrowing from the Treasury. As a practical matter, however, an institution that has survived for 40 years operating in a profitable fashion is not likely to be well regarded by any Administration or any Congress if it persistently

442

incurs losses. Despite competitive pressures, it would seem that Eximbank will be forced to raise its interest rates at least above its average cost of borrowings.

In light of these budget and income pressures, emphasis on finding a solution through negotiations has increased. A resolution has been introduced in the U.S. House of Representatives calling upon the President to "try to secure the agreement of other nations to reduce significantly the extent of export credit subsidies now granted" and to "make this issue a matter of high priority in our diplomatic and economic relations with the offending governments". The resolution suggests that the President should "consider employing whatever tools of trade policy stand at his disposal, consistent with domestic and international law, in order to counter and offset the economic consequences of excessive export credit subsidies granted by foreign governments, and to induce those governments to negotiate seriously to reduce those subsidies." The House resolution concludes that Eximbank "should establish as its first and dominant priority the use of its available resources to counter and offset the subsidies granted by those foreign governments, including the French, who have been most reluctant to negotiate a serious and meaningful reform" of the Arrangement. A similar resolution has been introduced in the U.S. Senate. Past exhortations to achieve success at the negotiating table had little effect on the European negotiating position. One can only hope for better success

443

in the future.

IV. STATUS OF SPECIAL SECTORS

The early negotiations on export credits focused on the aircraft and nuclear power sectors as the critical areas in which to seek harmonization. The difficulties in those sectors, however, proved so great that in the mid-1970s the negotiators threw up their hands and agreed to negotiate on all sectors but aircraft and nuclear. They went on to conclude the Gentlemen's Agreement in 1976, which is the basis for the current Arrangement, but had to exclude the aircraft and nuclear sectors from coverage. The exceptions remain to this day.

1. Aircraft (Duff)

There are two issues in the aircraft area, one involving large commercial jet aircraft and the other relating to all other commercial aircraft. The second issue deals with the rather narrow question of the appropriate repayment term for various types of aircraft. If a single-engine aircraft receives a repayment term of five years, should a multi-engine turbo-prop aircraft receive seven years? This inane issue has burdened the best and brightest minds in the export credit field. Hours, days and years have been spent on this subject and the classification system remains approximately where it was in 1975: seven years for large turbo-props and five years for everything else, although the

444

United States decided in 1978 that all turbo-props should receive a repayment term of seven years. This high degree of differentiation among various aircraft may have made some sense at a time when there was no general agreement on export credit terms, but since then the Arrangement has established general rules. The simplest and most sensible approach in the future would be to treat all but the large commercial jets as governed by the principles of the Arrangement. The savings in government travel budgets alone would be worth it.

The solution to the problem of the large commercial aircraft is much more difficult, yet oddly enough is an area which holds much promise. The governing rule is that of the 1975 OECD "Standstill" by which the major participants agreed not to offer more concessionary terms than were being offered at that time, generally up to 90% cover and repayment terms of 10 years for sales and 12 years for leases. The principle competition in the sale of airframes is between the United States and the European Airbus consortium, while in engines the principal competition is between the United States and Roll Royce of the United Kingdom. Informal rules of the road have been worked out for the engine competition, providing market-related interest rates. Discussions on the airframe competition towards a similar goal were slow in commencing but have moved quite far along in the last year. In the early years of the Airbus consortium, market penetration was all important to the success of the venture. As a result, the European governments that launched the consortium, namely the French and the Germans (more recently joined by the British), were not reluctant to offer financing at highly concessionary terms. One of the most celebrated cases involved Eastern Airlines which received several A-300 aircraft under one of the "wettest" leases of all times: no rent. In third country markets where U.S. aircraft competed, Airbus financing was no less attractive.

The U.S. response to this demarche came at a time when the United States balance of trade was highly unfavorable, when political winds were blowing in favor of exports, and when for the first time the principal U.S. capital goods export -- aircraft -- was facing real competition from overseas. Eximbank policy was to match the competition's official financing; not to improve upon it, but simply, if possible, to neutralize it. The Europeans were not in the beginning disposed to let Eximbank know what financing they were offering. In other sectors the system for exchanging information among the participants in the Arrangement worked fairly well, but aircraft as an excluded sector was not subject to the same rules. The Europeans either were not answering their mail from the United States or were simply saying "We have not been approached." Given this silence, Eximbank often had to assume that what the U.S. exporter and foreign buyer were saying about the Airbus financing offer was in fact true.

After a series of head-to-head competitive transactions, some won by the United States, some by the Europeans, the European side showed for the first time an interest in mitigating the budget cost of this competition. The Europeans began to find some value in the notion that, if each side intended to match the other, the matching might better occur at interest rates that would not be excessively costly. A dialogue began which continues to this day. The dialogue suggested a willingness on the Airbus side to reduce the level of subsidy by raising interest rates and reducing the amount of official financing. This willingness was demonstrated on August 3, 1981 when William H. Draper, III, the newly appointed Chairman of the Eximbank, announced that "new guidelines for official financing of commercial jet aircraft exports have been developed through successful discussions with European export credit agencies". He further stated, "The United States, France, Germany and the United Kingdom are each unilaterally increasing their export credit rates for competing aircraft and harmonizing their aircraft financing policies to reduce export credit subsidies. We regard the successful conclusion of our informal discussions on aircraft exports to be a major breakthrough in our continuing effort to limit export subsidization."

The new guidelines call for a minimum interest rate of 12% for credits denominated in U.S. dollars, 11.50% for credits denominated in French francs and somewhat lower than that depending on market conditions for credits denominated

447

in German Deutsche marks. Since the great majority of financing of aircraft exports is denominated in U.S. dollars, the dollar rate is the critical one. This understanding on aircraft represents a major advance in the negotiations on export credits: for the first time a minimum interest rate has been established for large commercial jet aircraft; moreover that interest rate is much closer to market rates than any other minimum rate applicable under the Arrangement. The U.S. Government has strong hopes that this breakthrough presages a willingness on the European side to raise interest rates in the overall Arrangement context.

The aircraft guidelines are also unusual in that they reduce the amount of direct credit support from the current 85% to 62.5% for official redits which are repaid over the full ten years of the repayment period (the traditional European repayment method) or 42.5% where the official credit is repaid over the last five years of the period (the traditional Eximbank approach). Either side may offer 62.5% or 42.5% of credit support as long as the appropriate repayment system is used. The understanding also imposes limitations on the amount of spare engines and spare parts which may be financed and provides for periodic reviews of its terms.

Finally, the aircraft guidelines break additional new ground in that they contemplate a serious look at the question of whether financing of aircraft on longer terms at

market rates might not be the best solution. Although the
European side has considerable political and technical
difficulties with longer terms, there could be benefits to
both sides from using longer terms at market rates.

The U.S. aerospace industry has suggested for some time
that longer repayment terms with market interest rates could
solve the aircraft sector's financing problems. One technique discussed is the equipment trust certificate, interna-
tionalized to permit the Europeans to use it as well.
Traditional equipment trust financing is a device that
enables many lenders to share in the security of a lien on
personal property (usually rolling stock in the railroad
industry). Regrettably (from the point of view of saving
government resources), lenders on international aircraft
transactions are not looking at the lien of the aircraft for
their security (if they were, they would not need export
credit agency participation); rather they are looking at the
guaranty of the export credit agency. The idea of shifting
aircraft support from direct loans to guarantees nonetheless
has much appeal, but it creates difficulties as well.
Longer repayment terms than currently followed are said to
be required; that is, 15 or 18 years instead of the now
standard 10 year maturity. A more iron-clad guaranty than
the one used by Eximbank is also said to be required.
Finally, it is said that Eximbank will need increased
guaranty authority to adopt this approach. The new aircraft
understanding will, however, provide a suitable environment

449

within which to discuss these and other ideas involving longer repayment terms for aircraft.

2. Nuclear Power Plants (Wallen)

One of the sectors to which the Arrangement does not apply is nuclear power plants. The Arrangement states that the terms of the 1975 OECD Standstill shall apply to nuclear power plants.

This Standstill has its origin in a discussion on different sector agreements that was held within the ECG Export Credits Groups during the first years of the 1970s. At that time, nuclear power plants represented a comparatively new product, and members thought that international discipline could be established before market conditions had been stabilized or a credit race had begun. (This was also the reason why a special agreement was made for ground satellite stations limiting repayment terms to eight years.) But nuclear power plants are enormously expensive and the first ones to be sold had high contract values and long credit terms. Here as in other fields the Europeans were inclined to push for shorter credit periods than the United States. The European Community sought a maximum repayment term of 10 or 12 years while the United States argued for a maximum credit period of at least 15 years.

After lengthy deliberations, a consensus on a Standstill was reached in 1975. All interested parties agreed to apply their best endeavors to reach a sector arrangement for nuclear power plants. To avoid a deterioration of credit terms in the meantime, the members of Export Credits Group agreed not to grant softer terms for nuclear power stations than their current practices. In practice this has meant financing up to 85%-90% of the contract and repayment terms up to 15 years. Matching is of course allowed.

Since the demand for nuclear power plants has diminished greatly in the last two years, the few new orders placed each year are intensely fought over. Intense competition, plus the large amounts required for each contract, have caused export credits for nuclear power plants to constitute large portions of Eximbank's annual authorizations. Presumably this is also true for the other principal players in the nuclear game, France, Germany and Canada.

3.   Ships (Wallen)

The evolution of international discussions and common guidelines on export credits for ships has had great relevance for the development of the Arrangement. In 1969, the Understanding on Export Credits for Ships was adopted within the OECD. The United States did not take part in the discussions within Working Party 6 (WP6) and has not become a member of the Understanding. There are various reasons for U.S. abstention, but one was the absence of U.S. exports of ships. The Understanding was changed several times during the 1970s. Originally, the maximum credit length was 8 years, the minimum downpayment was 20%, and the minimum

451

interest rate was 6%. During the late 1970s, the corresponding guidelines specified 7 years repayment term, a 30% minimum downpayment and an interest rate of not less than 8%. From 1 December 1979, the maximum credit length was changed to 8.5 years and the minimum downpayment back to 20%. The 1979 changes were not mainly made to reflect increasing problems in the shipbuilding market -- which are really not new -- but were more connected with the development of the Arrangement. When the Arrangement was established in 1978, it was necessary to draw a borderline between the export of ships and the export of goods in general, as the existing Understanding on ships could not easily be abandoned. Therefore it was stipulated in the Arrangement that terms of the Arrangement should not apply to ships covered by the OECD Understanding on Export Credits for Ships. But the Arrangement also stated that Participants should apply the terms of the Arrangement to ships not covered by the Understanding on ships (for example ships below 100 gross tons), and it was further stated in the Arrangement that if a Participant intends to support terms for any type of ship to which the Understanding applies which could be more favorable than the terms permitted by the Arrangement, the Participant should give prior notification to all other Participants of such terms.

The ensuing distinction between ships covered by the Understanding and other kinds of goods has created problems. While the Understanding did not permit the sale of a large

452

tanker at longer credit than 7 years (now 8.5) and with a smaller downpayment than 30%, (now 20%), it was possible to sell a small fishing vessel to a developing country on 10 year terms and with as little as 15% downpayment. In fact, during the crisis within the shipbuilding field, most exports of ships to LDC's have been made at aid credit terms and the differences between the Understanding and the Arrangement have played a relatively small role. Nevertheless, over the years strong demands for harmonization of terms have been heard, and it seems that the withdrawal of Spain from the Understanding has at least one root in the fact that ships are not covered by the Arrangement.

The efforts made within WP6 to transform the Understanding to conform to the Arrangement (or to abandon the Understanding) have not been entirely successful. To an important degree this stems from the fact that shipowners can easily change flags. If a factory in a European industrialized country wishes to buy equipment, it must import it to the place where the factory is situated. This means, among other things, a maximum credit length of 5 years under the Arrangement. But a shipowner always can have a branch in an LDC, which, according to the Arrangement, could buy a ship at a credit term of 10 years. For this reason there is only one rule on the maximum credit length for ships in the Understanding, namely 8.5 years.

But it cannot be denied that the exclusion of ships from the Arrangement creates many problems. WP6 has devoted much time and trouble in trying to draw exact borders between different types of floating objects, for example, drilling rigs with or without their own propelling machinery. Such useless work would be unnecessary if common rules could be adopted. Another problem is that all major countries in Europe and Japan adhere to the Understanding, while the United States does not.

V. ATTEMPTS TO LINK EXPORT CREDITS WITH OTHER ISSUES (Duff)

Export credit agencies have from time to time gone "off cover" in a country for reasons of creditworthiness. In recent years, Turkey, Zaire, Peru, Nicaragua and Poland, among others, have seen a slowdown or cessation of export credits as they tried to work their way through difficult economic times. In addition, many countries of the world never receive export credits because their level of economic activity and creditworthiness are so low that exporters find little demand for their goods and, even when they do, credit insurers and lenders are unwilling to take the risk.

In recent years attempts have been made to reduce or eliminate export finance in certain countries solely for political rather than economic reasons. The prime example is the provision inserted in the U.S. Eximbank's charter in the late 1960s prohibiting any loans to Communist countries without a Presidential determination that the loans are in the national interest (Section (2)(b)(2) of the Eximbank statute, found at 12 U.S.C. 635(a)). With the advent of

454

detente in the early 1970s and the Nixon-Kissinger view that both competition and cooperation with the Soviet Union were necessary elements of U.S. policy, President Nixon determined in 1973 that it was in the national interest for Eximbank to extend credits to the Soviet Union. For a brief period Eximbank accomplished the goal that gave rise to its creation in 1934 by President Roosevelt: the expansion of U.S.-Soviet trade. The Bank extended credits amounting to $469 million before passage of the Trade Act of 1974, which contains the Jackson-Vanik Amendment. This Amendment bars the extension of Eximbank credits to a non-market exonomy country which prohibits its citizens from emigrating freely unless the President of the United States finds that a waiver of the prohibition will help the objectives of the Act and receives assurances that the emigration practices meet the requirements of the Act. Given the current atmosphere between the two countries and the cutback in Eximbank resources, it is hard to imagine an early opening of U.S. Eximbank credits to the Soviet Union.

The situation with the People's Republic of China is entirely different. The rapprochement with the PRC which was carried forward by the Carter Administration brought with it a Presidential determination that Eximbank credits to the PRC were in the national interest. Vice President Mondale went to China in August 1979 and indicated that up to $2 billion of Eximbank credits were available over a five year period. Fortunately from the Bank's budgetary point of view, the great buildup in China has dramatically slowed and the demand for Eximbank resources has been small. In fact, although several preliminary commitments were issued by the summer of 1981, no credits had been authorized by the Bank.

Other Presidential determinations have been made under the Bank's statute to permit credits to certain Communist countries: Yugoslavia (1968), Romania (1971), Poland (1972), and Hungary (1978).

Other countries have been effectively off limits to the Bank from time to time for political reasons. During the U.N. sanctions, it was illegal for U.S. exporters to sell to Rhodesia and hence Eximbank support was non-existent in that market; today Zimbabwe is an open market for the Bank. A 1978 amendment to the Bank's charter bars Eximbank assistance to the South African Government and limits such assistance to South African private enterprises that are able to meet certain criteria such as equal pay for equal work. The U.S. Secretary of State must certify that these criteria are met; to date no enterprise in South Africa has received certification.

The idea has thus grown up, principally in the United States, that export credits are a benefit conferred by government. Since this benefit is not available as an entitlement program, important policy objectives not directly related to the narrow field of export credits could be served by linking export credits to other desired goals of the U.S. Government. This notion reached its peak in the human rights movement, but before discussing that linkage it might be worth pointing out a narrower but nonetheless important qualification on the use of Eximbank credits.

Since 1968, the Bank's statute in one form or another has required the Board of Directors, in considering whether to authorize a loan or guarantee, to taken into account "any serious adverse effect of such loan or guarantee on the competitive position of United States industry, the availability of materials which are in short supply in the United States, and employment in the United States" (Section 2 (b)(1)(B)). This provision requires the Eximbank Board of Directors to balance the negative effect on the U.S. economy from any output of the project imported back into the United States against the benefits derived by the U.S. economy. A steel case in Trinidad and Tobago in 1977-78 prompted a bill in the U.S. Congress that would have prohibited Eximbank support for the project, the output of which might return to the United States, if a surplus of that type of output existed in the United States. This bill was defeated in 1978 by a handful of votes in the House of Representatives. Hence, the balancing provision of 1968 remains as the standing guidance for the Board of Directors. The 1978 initiative was probably defeated because, in almost every case, the project will go forward whether or not Eximbank supports it, usually with export finance from other countries. Thus any negative effect on the U.S. economy will occur whether or not Eximbank supports the transaction. But benefits to the United States will occur only if the U.S. exporter is successful, and this will usually happen only if Eximbank supports the transaction.

Whenever world economic growth slows down, pressures in all industrialized countries increase to keep out "harmful" imports. These imports are particularly galling to protectionist sentiment if their production has in part been financed by official credits supplied by the importing country. While the U.S. Eximbank may be the only export credit institution with a specific statutory mandate, most export credit agencies must look carefully when they are financing projects resulting in imports to their own economies. None of them, however, lives in quite the public fishbowl that houses the U.S. Eximbank.

The most celebrated issue linked to export credits is "human rights". In 1977, the U.S. Eximbank's statute was amended to require that "...the Board of Directors... shall also take into account, in consultation with the Secretary of State, the observance of and respect for human rights in the country to receive the exports supported by a loan or financial guarantee and the effect such export may have on human rights in such country" (Section 2(b)(1)(B)). The practical workings of the statute meant that all transactions had to be cleared by the State Department for human rights considerations. Only a very few transactions were actually turned down for human rights reasons. A much publicized Argentinian transaction was deferred because of

U.S. concern for human rights, and this handling created tremendous notoriety in Argentina.

In 1978, the Congressional proponents for a stronger provision on human rights in the Eximbank charter moved to prohibit Eximbank loans to any country that violated human rights. This provision was resoundingly defeated. Out of the legislative debate emerged a provision that had the effect of almost eliminating human rights as a factor to be considered by Eximbank. The substitute provision reads:

> Only in cases where the President determines that such action would be in the national interest and where such action would clearly and importantly advance United States policy in such areas as international terrorism, nuclear proliferation, environmental protection and human rights, should the Export-Import Bank deny applications for credit for nonfinancial or noncommercial considerations. [Section 2 (b)(1)(B)].

This provision is the opposite of the original human rights approach since only in a most extraordinary case, one requiring Presidential determination (now delegated to the Secretary of State), can the Eximbank deny a transaction for other than financial or commerical reasons. The only instance where a Presidential determination has been made under this provision was in 1980 in connection with the U.S. investigation of the murder of the Chilean diplomat Orlando Letelier. The U.S. Government had requested the Government of Chile to extradite individuals who were alleged to be implicated in the murder. When the Supreme Court of Chile refused to permit such extradition, the U.S. Government responded by, among other things, making a determination that it was in the national interest for Eximbank to cease

459

extending credits to Chile. One of the early acts of the Reagan Administration was to rescind this action so that Chile is now eligible for Eximbank support.

The human rights issue had a short, meteoric life as it touched Eximbank. Even ardent proponents of linkage between human rights and export credits came to wonder whether it provided much leverage over another country's actions. Thoughtful observers have questioned whether a human rights policy conducted through newspaper headlines can ever be effective. Whatever the merits of the human rights campaign, its public linkage to the availability of export credits was not particularly helpful.

Another great movement of the 1970s spilled over into the export credit field. Environmentalists had been exercised for some time that Eximbank credits were not receiving proper environmental review. In the late 1960s, the United States had passed a law, the National Environmental Policy Act (NEPA), calling for an environmental review prior to the taking of any major federal action. The review was called an "environmental impact statement"; these statements gave all concerned parties the opportunity to assess the environmental impact of each proposed major action by the U.S. Government. Until the mid-1970s, no one claimed that NEPA was meant to cover acts of the U.S. Government taking place outside the boundaries of the United States. But in late 1976, Eximbank was sued by an environmental group which alleged that Eximbank should adopt procedures to ensure that environmental effects were considered in its decision-making process and should publish environmental impact statements before authorizing loans or guarantees, to borrowers in foreign countries. The lawsuit forced the U.S. Executive Branch to agree on a uniform position. After a year of internal negotiations, a compromise was reached resulting in the issuance of an Executive Order by President Carter (Executive Order 12114 issued January 4, 1979). The effect of the Order is to require Eximbank to review the environmental consequences of a proposed loan or guarantee only in a limited number of cases. The Order thus represents a fair compromise between two different objectives: environmental protection and export credits.

VI.   SECURITY REQUIREMENTS (Duff)

An area of export credit competition which has not been addressed in international harmonization efforts to date -- and which would probably elude resolution -- is the question of security requirements. In other words, what form of guarantee or other security will the export credit agency require as a condition of going forward with a particular transaction? In addition to undercutting the competition's interest rate, an export credit agency can also ask for less in the way of security. This has gone on to some extent in the past, but by and large the differences in security requirements among competing export credit agencies have tended to flow mainly from different historical and

461

institutional perspectives rather than from a desire to undercut the competition.

The Europeans, having come to the business as insurers, for example, have tended not to analyze the economics and cash flow of a project but simply to satisfy themselves that they were doing business in a country that was an acceptable risk. If they spread that risk among many acceptable countries, their chances of coming up short were not too worrisome. The United States, Canada, and Japan on the other hand have tended to be much more security conscious and have worried about the viability of each project. Even where they were protected by a government guarantee, experience showed that severe difficulties could arise with a bad project in a creditworthy country.

The post-Iranian world will undoubtedly find more emphasis on requiring sovereigns to waive their immunity, to agree to the lender's domestic law as the governing law, and to submit to the lender's jurisdiction. This will come at a time when many government-related borrowers are being instructed by their governments to borrow on their own without benefit of the government guaranty. More and more large projects are being presented -- particularly in Latin America -- without home government backing.

In the shakier and more debt-prone world of the 1980s, reschedulings will at least continue apace and will probably increase. The Paris Club rescheduling system has worked quite well; by and large it is an accepted and flexible

462

procedure. Clearly, however, the extension of export credits in the 1980s will be a riskier business than before. Security conditions will become correspondingly more important.

VII. OUTLOOK FOR THE 1980s (Wallen)

1. Possibility of International Agreement

Economic events in the 1970s, especially the successive large increases in the price of oil, have drastically altered export conditions for the industrialized countries. These events have increased the competition and at the same time made exporting more hazardous. Although the Middle East and other oil rich countries have become bigger and better markets than before, most developing countries and the Eastern European countries have not expanded their import capabilities at the same pace. Thus at a time when exporting has become even more important to most western countries -- to solve their own balance of payments problems -- many traditional markets have become relatively weak.

It might seem that this development would increase the willingness among the main exporting countries to cooperate in avoiding a self-defeating export credit race, from which no one would gain but the buyers. And to some degree this was the case in the middle of the 1970s. The purpose behind the Consensus and the Arrangement was clearly stated to be the prevention of a credit war. But one can question whether this purpose has been achieved. In many cases, the

Consensus and the Arrangement have prevented the lengthening of credit periods on medium-size transactions, especially to industrialized countries and to Eastern European countries. The Consensus and Arrangement have probably also prevented competition leading to even lower interest rates than the minima of the matrix.

Experience with the Consensus and Arrangement is not, however, completely positive. The reasons are varied. To begin with, one immediate result of agreement on common guidelines was to increase the degree of subsidization. Even countries that had not earlier subsidized interest rates or had not subsidized so extensively, felt forced by the acceptance of the guidelines to enable their exporters to offer finance at the guideline minimum rates.

As market rates have become much higher over time, the general volume of subsidization has further increased. This volume might not have been so large without the Consensus and Arrangement. The rigidity of these agreements has perhaps eliminated a natural adjustment of export credit rates to market interest rates. On the other hand, in many individual cases the Consensus may have eliminated a real credit race.

Another problem with the present guidelines stems from various technical inefficiencies. Most participants express satisfaction that derogations have been quite limited over the years. But the discipline of giving prior notification does not always work. According to the guidelines, participants should give prior notification as soon as they "intend" to support terms deviating from the guidelines. But it has happened that prior notification is not given until a firm commitment has taken place, for example by signing a contract or letter of intent. The basic purpose of the prior notification procedure -- namely, to discourage derogations because of the possibility of matching -- can be destroyed if notification is withheld. And this threat now grows progressively greater.

Other technical inefficiencies could be mentioned. More interesting, however, are the fundamental imperfections existing within the Arrangement that create the gravest doubts regarding its justification and its future.

As mentioned earlier, there has been a long fight whether and to what degree mixed credits should be excepted from the derogation procedures. As a consequence of European Community resistance, the present guidelines still accept a prompt notification procedure, even when the grant element is as low as 15%. (Prompt notification usually amounts to notification after the contract is signed.) This means that, whenever a participant really wants its exporter to win a contract in a developing country, it can achieve that goal comparatively cheaply by adding a 7-8% grant element to the permitted level of Arrangement subsidization. This can be easily accomplished by reducing the minimum interest rate level or by lengthening the credit period. Thus, the use of mixed credits with a 15% to 25% grant element is rapidly spreading among Participants. With greater use, this comparatively easy way to act against the spirit of the Consensus becomes increasingly difficult to give up.

It is deplorable that it has not, so far, been possible to eliminate the mixed credit. This sad development poses a mortal threat to the basic Consensus concept, namely that all Participants should in their own common interest agree not to go beyond certain minima and maxima terms except in very special cases. And in those special cases matching should be allowed or "genuine aid" should be involved. According to the basic Consensus concept, in normal cases export credit subsidization should be equalized between Participants, and price and quality should serve as the decisive factors.

We are approaching the heart of the matter when we find that different Participants may have accepted the Consensus and Arrangement with different aims. While most Participants seem to have thought that export credit subsidization should be abandoned as a competitive weapon, and have found it natural to accept the burden of concerted action and discipline to reach this goal, other Participants may have wished the system to allow circumvention whenever their own export industry might thereby derive an advantage. As long as the system has such "holes in the net," it may be doubted whether the Arrangement is worth retaining; and in a period when circumvention is spreading this doubt grows. The

466

effort to reach a harmonization of subsidy levels has by now become quite costly -- since the cost depends on the difference between market and minimum interest rates. One can wonder whether these costs are justified if some Participants use circumvention as an additional competitive weapon. Further doubt as to the viability of the Arrangement arises since its present structure favors those Participants who engage in circumvention: circumvention yields greater gains when other Participants loyally live up to the basic Consensus concept. More and more Participants are becoming aware of the advantages of circumvention and are starting, for example, mixed credit schemes of their own.

Mixed credits are not the only fundamental problem for the application of the Consensus. Even more sophisticated and more difficult to analyze is so-called side financing. Side financing is private financing or other private arrangements provided outside and above the official support. If subsidization did not exist, side financing would be quite ordinary and quite acceptable financing; it would reflect the economic strength of the exporter and the price and quality of his offer. But when side financing enters into a field where heavy subsidization is already used, it can upset the basic concept underlying maxima and minima terms for length of credit, downpayment, and interest rate. As stated before, this concept is the approximate equalization of the export credit weapon between competitors. There is an essential difference between private financial arrangements in a case where a platform of official subsidization already exists, and in a case where such subsidization does not exist. In the one case, private provenders of side finance can look to an additional source of indirect security that arises from the soft terms of the official export credit agency and therefore the greater capability of the exporter of the project to service the private loan; in the other case, private provenders of side finance can only look to the security of the exporter and the project. This difference between the two cases is not generally accepted. Some Participants believe that private side financing is acceptable irrespective whether there is official support or not. But when a Participant supports an export transaction formally on Arrangement terms, but at the same time allows side financing in such a way that the cash payment or the length of credit are non-conforming, the Participant seems to circumvent the Arrangement.

For this reason some variants of side financing have been especially discussed, namely, those in which the exporter combines officially supported financing with non-supported financing to produce an especially favorable credit package. The dubious feature of these combinations is the fact that export credit insurers, who normally supervise the observance of Arrangement rules on credit length, are misled when they cover only one of two combined financing contracts. Hopefully, the Export Credits Group will find means to stop the use of such deceptive arrangements.

So far, only a few countries have tried to regulate side financing that involves recourse to the exporter. No country intends to limit the role of international banks in arranging side financing that involves no recourse to the exporter. Those Participants who would like to limit at least some variants of side financing probably also believe that a reduction of subsidization would alleviate the abuse of side financing. In the eyes of those Participants, the present large degree of subsidization, which results from the rigid minimum interest matrix and the generally very high market interest rates, creates the basic problem.

These technical and fundamental problems within the Arrangement -- the inefficiencies in discipline, the rigidity, Participants' different aims, the "holes in the net" involving mixed credits and side financing -- might lead to the conclusion that the Arrangement is a compromise that does not in any relevant respect achieve the general aim of reducing subsidization. The basic compromise between European low interest rates and American long credit terms was, from this point of view, questionable. And the low level of the interest rate matrix, which created a demand for subsidization down to that level and which forced many Participants to introduce schemes to match others' subsidies, was another doubtful result. Finally, the rigidity of the Arrangement, especially the matrix, is most questionable.

The Consensus was built on the assumption of approximate equalization of subsidies. One may argue (as has been done in the OECD interest rate study) that nothing can be as self-destructive to this goal as the maintenance of subsidization at an unchanged high level. In our opinion, the introduction of the Consensus created, as a natural and logical consequence, the need for progressive steps to reduce the element of subsidization. But these steps have not been taken, leaving all Participants providing high subsidies without thereby gaining anything but the sometimes doubtful assurance that other Participants will adhere to a very costly and self-destructive subsidization.

What is then the outlook for the Arrangement over the coming years? After reviewing all the negative aspects, one might conclude that we will soon see the end of our Arrangement. If there is no success in changing the Arrangement for the better in the relatively near future, the Participants should explore the possibility of taking quite new initiatives, perhaps bilaterally or with the exclusion of some countries. The prospect of reaching a better result in a smaller Concensus group are, however, not bright. All buyers will know that those countries who would not take part in the new Consensus could extend soft credit terms that had to be matched by others. In other words, the problem that exists today with Brazil and South Korea, countries that are outside the Arrangement, would be greatly magnified.

470

Most Participants probably view a total abandonment of common guidelines in the export credit field as a worse alternative than keeping the present Arrangement. This general feeling gives a strong position to those Participants who see the Arrangement more as a means to realize their own aims than as a means to reach common goals.

We can see various different scenarios ahead. The most probable seems to be the survival of a rather weak Arrangement. Hopefully the Participants will solve the sub-matrix problems mentioned at the beginning of our paper. This might in turn lead to an increase of the matrix rates. Of course, a vast majority of the Participants would like to see an automatically moving matrix, but for the moment such an arrangement seems far away. The structural and definitional problems may not be impossible to overcome for most Participants, but for the Community, even a formal recognition of the "pure cover" concept might create problems.

The fundamental mixed credit problem ought to be solved by increasing the grant element below which prior notification should be given. But this is not easy to achieve. The present spread of mixed credit systems can lead in two directions: (1) The most reasonable but surely not the most probable outcome is that all Participants will see the self-destructive results of the present combination of high subsidization and easy circumvention and will then agree to change the present system; or (2) No such reasonable conclusion will be reached and we will continue a rather

471

disappointing credit race in which official export credits increasingly displace true aid and World Bank lending. The increasing risk is that, as LDCs and aid officials become accustomed to mixed credit arrangements, and as those arrangements gather support from the export community, there will be no strong compulsion to change the present system.

We have hardly touched the problem of the transfer of resources to LDCs. Yet this is a major problem, since both France and Japan largely defend their present attitudes by the fact that the LDC markets are weak and that providing credit at soft terms is better than pushing certain LDCs to earlier default by harder terms. This method of reasoning may seem attractive. One can nevertheless doubt whether a growing mixture of trade and aid is the most reasonable answer to the payment problems of LDCs, especially if it leads to a weakening of the World Bank and a reduction of a genuine bilateral aid.

What would happen if the Arrangement were totally abandoned is an open question. Without the Arrangement, a credit race might well emerge of a different type than the one which existed before the era of the Consensus. The worst thing, perhaps, is that it would start from a higher level of subsidization than existed some years ago -- a level created by the Consensus itself. A new credit race might lead to a lengthening of credit periods and the use of "grace periods". Minimum interest rates are already so low that a rapid race in this area is perhaps not so much to be

472

feared.

But in relation to LDCs, a lengthening of credit periods and more frequent use of grace periods would mean the same as more use of mixed credits close to the 15% grant element level. Thus, one can well imagine a scenario where the Arrangement remains formally "alive" but in reality has no restraining effect in LDC markets. The main difference between an "alive" if moribund Arrangement, and no Arrangement, is that when the Arrangement is still valid Participants will receive information through the prompt notification mechanism about all mixed credit cases. As this example illustrates, probably the most positive feature in maintaining the Arrangement is the valuable transparency which it provides.

2.   Official Insurance and Credit-worthiness

As a natural consequence of the economic environment of the 1970s, the overall debt of LDCs and Eastern Europe increased drastically. We have briefly touched upon this problem in the context of the Arrangement. This development has caused payment problems in many countries and debt reschedulings have become more frequent in recent years. In many cases, deficits have become so large that countries cannot fulfill their obligations even with long postponements. This development has led in turn to claims for insurance against protracted default and other political risks. Many of the official insurance institutions now show accumulated deficits, and the reserve position is very weak in some of the smaller institutions. According to GATT rules, which were reinforced by the Agreement on Subsidies and Countervailing Measures, these circumstances should lead to a serious reconsideration of present underwriting policies and possibly a reduction in high risk insurance. As this would imply a reduction in export possibilities it is not very likely that governments would let their insurance institutions drastically decrease their activity. On the other hand, the general economic decline of many markets should to some extent influence the willingness of official institutions to take risks -- otherwise the losses will probably soon become too heavy a burden on governmental budgets.

As in export credit subsidization the large exporting countries' underwriting policies are diverging. Also it seems that some countries are prepared to accept much worse risks than others. As in export financing, the countries with the biggest economic problems at home may lead the race, with a majority of competitors not far behind.

The most probable outlook is that most industrialized export countries will continue to write very risky export credit insurance activities, with consequent heavy subsidization in this field as well as in the finance field. In the short term, governments may find it preferable to produce and export goods to high risk markets than to accept immediate unemployment.

VIII. POSSIBLE U.S. OPTIONS (Duff)

Export credits appear more and more like a runaway horse which the industrial nations are willing to ride wherever it takes them. Total capital good exports financed through officially-supported export credits have increased fourfold over the last decade. Due to the high market rates of interest in recent years and the practice followed by many industrial nations of offering export credits at the Arrangement minimum rates, the subsidy factor has increased sharply. Although this has caused the most committed subsidizers to become a little more interested in basic reform, the only changes these governments seem willing to countenance is a modest increase (about 1%) in the minimum interest rates.

At a time when all governments in the industrial world are -- or should be -- looking for a way to reduce public expenditures, it is hard to imagine those very same governments permitting a system to exist which during 1980 costs them in the aggregate a minimum of $4 billion and perhaps as much as $5.5 billion. It is also hard to imagine these same governments which daily transact financial business in the marketplace clinging to the idea that the real world will somehow go away and export credit "harmonization" will better be achieved if all currencies are treated the same with a single minimum interest rate.

What should a government do which wants to stop the runaway horse? The obvious answer has been to convince others to stop increasing the subsidy. The argument is transparent in its simplicity: all countries are better off if all refuse to subsidize. Efforts to persuade others of the validity of this argument have been going on for years but have been particularly intense since 1974.

By European standards the results have been monumental: a single document setting down the rules has been created, maximum repayment terms have been established, minimum interest rates have been fixed, notification procedures have been promulgated. From the U.S. point of view the results have been negligible: a building block has been created upon which no one is building. The minimum interest rates today are almost precisely the same as they were in 1975, although the market rates for most currencies have increased by more than 50%. True, repayment terms are fixed, but they are artificially short in the U.S. view. The notification procedures work only as well as the notifier is willing to make them work and oftentimes that is not very well.

Whatever happens, the negotiations will go on; no one dare stop trying. Much of the burden on this point falls upon the United States. Although other countries are committed to the goal of reducing or eliminating the subsidy element in export credits, none is so ideologically committed and institutionally required to seek a reduction of subsidies as the United States. Nor, it must be said, none -- save, possible, Japan -- is as well placed economically to accomplish the goal.

476

What then can the United States do? The provision of more budgetary resources for Eximbank is one policy option. This at least has the virtue of letting the U.S. side look less like a paper tiger. But would greater Eximbank resources cause the Europeans to agree to a reduction in their subsidies? Eximbank in the latter half of the 1970s generally authorized somewhere between $3.0 and $5.5 billion a year; if that latter figure were to treble to say $15 billion a year, a fair guess is that negotiations would move pretty fast to a reasonably sensible conclusion. If a major player in the game appeared with a bankroll large enough to participate heavily in every major transaction, there would be ample incentive for the Europeans to negotiate.

Even the most ardent advocates for Eximbank are not seeking increases of that magnitude. In fact, such an increase is not a good idea nor is it one that will attract much support in a time of budget-cutting. A cousin of the increased resources argument is the argument that Eximbank should be removed from the Federal budget, thereby, it is said, freeing up large resources for Eximbank. The Federal budget is a cash budget and it is not illogical that cash disbursements -- whether for military hardware, for transfer payments or for Eximbank loans to foreign borrowers -- are lumped together. Starting from scratch, a more artful way to group similar types of cash disbursements could be devised; in fact, a budget which brings together all credit extensions is probably not far off. But no matter how the

477

grouping is done, both the executive and the legislative branches have valid reasons to control the amount of disbursements by Eximbank in any fiscal year. Thus, even in the early 1970s when Eximbank was excluded from the Federal budget, the Office of Management and Budget still set a target figure of authorizations which the Bank was not to exceed in a given year, and the Congress imposed then -- as it continues to do now -- an annual ceiling on authorizations. Thus, whether in or out of the budget, annual limitations will be imposed on the Bank.

Another approach to the negotiations might be: if you can't lick 'em, join 'em. The Europeans by and large do not have the budget problems of the United States because they provide a direct subsidy to the lending banks and all that appears in the budget account is the amount of the subsidy, not the full loan. Eximbank could adopt the ECGD approach and simply subsidize the private extenders of credit. In 1977-78 a scheme was proposed whereby Eximbank, in order to be competitive, would make up the difference to the lending institution between the rate at which funds were actually lent and the rate the lender would otherwise have received in the marketplace. Even in that time of export promotion and less intense budget-cutting enthusiasm, the idea did not attract much of a following. It was said that the United States had coped in the world of export credits for 40 years without resorting to a direct tap on the public "fisc" and it seemed a shame to reverse that policy. Moreover, the concept of the large money-center banks receiving a direct subsidy from the Federal Government was politically unappealing. Finally, the cost was seen to be potentially enormous.

The idea still lingers, although the impetus today is not so much budget-saving but rather devising a mechanism that can be directed at the French. On April 10, 1981, Congressman Stephen Neal introduced a bill that would create a fund of $1 billion to subsidize private financing of exports -- in short, an ECGD interest "make up" scheme. The fund obviously goes farther than Senator Heinz's bill to increase Eximbank authorizations by $1 billion, in that the Neal bill could support authorizations of substantially more than $1 billion (estimated by Mr. Neal at as much as $5 billion). The use of this fund by Eximbank would be subject to a veto by the Secretary of the Treasury and the fund would only be directed at transactions where there is intense, particularly French, competition. The bill provides timing mechanisms so that its use would be geared to the progress, or lack of progress, in the Arrangement negotiations.

Despite reports to the contrary, Eximbank still has budgetary authority with which to operate. Given the adoption of appropriate policies, it can offer reasonably competitive financing packages in the most competitive cases. But this itself has not so far proved sufficient to bring success at the bargaining table. Can the Eximbank

479

resources be targeted against the offending countries so as to cause them to negotiate more forthrightly? Not to mince words, can a targeted approach be used against the French? Two major sectors where the United States and France meet head-on are aircraft and nuclear power plants. Since progress as earlier described has been made in the aircraft area, this leaves the nuclear sector and perhaps telecommunications and subway equipment as sectors where the French are strong. Further use of matching mixed credits could be attempted.

Even if all of these things were done, there would still remain a substantial demand for Eximbank resources from U.S. exporters who were facing official export credit competition at the same subsidized rates as the French were offering but not from the French. Should these exporters be denied access to Eximbank resources because their competition was not French? One suspects that such an approach would not last very long: the ingenuity of U.S. sellers and foreign buyers would quickly find a French competitor in every transaction.

Another negotiating approach might be to play the card that has been talked of for so long: extending maturities. It seems clear that as long as the United States is willing to live with the present Arrangement, the Europeans will not find much incentive to make changes. If the United States were to announce that the failure of negotiations meant the failure of the Arrangement and that the United States was leaving, there would be tremendous pressure to pull the negotiations together. This announcement would resemble a small nuclear blast and most people are reluctant to deploy even the smallest nuclear weapon. But much the same kinds of potential benefits -- with somewhat fewer risks -- could be obtained if the United States said that it intended to stick with the Arrangement but that until Arrangement interest rates come more in line with market rates the United States will offer repayment terms justified by the economics of the project, even if longer than the Arrangement guidelines. The Europeans clearly do not want longer terms. The United States has threatened this prospect off and on over the last five years. Given the substantial lack of progress in the negotiations, it is hard to see why the time has not come to make good on that threat.

IX. <u>NOTES</u>

[1] The views expressed are those of the authors and do not necessarily reflect those of their respective institutions. The author is indicated at the beginning of each section.

CHAPTER NINE

INTERNATIONAL BANKING IN A MULTICURRENCY WORLD

H. Robert Heller

Vice President for International Economics
Bank of American N.T. and S.A.

CONTENTS

TABLES

		Page

I. INTRODUCTION

Profound changes in the world economy and in the international financial system during `the 1970s have also brought a quantum change in the character of international banks and the services they provide. In particular, the role of the U.S. dollar and other key currencies has changed substantially.

This paper deals with the causes of these changes and their implications for the future of the international banking system. I will begin by reviewing some basic economic trends that significantly affect international banking activity. The focus in the main body of the paper will be on the fundamental changes that have taken place in the commercial banking system as the international financial system moved from a dollar standard to a multiple currency standard. I will also briefly comment on related developments in international bond markets and official foreign exchange reserve holding patterns. The paper will conclude with an assessment of the effects of these various developments on commercial banks.

II. THE UNITED STATES IN THE WORLD ECONOMY

Developments in international financial markets cannot be seen in isolation from general trends in the world economy. In particular, trends in the relative importance of the closest competitors to the United States are of great significance in the evolution of the international financial

486

system from a dollar standard to a multicurrency financial environment. The most important countries are not only the largest economies in the free world, but also their currencies dominate international financial markets. Almost all of the world's largest banks are headquartered in these countries as well.

The share of the United States in the world economy has consistently declined during the post-World War II period, while the relative importance of its closest competitors has been enhanced. Table 1 shows that the share of the United States in World GDP declined from 45 percent in 1950 to 25 percent in 1980. During the same period the share of the four main competitor countries increased from 16 percent to 27 percent. Also noteworthy is the rising importance of all other countries, which increased their share of World GDP from 39 percent in 1950 to 48 percent in 1980, with all the increase coming in the 1970s.

Exchange rate changes probably did not distort the relative decline of the importance of the U.S. economy over the thirty-year time span covered here. While exchange rate changes may not fully reflect inflation differentials over relatively short time periods, it stands to reason that over longer periods this possible source of distortion is minimized.

Nevertheless, the breakdown of the adjustable parity system in the early 1970s did distort the time pattern of the relative decline of the U.S. economy. Especially during

TABLE 1

GDP: World and Selected Countries
($ billions)

Year	1950	1960	1970	1980
World	632 (100%)	1,118 (100%)	2,481 (100%)	10,705 (100
United States	285 (45%)	479 (43%)	978 (39%)	2,626 (25
France	29 (5%)	61 (5%)	146 (6%)	600 (6
Germany	23 (4%)	73 (7%)	188 (8%)	780 (7
Japan	14 (2%)	43 (4%)	197 (8%)	1,039 (10
United Kingdom	36 (6%)	72 (6%)	122 (5%)	510 (5
All others	245 (39%)	390 (35%)	850 (34%)	5,150 (48

the later 1960s the dollar had become increasingly over-
valued, and hence the relative importance of the United
States economy as represented in the 1970 data shown in
Table 1 is exaggerated.

III. FLEXIBLE EXCHANGE RATES AND PORTFOLIO DIVERSIFICATION

This brings us conveniently to the first reason for the
ascendancy of other currencies in international banking and
finance: the breakdown of the dollar exchange standard that
provided the anchor of the Bretton Woods system of fixed,
but adjustable, parities. Under the dollar exchange standard there was very little reason to hold diversified
currency portfolios as all major currencies were freely
convertible into dollars. The likelihood of a dollar
depreciation in terms of other currencies was rather remote,
while the likelihood of a depreciation of other currencies
was considerably greater. Little gain could therefore be
expected by currency portfolio diversification and the
dollar's role in international banking was supreme. The
vast majority of all foreign assets of the European banks
covered by the BIS survey was denominated in dollars. For
instance, in 1969 these banks held 4.4 times as many dollar
assets as other foreign currency assets abroad. With the
abandonment of the dollar standard, the dollar component was
reduced drastically to a 2 to 1 ratio by 1979. Most of the
adjustment in the currency portfolio took place rather
rapidly between 1969 and 1971, when the ratio reached 2.5

(see Table 2).

While it is true that these data are affected by the change in the exchange rate itself, this factor accounts for only a small fraction of the change in the ratio observed. For instance, between the end of 1969 (pre-Smithsonian parities) and the end of 1980, the effective exchange rate of the dollar lost only 16 percentage points while the ratio of dollar to foreign currency assets fell by 55 percentage points -- that is, the U.S. dollar component was cut more than in half.

While the diversification process is still proceeding, its speed seems to have slowed considerably, and it may well be reasoned that a new equilibrium position for the dollar in the world economy is being approached asymptotically.

IV. MONEY AND THE ECONOMY

If all other things were equal, one might expect that currency use -- and therefore the size of the various national money supplies -- would stand in proportion to the size of the national economies. Two key factors distort this simple relationship: different velocities and external currency usage.

Monetary institutions and payments habits differ widely among counries, and consequently we find that the velocity of circulation of money also differs among countries, thereby breaking any direct international correspondence between the volume of money and the size of the economy.

490

TABLE 2

External Assets Composition of European Banks
($ billions)

End of Year	Dollars	Other Foreign Currencies	Ratio of Dollars To Other Foreign Currencies
1966	16.1	4.2	3.8
1967	19.9	5.0	4.0
1968	30.4	7.4	4.1
1969	47.6	10.7	4.4
1970	60.4	17.9	3.4
1971	71.7	28.7	2.5
1972	98.0	33.8	2.9
1973	132.1	55.5	2.4
1974	156.2	58.9	2.7
1975	190.2	68.0	2.8
1976	224.0	81.3	2.8
1977	268.4	116.4	2.3
1978	339.5	162.5	2.1
1979	428.0	212.0	2.0

The second factor, external currency usage, also tends to bring about a discrepancy between the size of an economy and the total worldwide usage of its currency.

The dynamics of this relationship are not well understood, but certain basic elements may be discerned. While the supply of a currency is under the control of the monetary authorities issuing it, the demand for a currency is related -- among other factors -- to its use as a transaction medium and as a store of value. In both uses a currency that is stable in value offers advantages over a currency that does not enjoy this quality.

A currency for which the monetary authorities increase the supply only commensurately with increases in demand for it will by definition be stable in value. Only when the money supply is expanded at a more rapid rate than the demand for the currency will the excess supply result in a loss of domestic and international exchange value, with ensuing inflation and depreciation.

A currency with a stable value offers attractions not only to domestic, but also to foreign economic units. Consequently, the total demand for the currency by domestic and international holders expands. That is, the domain of the currency will be enlarged. Under such circumstances it is entirely possible that measured monetary expansion rates will be rather high, and that most of the increases in the money supply will be effectively hoarded and thereby sterilized or taken out of active circulation. Alternately,

492

the money may be used abroad for transactions unrelated to the domestic economy. This also implies an effective sterilization for domestic policy purposes. Here we have an example of a truly virtuous circle, where a currency's initial stability sets forces into motion that further enhance its attractiveness. By increasing the demand for the currency, these forces will lead to further appreciation of the currency which not only reduces measured domestic inflation, but also further enhances the status of the currency as a speculative vehicle for potential gain.

While difficult to document, such episodes of excess demand may well have been instrumental in the sharp rise in the external value of the DM, yen, and Swiss franc during the early 1970s.

This interpretation is consistent with the higher monetary growth rate that was experienced in the 1970s in Germany in comparison to the United States, while at the same time inflationary pressures in the United States were greater than in Germany and the Deutsche mark appreciated in value relative to the dollar.

National income grew only slightly faster in Germany than in the United States, and the demand for money due to the marginally more rapid expansion of the domestic German economy contributed to more robust demand for the Deutsche mark than the dollar. But this factor alone was clearly insufficient to account for the inflationary differences between the two countries.

493

This framework of analysis also allows us to explain the apparent contradiction between the fact that during the 1970s the international use of the dollar as an investment currency continued to expand while its value in the exchange market declined. The persistent international expansion of the domain of the dollar was evidence for its great international usefulness, but the decline of its exchange value reflected the fact that the dollar supply increased even faster than the continued expansion in the demand for dollars. Domestic U.S. inflation and exchange rate depreciation tell the same story.

The other important currencies were also created at excessively high rates as evidenced by domestic inflationary pressures. But, for reasons already discussed, the international demand for these currencies increased faster than that for the dollar, and hence the international value of these currencies increased relative to the dollar.

V.   INVOICING PATTERNS IN INTERNATIONAL TRADE

Invoicing patterns in international trade are an important factor in determining currency usage. While the U.S. dollar formerly occupied a virtually exclusive position of preeminence in world trade, other currencies now play a significant role as well.

A distinctive pattern in the use of various currencies in world trade has begun to emerge. Table 3 details the proportions of world trade denominated in various

494

TABLE 3

Proportions of Domestic and Foreign Currency
Denominations in Trade Contracts: 1976
(percent of the total)

ports ports t available	Own Currency		US $		DM	S.F.	Ł	F.F.	Yen
	X	M	X	M	X	X	X	X	X
	90	–	90	–	–	–	–	–	–
y	87	42	5	31	87	–	–	–	–
rland (1977)	83	41	7	–	–	83	–	–	–
1977)	69	–	17	–	–	–	69	–	–
	68	32	9	29	–	–	–	68	–
(1973)	67	26	14	22	–	–	–	–	–
a	55	25	10	16	–	–	–	–	–
k	54	25	12	23	–	–	–	–	–
lands	50	31	13	23	–	–	–	–	–
n	47	26	12	25	–	–	–	–	–
	39	16	31	43	–	–	–	–	–
d	16	–	22	–	–	–	–	–	–
	30	1–2	68	90	–	–	–	–	30
aland lia	20–30	–	75	70–80	–	–	–	–	–
America	0	0	85	–	–	–	–	–	–
	0	0	95	–	–	–	–	–	–
	0	0	70	–	–	–	–	–	–
					1977	1977	1977		
total			52	52	14	2	6–7	6.5	2.3

Hans-Eckart Scharrer, "Die Wahrungsstruktur im Welthandel," Wirtschafts Dienst, September 1979 (Table prepared by T. Nakamura)

495

currencies. The following observations can be made:

(1) Exports of industrial commodities tend to be denominated in the currency of the exporting country. This tendency is particularly apparent in strong-currency countries like Germany and Switzerland where respectively 87 and 83 percent of exports are denominated in DM and Swiss francs.

(2) Trade in raw materials (especially LDC trade) still tends to be denominated in dollars because world prices tend to be quoted in dollars. The currency of quotation is dominant.

(3) To the extent that trade is denominated in currencies other than the exporting country, the importing country's currency dominates. Otherwise, the dollar remains the preferred currency.

(4) The existence of forward exchange markets is a precondition for the use of that currency in trade contracts.

Given the trends in the world economy, it is likely that the dollar will play a diminishing role in trade among the industrialized countries and will eventually also be challenged in its role for manufactured goods trade among the developing countries. For raw material and commodity trade the dollar will continue to be used, but may eventually be challenged by composite currency units such as the SDR.

As international trade is increasingly denominated in

496

currencies other than the dollar, international banks also increasingly offer trade financing in the various currencies. The tendency to finance exports in the currency of the exporting country is strengthened by the existence of various governmental export financing or guarantee agencies that insist on utilizing the currency of the exporting country.

VI. THE CURRENCY COMPOSITION OF INTERNATIONAL BANK LENDING

Bank activity in the international markets expanded rapidly during the 1970s. During that decade there were also marked changes in the currency composition of the balance sheet of international banks. Between 1969 and 1979 the dollar component of interntional assets reported by European banks decreased rather steadily from 82 percent to 67 percent. The same pattern is evident if one includes the various off-shore centers. Of course, due to the strong presence of U.S. banks, the dollar compenent is slightly larger there.

Overall, the balance sheet of European banks at the end of 1979, showed the following foreign asset composition;

U.S. dollars	66.9 percent
Deutsche mark	19.4 percent
Swiss francs	6.0 percent
Pounds sterling	1.8 percent
Dutch guilders	1.3 percent
French francs	1.2 percent
Other currencies	3.4 percent
Total	100.0 percent

Perhaps even more instructive is the currency composition of foreign assets observed in the various countries.

497

Table 4 shows that Germany and Switzerland are the only countries where domestic currency lending dominates in international banking activity. For banks located in Germany's immediate neighbors, Austria, Luxembourg, and Denmark, the "other currency" category dominates -- presumably indicating that most of the international lending is taking place in German marks as well.

Among those many countries where U.S. dollar lending still dominates the international banking business, it is noteworthy that the "other" foreign currency component of foreign lending has often become very significant, for example in Belgium, France, the Netherlands, Sweden, and the United Kingdom.

Overall, we can observe that currencies other than the U.S. dollar play in increasingly important role in international lending. In particular, the hard currency countries of Germany and Switzerland are assuming a more important role.

Since international banks engage in rather precise currency matching, the developments described above are mirrored almost exactly on the liability side of the balance sheet.

VII. INTERNATIONAL BOND MARKETS

International bond markets also reflect increasing currency diversification. Only approximately half of all international bond issues are now denominated in dollars,

498

TABLE 4

Currency Composition of External Bank Assets: 1979

	Assets denominated in (amounts in $ billions)			Percentage Composition of Assets		
	Domestic currency	U.S. dollars	Other foreign currency	Domestic currency	U.S. dollars	Other foreign currency
Dollar dominated						
Belgium	3.3	23.3	16.3	7.7	54.3	38.0
France	23.2	71.7	28.7	18.8	58.0	23.2
Italy	1.3	21.2	7.1	4.4	71.6	24.0
Netherlands	11.4	23.0	21.5	20.4	41.1	38.5
Sweden	1.0	3.0	1.8	17.2	51.7	31.0
United Kingdom	15.5	211.8	58.2	5.4	74.2	20.4
Canada	0.6	22.9	2.0	2.3	89.8	7.8
Japan	11.4	30.4	3.7	25.1	66.8	8.1
United States	133.6	(N.A.)	2.4	98.2	(N.A.)	1.8
Domestic currency dominated						
Germany	47.6	14.4	7.4	68.6	20.7	10.7
Switzerland	27.2	21.5	10.4	46.0	36.4	17.6
Other currency dominated						
Austria	4.2	6.6	7.1	23.5	36.9	39.6
Luxembourg	1.4	29.3	50.1	1.7	36.7	62.0
Denmark	0.2	1.9	2.0	4.9	46.3	48.8

Source: BIS, Annual Report 1980

499

but the total value of the dollar issues averaged 58 percent over the 1975-79 period. This reflects to a large extent the depth of the international dollar market (see Table 5), causing large issues to be denominated in dollars. Nevertheless, the Deutsche mark issues accounted for 28 percent of the volume over the 1975-79 period.

Global totals are somewhat misleading as far as basic trends are concerned. Table 6 shows that U.S., Canadian, and European borrowers dominate the dollar component. The other developed countries (Australia, Japan, New Zealand, and South Africa) as well as the developing countries (shown as "rest of the world" in Table 5) issued almost as many DM denominated bonds as U.S. dollar bonds during the period from January 1976 to June 1980.

The international bond market is also highly sensitive to exchange market developments. During the dollar weakness of 1978 there was a pronounced decrease in activity in the new issues dollar market.

We may conclude that the basic trend towards increasing diversification into non-dollar currencies and in particular the Deutsche mark has also characterized the international bond markets.

However, it is unlikely that a further significant deterioration of the position of the U.S. dollar will take place. The large size and depth of U.S. financial markets will continue to make them attractive to international borrowers and lenders, and therefore a continued secular

500

TABLE 5

International Bond Issues by Currency

	1975		1976		1977		1978		1979	
	Principal amount (millions)	Number of Issues	Principal amount (millions)	Number of Issues	Principal amount (millions)	Number of Issues	Principal amount (millions)	Number of Issues	Principal amount (millions)	Number of Issues
Dollars	$2.823	86	$7.538	166	$9.928	193	$5.512	107	$9.198	149
Deutschemarks	DM4.325	47	DM5.360	53	DM9.535	78	DM11.035	94	DM5.080	45
Guilders	Dfl 1.460	23	Dfl 1.095	18	Dfl 1.670	9	Dfl 845	11	Dfl 549	8
Canadian dollars	Can$575	23	Can$1.370	47	Can$575	20	-	-	Can$479	12
Yen	-	-	-	-	Y 30,000	2	Y 15,000	1	Y 25,000	2
Special Drawing Rights	-	-	-	-	-	-	SDR25	2	SDR 70	2
Totals	(Dollar equivalent) $6,926	224	(Dollar equivalent) $11,937	304	(Dollar equivalent) $15,648	327	(Dollar equivalent) $12,709	252	(Dollar equivalent) $14,315	257

Source: "Market Commentary", Euromoney, February 1980, p. 145

TABLE 6

International Bond Issues by Borrower: 1976-June 1980
(In $billions)

Country or Region	U.S. dollars	Deutsche mark
United States	5.3	.4
Canada	3.9	.8
Western Europe	16.6	9.1
Japan, Australia, New Zealand, and South Africa	4.8	3.7
Rest of world	3.8	3.2
International institutions	5.3	3.2
World total	42.0	20.4

Source: BIS, Annual Reports

decline of the U.S. dollar share in international bond markets is not be expected. The current situation may well be characteristic of the situation prevailing ten years from now.

VIII.   OFFICIAL FOREIGN EXCHANGE RESERVE HOLDINGS

Central banks play a large role in international financial markets as holders of foreign exchange reserves. Two conflicting motives have a powerful influence on the currency composition of their assets: the intervention motive and the portfolio motive.

Central banks acquire their foreign exchange reserves through foreign exchange market intervention or through direct borrowing. If foreign exchange is acquired as a result of intervention designed to prop up the value of the foreign currency, relatively weak currencies will be acquired. In contrast, every central bank has a motive to amass a liquid and stable portfolio of foreign reserve assets. This portfolio motive will lead it to desire strong currencies.

Actual portfolios will reflect the combined effects of the intervention motive and the portfolio motive. The weight of both factors will vary among countries, with exchange arrangements heavily influencing the composition of a country's foreign exchange reserves. It stands to reason that a country that pegs its currency to the U.S. dollar will also hold a very large proportion of its exchange reserves in the currency to which it pegs. Two influences

come into play here: First, the already mentioned intervention motive which mandates that a country hold readily
available assets for purposes of intervening in the foreign
exchange market. Second, a country will desire to avoid
sharp fluctuations in the value of its external assets and
therefore the portfolio motive will also argue in favor of
holding a large proportion of the foreign exchange reserves
in the currency to which the country pegs.

Ten years ago virtually all currencies were pegged to
the U.S. dollar, but the situation changed drastically
during the 1970s. Only 41 currencies were pegged to the
dollar in 1980. Even more significant is the fact that the
list of countries whose currencies are still pegged to the
dollar does not include a single major industrialized
country.

The increasing tendency towards currency portfolio
diversification among central banks is particularly apparent
for official foreign exchange deposits with commercial
banks. In 1976, U.S. dollar deposits accounted for 72
percent of all official deposits with commercial banks
outside the United States, but by the end of 1979, the
dollar share had decreased to 59 percent. Deutsche mark
deposits account for slightly more than half of all official
non-dollar deposits held at commercial banks (Table 7).

Overall, offical Eurodollar holdings amounted to $10.5
billion in 1970, while other Eurocurrencies were only $0.4
billion. By 1979, non-dollar Eurocurrency holdings had

TABLE 7

Official Deposits with Commercial Banks[1]
($ billions)

Currency	1976	1977	1978	1979
Deutsche mark	9.3	14.2	19.9	27.5
Swiss francs	4.1	4.5	5.2	6.6
Yen	0.7	1.8	4.9	5.1
Pound sterling	1.5	1.9	1.9	3.4
Other non-dollar	2.6	3.2	4.7	7.9
Total non-dollars	18.2	25.6	36.6	50.5
Dollars at non-U.S. banks	47.2	53.0	52.8	73.3
Deposits with off-shore branches of U.S. banks	4.5	4.4	5.7	6.4
Total	69.9	83.0	95.1	130.2

[1] Europe, Canada, and Japan

Source: BIS Annual Report and IMF, Survey, June 3, 1980

505

expanded to over $50 billion, while the dollar component was approximately $80 billion.

Perhaps even more remarkable has been the shift in official deposits from U.S.-based banks to foreign-based banks as the preferred depository of foreign central banks. Official dollar deposits at off-shore branches of U.S. banks were $6.4 billion at year-end 1979 and $11.8 billion at domestic U.S. banking offices, for a total of $18.2 billion. By contrast, some $73.3 billion in dollars were held at non-U.S. banks by official foreign institutions.

IX. RELATIVE SIZE OF BANKS

The change in the relative size of the U.S. dollar area and the decreasing utilization of the U.S. dollar in comparison to other currencies has profound implications for the relative size of banking institutions in the United States and abroad.

Table 8 shows the dollar value of deposits at the 20 largest commerical banks in the world. While at the end of 1969 the world's three largest banks were American, only one U.S. bank was in the top three in 1979. Even more startling is the fact that in 1969 nine U.S. banks were among the top thirty, but in 1979 only three were left in that league. American, British, and Canadian banks had been replaced by French, German, and Japanese banks as holding the largest deposits.

These   trends   show   very   clearly   the   increasing

506

TABLE 8

Deposits at Top 20 Commercial Banks of the World
($ billions; number of banks in parentheses)

Headquarted in	1969	1979
United States	95.5 (7)	266.9 (3)
United Kingdom	29.4 (3)	131.9 (2)
France	16.3 (2)	379.7 (4)
Germany	16.3 (2)	278.7 (4)
Japan	14.3 (2)	350.7 (6)
Canada	24.3 (3)	0 (0)
Italy	8.8 (1)	0 (0)
Brazil	0 (0)	49.2 (1)

Source: American Banker

507

importance of commericial banks in the five large countries whose currencies have attained a position of increasing importance in international finance. Currency usage in international trade, finance, and reserve holding patterns exert a pro- found influence on the competitive position of commercial banks in the various countries. Along with the change from a dollar-centered international monetary system to a multi-polar key-currency system, the commercial banking system has changed from domination by American banks to a broadly diversified international banking system that is truly multinational in character.

X.   CONCLUSION

While the United States is still the most important economic and financial center in the world economy, rapid econimic growth abroad and the spread of financial sophisti- cation have resulted in an increasing pluralism and interde- pendence. This has found expression in a decline in the share of the world GDP produced in the United States, and has brought a fundamental change in the role of the dollar from a position of unchallenged eminence to that of a senior partner among equals. These tendencies are reflected in the currency composition of payments for international trade, lending patterns of commercial banks, the international bond markets, and the currency composition of official foreign exchange reserves. These developments have also enhanced the role of non-U.S. based commercial banks and brought about a greater balance in the nationality mix of the internationally active commercial banks.

INTERNATIONAL BANKING IN A MULTICURRENCY WORLD

H. Robert Heller

COMMENT

Robert Z. Aliber

University of Chicago

TABLES

Page

The thesis of Robert Heller's paper is straightforward. He seeks to predict the changes in the market share of U.S. banks in the international marketplace in the 1980s from observable trends in the growth of national incomes in the United States and abroad, and from the demand for assets denominated in the dollar relative to the demand for similar assets denominated in various foreign currencies. Heller's paper involves an exercise in the analysis of the determinants of market shares. His implicit proposition is that the share of U.S. owned banks in the international market for deposits and loans will decline if there is a worldwide decline in the demand for dollar assets and in the U.S. share of world GNP. Apparently he believes that comparative advantage is not important in producing banking services or that, alternatively, banks headquartered in each country have a comparative advantage in producing deposits denominated in their domestic currency.

This comment focuses on the interpretation and relevance of the tables in Heller's paper. His first table shows -- or purports to show -- that the U.S. share of world GNP has fallen from 45 percent in 1950 to 39 percent in 1970 to 25 percent in 1980. Heller asserts that "Exchange rate changes probably did not distort the relative decline of the importance of the U.S. economy over the thirty-year time span covered here." This proposition is readily testable. It might be noted that although changes in exchange rates reflect changes in relative national price levels (e.g.,

Purchasing Power Parity is generally valid), changes in exchange rates may also reflect structural changes or changes in the terms of trade. Over the 1970s decade, the depreciation of the dollar relative to the German mark, the British pound, the French franc, and the Japanese yen was substantially greater than might be inferred from changes in relative national price levels. Thus, part of the decline in the U.S. share of world GNP reflects the exchange rate effect. This point is captured by contrasting the implicit growth rates for national income shown in Heller's table with the explicit growth rate in their own currencies for each of these countries. Thus, in Table 1 below, the first column shows the growth rate of money GNP for the 1950 to 1980 period implicit in Heller's data, while the second column shows the growth rate for the 1970 to 1980 period using the same data. The third column shows the growth rate in money income for each of these countries for the 1950 to 1980 period in its own currency, while the fourth column shows the same data for the 1970 to 1980 period. The fifth column looks at the ratios of column (1) and column (3), and the sixth column looks at the ratios of column (2) and column (4).

If Heller's proposition that the changes in the exchange rates do not distort the relationship between the growth of incomes in the various countries is correct, the ratios in columns (5) and (6) should not differ from unity. They differ, however, and not by a trivial amount; thirty

513

TABLE 1   AVERAGE ANNUAL GROWTH RATES OF GROSS NATIONAL INCOME, 1950 – 1980

	(1) GNP, $, 1950/80	(2) GNP, $, 1970/80	(3) GNP, LC, 1950/80	(4) GNP, LC, 1970/80	$(5)=\frac{(1)}{(3)}$	$(6)=\frac{(2)}{(4)}$
United States	7.7	10.4	7.8	10.8	100	100
France	10.6	15.2	10.0	11.2	106	152
Germany	12.5	15.3	9.6	8.3	130	184
Japan	15.4	18.1	12.9	13.1	119	138
United Kingdom	9.2	15.4	9.2	15.8	100	97

Source: INTERNATIONAL FINANCIAL STATISTICS

percent of the increase in Germany's income in dollars in the longer period, and eighty-four percent in the shorter period, reflects the exchange rate effect.

During the 1970s, Heller's data suggest a decline in the U.S. share of national GNP of fourteen percentage points, whereas in the previous two decades the decline had been six percentage points. The fact that much of the decline in the 1970s decade reflects the changes in exchange rates and does not solely reflect the changes in relative national GNP, is evident from the high values of the ratios in column (6).

Even if the U.S. share of world GNP declined in the 1950-1980 period, it does not follow that the U.S. share of world GNP will continue to fall. Much of the change in national shares of GNP can be explained by a prolonged adjustment to the structural imbalances that resulted from World War II. Thus, the U.S. share of world GNP in 1950 was unusually high, and reflected the much more rapid growth of U.S. GNP than the GNP in other industrial countries during and immediately after World War II.

The second table in Heller's paper shows the decline in the share of dollar-denominated deposits in the aggregate of offshore deposits denominated in all currencies. Heller repeats the story that central banks seek to diversify the currency mix of their assets. True, the non-dollar holdings of foreign central banks have increased. But such holdings are not evidence that individual central banks are diversifying. Some may find their interests served by concentrating all their assets in a currency other than the dollar. It is true that individual investors often diversify to reduce risks, but central banks may be less concerned with the particular risk associated with concentrating their assets in a single currency (more on this subject later).

At the end of 1969, offshore deposits denominated in currencies other than the dollar were 18.4 percent of the aggregate of offshore deposits; at the end of 1979, the comparable figure was 33.1 percent. But virtually all of the increase in the non-dollar component of offshore deposits is due to the appreciation of the mark and other currencies. The mark had appreciated from 3.69 marks per dollar at the end of 1969 to 1.73 marks per dollar at the end of 1979; the decline in the mark price of the dollar would have led to an increase in the non-dollar component of offshore deposits to 32.4 percent.

But assume there had been a measured and significant decline in the share of offshore dollar deposits to offshore market deposits. The implication of Heller's argument is that the foreign or global demand for the dollar had declined. Yet this inference is inappropriate. Rather, all that can be inferred is that the incentive to hold offshore mark deposits had increased relative to the incentive to hold offshore dollar deposits. Thus, changes in the market shares of dollar and non-dollar deposits are much more likely to reflect changes in the risk and return relationship between domestic and offshore deposits denominated in the same currency, rather than the changes in the demands for offshore deposits denominated in different currencies.

The third table in Heller's paper shows the currency of invoicing for exports and imports of major industrial countries for 1976. Heller suggests that there has been a relative decline in the use of the dollar as a currency of invoicing. Perhaps, but if so, any inference about the decline in the use of the dollar as an invoicing currency would have to be based on time-series analysis rather than on cross-sectional analysis. Assume, however, that the data shows that the role of the dollar in invoicing bilateral U.S.-Japanese or U.S.-Italian trade had declined. What is the appropriate inference? Heller would suggest that the foreign demand for dollar balances would decline. The appropriate inference, however, is that there have been changes in interest rate differentials relative to anticipated exchange rates. The choice of a currency for financing trade reflects the desire to minimize the financing costs; the currency of invoicing reflects the currency of financing. If there is a persistent tendency to invoice exports of manufactures in the seller's currency, the appropriate inference is that interest rates in this currency are below those in the importer's currency. Further, the expectation that the dollar would appreciate relative to the yen (with interest rates constant) would lead the exporter to shift from financing U.S.-Japanese trade in yen to financing in dollars, and to a corresponding change in the currency of invoicing.

Heller discusses changes in the currencies used to denominate international bond issues. He suggests that there has been a decline in the use of the dollar for denominating offshore bond issues. The data in his Table 5 do not confirm this conclusion. The share of dollar denominated bond issues has varied; in 1975, the share was 41 percent; in 1976 and 1977, 63 percent; in 1978, 43 percent; and in 1979, 64 percent. Suppose, however, that the data had shown a decline in the share of dollar-denominated bond issues to total international bond issues. What is the appropriate inference? The choice of currency for denominating bond issues involves interest rate differentials, anticipated exchange rates, and the borrower's foreign exchange exposures. The share of international bonds denominated in the dollar has tended to decline when the dollar is weak and depreciating, and increase when the dollar is strong and appreciating, which suggests that interest rates on dollar debt are judged relatively high when the dollar is weak and relatively low when the dollar is strong.

The next to last table in the Heller paper deals with official deposits placed in commercial banks, and distinquishes between dollar deposits placed in non-U.S. banks and all deposits placed in offshore branches of U.S. banks. In the 1976-79 period, the share of non-dollar deposits to dollar deposits at non-U.S. banks has increased from 27.8 percent to 40.8 percent. The appropriate inference is obscure. Many of these foreign official institutions have agreed not to hold offshore dollar deposits; to the extent they want dollar deposits, they will place these deposits in the United States. Moreover, many foreign central banks hold much of their dollar assets in the form of marketable dollar securities which have no ready counterpart abroad. Hence, the data in the table are incomplete for judging whether foreign central banks have reduced their demand for dollar assets relative to their demand for comparable assets denominated in other currencies. Moreover, the table shows only a very modest decline in the share of official deposits placed with offshore branches of U.S. banks relative to dollar deposits placed with non-U.S. banks.

The concluding table in the Heller paper shows that the share of the large U.S. banks in the world market for banks deposits has declined. There are now fewer U.S. banks in the top ten and the top thirty than there were a generation ago. Much of the decline in the U.S. share almost certainly reflects the exchange rate effect, and the impacts of a depreciated dollar. Some of this change reflects the fact that mergers among top banks abroad have been more extensive than mergers among top U.S. banks. However, some of the foreign banks are headquartered in more rapidly growing

countries abroad, so an increase in their size may reflect
the increased importance of their national market economies.
Finally, the market share of the U.S. banks might have
decreased because their foreign competitors are more efficient in their roles as financial intermediaries; certainly
the rapid growth of foreign banks in the United States is
impressive.

There may be trends in the international economy that
will lead banks headquartered in the United States to have a
declining share of the world market for deposits and loans.
Such a development might reflect the fact that U.S. banks do
not have a comparative advantage, or that they are handi-
capped by restrictions in the United States or abroad. The
data presented by Heller do not provide any convincing
evidence that U.S. banks are at an economic or regulatory
disadvantage.

There is little evidence in the Heller paper to support
the contention that there will be significant changes in the
national banking environment in the 1980s. It is possible
that the relative importance of the dollar as a reserve
asset will decline, and that U.S. banks will account for a
smaller share of world banking. Yet there is little data in
the paper to suggest that such changes have occurred, or why
they have occurred, or whether they will continue to occur.

A rationale often advanced for the supposed decline in
the foreign demand for dollars is that foreign central banks
wish to hold a diversified currency mix of assets. This

rationale applies a model devised to explain investor behavior in a competitive system to explain the demand for reserve assets. The general inference of this model is that investors should diversify to reduce the risk of their portfolio, and hence, to reduce the variability of their income streams. How relevant is this model to central banks? Central banks do not compete among themselves to minimize their risk and maximize their return. Moreover, variations in returns realized by individual investors occur primarily as a result of variations in share prices; variations in returns to central banks occur as a result of changes in exchange rates. This difference in asset composition points up further differences between the outlook of central bankers and the outlook of individual investors. Returns to a central bank should be deflated by the changes in the prices of the nation's imports and of exports, since the central bank should be concerned about net real income. Taking this deflation into account, changes in exchange rates will affect net real income only if there are non-offsetting deviations from Purchasing Power Parity and Fisher Open. These deviations might be significant for only one or two years. By contrast, the individual investor maximizes his nominal return without regard to the connection (if any) between share prices and his earnings or expenditure stream.

The evidence that central banks act as diversified investors is limited. Certainly there is no evidence of such behavior for the pegged exchange rate period. U.S. behavior does not suggest that reserve diversification is an important goal. If central banks hold reserves denominated in several different currencies, it might be less an act of diversification than an effort to profit from changes in exchange rates, or an attempt to shift permanently from holding assets denominated in one currency to holding assets denominated in some other currency.

INTERNATIONAL BANKING IN A MULTICURRENCY WORLD

H. Robert Heller

REPLY TO THE COMMENT OF

Robert Z. Aliber

Given the substantial disagreements between Professor Aliber and myself, it is worthwhile to further clarify my views on the issues raised by Professor Aliber.

First of all, I very much believe that banks headquartered in a specific country have a comparative advantage in providing banking services denominated in that currency. The bank's equity will be denominated in that currency, giving it a stable base in that currency. It is also generally easier to raise long term funds in the form of bond issues in the home country, although increasingly banks have successfully tapped foreign bond markets. In addition, the bank can call upon the resources of the home country's central bank in times of difficulty -- a privilege not always accorded to branches of foreign banks. Finally, a foreign bank may be subjected to additional regulations and -- in extreme cases -- even absolute ceilings on its business. The recent Canadian legislation is an excellent example for this type of regulatory constraint. Thus, I would conclude that banks do indeed tend to have a comparative advantage in domestic currency banking activity.

However, it is also clear that other factors may at times overcome this natural advantage. For instance, foreign banks may have more sophisticated management, broader experience, or greater financial resources. But these offsetting factors will be subject to erosion and will therefore be only temporary in nature.

One exception to this general rule is provided by the global network banks that offer specialized services transcending national borders. Typically, these services cannot be provided by purely domestic banks, and they tend to complement rather than compete with the services provided by domestic banks.

It is difficult to judge from Professor Aliber's comments whether be believes in Purchasing Power Parity (PPP) or not. In the next to the last paragraph of his comments he declares that:

> ...changes in exchange rates affect net real income only if there are non-offsetting deviations from Purchasing Power Parity...these deviations might be significant for only one or two years.

I would very much agree with this statement, although I only claimed that PPP would hold "over the thirty-year time span covered" by my data. Yet, Professor Aliber argues in his discussion of my Table 1 that the opposite was true in the 1970s:

> Over the 1970s decade, the depreciation of the dollar relative to the German mark, the British pound, the French franc, and the Japanese yen was substantially greater than might be inferred from changes in relative national price levels.

I find it difficult to reconcile his two statements.

Professor Aliber sees no reason why the share of the United States in world GDP should fall in the future. He argues that the 1950 data for Europe and Japan were distorted due to World War II. I have little difficulty with that. But the developing countries are likely to grow faster than the United States in the coming decades, thereby further reducing the U.S. share of world GDP in years to come.

Regarding currency diversification, Professor Aliber agrees that:

> True, the non-dollar holdings of foreign central banks have increased. But such holdings are not evidence that individual central banks are diversifying.

Unfortunately, data on individual central bank portfolios are not published and hard evidence can therefore not be cited for individual countries. But hard evidence does exist for the tendency of all central banks together to diversify their portfolios, and a decade of experience with central banks leads me to conclude that this trend is representative of the vast majority of central banks.

Next, Professor Aliber claims that:

> ...virtually all of the increase in the non-dollar component of offshore deposits is due to the appreciation of the mark and other currencies.

The data published regularly by the Bank for International Settlements show that external Deutsche mark deposits at European banks increased from $20 billion in 1972 to $125 billion in 1980. Holding the exchange rate constant, DM deposits rose from approximately $40 billion to $125 billion over the same period. Moreover, for the years 1978 and 1979, the increase in all non-dollar deposits amounted to $26 billion and $61 billion respectively, excluding exchange rate effects (BIS 50th Annual Report, 1980, p. 123).

Professor Aliber then turns to a discussion of the factors determining the currency of invoicing. He contends

526

that:

> If there is a persistent tendency to invoice exports of manufactures in the seller's currency, the appropriate inference is that interest rates in this currency are below those in the importer's currency.

This statement ignores the crucial difference between real and nominal interest rates. Nominal interest rate differentials reflect differences in inflationary expectations and are also reflected in forward rates. Thus, little advantage should accrue to traders from invoicing in strong currencies on a persistent basis.

Professor Aliber argues that because my data on foreign exchange holding patterns pertain only to central bank deposits at commercial banks, the analysis presented is incomplete. As the title of the paper suggests, it deals only with banks. All forms of official foreign exchange reserves have been discussed in detail in my paper on "Reserve Currency Preferences of Central Banks", published jointly with Malcolm Knight in the Princeton Essays in International Finance (1978).

Nevertheless, I find it gratifying that after all of Professor Aliber's argumentation we seem to agree on the key conclusions. In his own words:

1. There are now fewer U.S. banks in the top ten and top thirty than there were a generation ago.

2. ...some of the foreign banks are headquartered in more rapidly growing countries abroad, so an increase in their size may reflect the increased importance of their national market economies.

3. There may be trends in the international economy that will lead banks headquartered in the United States to have a declining share of the world market for deposits and loans.

These are precisely my own conclusions.